Food and Agricultu Tourism

This book fills a gap in the growing academic discipline of food and agricultural tourism, offering the first multidisciplinary approach to food tourism and the role it plays in economic development, destination marketing, and gastronomic exploration. It provides a comprehensive introduction to the discipline by considering food tourism in connection with both cultural values and important issues in agriculture, food consumption and safety, and rural heritage and sustainability.

The book is divided into four parts. Part I defines the elements of food tourism and explains its relationship with sustainability. Part II provides an overview of rural development and demonstrates the impact of industrialization and globalization on eating habits. Part III focuses on food tourism studies and market segmentation techniques to help students understand customer needs regarding food tourism products. Finally, Part IV looks at the financial, policy, and legal requirements relating to food tourism development, providing hands-on tools for students entering food tourism businesses or industries.

Complemented by a wide range of international case studies, key definitions, and study questions, *Food and Agricultural Tourism* is essential reading for students of tourism, geography, and economic development studies.

Susan L. Slocum is an Assistant Professor in the Department of Tourism and Event Management at George Mason University, Manassas, Virginia. Sue has worked on regional planning and development for 15 years and worked with rural communities in Tanzania, the United Kingdom, and the United States. Her primary focus is on rural sustainable development, policy implementation, and food tourism, specifically working with small businesses and communities in less advantaged areas. Sue received her doctoral education from Clemson University and has worked at the University of Bedfordshire, UK, and Utah State University.

Kynda R. Curtis is a Professor and Extension Agriculture and Food Marketing Specialist in the Department of Applied Economics at Utah State University, Logan, Utah. She received her Ph.D. in Economics from Washington State University in 2003. Her research interests include international agriculture/food marketing, consumer demand for specialty foods, and behavioral economics. As an Extension Specialist, Dr. Curtis assists small-scale growers in developing new markets for their products and assessing the feasibility of new products and value-added processes. Dr. Curtis has received several awards including Extension group program awards from the Agricultural and Applied Economics Association (AAEA) and the Western Agricultural Economics Association (WAEA) and the AAEA Presidential Recognition Award.

Food and Agricultural Tourism

Theory and Best Practice

Susan L. Slocum and Kynda R. Curtis

Routledge
Taylor & Francis Group

LONDON AND NEW YORK

First published 2018
by Routledge
2 Park Square, Milton Park, Abingdon, Oxon OX14 4RN

and by Routledge
711 Third Avenue, New York, NY 10017

Routledge is an imprint of the Taylor & Francis Group, an informa business

British Library Cataloguing-in-Publication Data
A catalogue record for this book is available from the British Library

Library of Congress Cataloging-in-Publication Data
A catalog record for this book has been requested

ISBN: 978-1-138-93109-1 (hbk)
ISBN: 978-1-138-93110-7 (pbk)
ISBN: 978-1-315-67994-5 (ebk)

Typeset in Frutiger
by Keystroke, Neville Lodge, Tettenhall, Wolverhampton

Contents

Images

Figures

Tables

Preface

Just as we humans must procreate, and just as our bodies will all eventually pass from this state of living, we all must eat to sustain ourselves. Yet how we eat, and what we eat, and when we eat, and with whom we eat, all uniquely vary from place to place, group to group, time to time—thanks to long standing geographic, economic, social, and cosmological differences throughout the world.
—Di Giovine and Brulotte (2014. p.1)

While we recognize that tourists must eat and drink while traveling, food and beverage offer much broader functions than simple sustenance. Food and beverage are tied to a region's heritage, history, and culture. While traditional tourism has allowed visitors to see, smell, and hear a society, food tourism provides unique opportunities to taste culture, adding a deeper experience to the tourism product.

Food tourism is a growing field of both research and practice. Numerous books and academic articles have guided the information in this textbook. Beginning with *Food tourism around the world: Development, management and markets* (Hall et al., 2003), the food tourism discipline has exploded to include recent additions like the *Journal of Gastronomy and Tourism* in 2014. Universities worldwide offer both undergraduate and graduate courses related to food tourism, agritourism, and culinary tourism. This research has informed numerous governments and communities as they recognize the value of their local food culture to tourists and the economy. Food, as part of a destination's marketing message, is on the rise, and there is evidence that some tourists travel specifically to explore culinary culture (Everett & Aitchison, 2008).

Yet many of the available food tourism texts provide a one-sided approach to food tourism, either from an agriculture perspective or a tourism perspective. Research has shown that the organizational structures and industry cultures within tourism and agricultural practice (as well as policy-making) are diverse, and collaboration between these industries is fragmented (Everett & Slocum, 2013). This textbook addresses this gap by taking a multidisciplinary approach, covering theories and concepts from tourism, agriculture, economics, and rural development. Some concepts—such as the commodification of culture or the theory of comparative advantage—may already be familiar to students of either tourism or economics. Other models—such as market segmentation strategies and business planning—are, hopefully, common to all disciplines. By introducing industry-specific ideas and applying them broadly to food tourism, the goal of this textbook is to help students better understand the theoretical underpinnings and operational realities of the industries with which they must partner to be successful in food tourism development and expose them to the rationale driving various policy and market decisions.

While *Food and Agricultural Tourism: Theory and Best Practice* is not the only textbook on the market, the authors hope this book offers a fresh perspective on the subjects that comprise food, agriculture, and tourism studies. This textbook is designed for upper-level undergraduate courses in tourism, agribusiness, agricultural economics, and geography; the book is organized so that each chapter begins with an overview and a list of learning objectives. Definitions and concepts are highlighted throughout the text. Study questions and a glossary of defined terms follow the main text. Finally, case studies at the end of each chapter provide concrete examples of the theoretical material.

Chapter 1 introduces food tourism as an economic endeavor and begins with a description of the economic sectors of tourism, agriculture, and rural development. It includes an overview of economic impacts, what they mean, and how they are determined so that students understand the values and implications of common economic impact reports. Concepts include direct, indirect, and induced effects; leakages; multipliers; input/output modelling; and tourism satellite accounts. The chapter concludes with a brief introduction to food tourism.

Chapter 2 highlights the link between globalization and tourism in order to introduce sustainable tourism. It covers both environmental and social externalities that tourism and agriculture can have on communities and how food tourism can alter these impacts. The chapter explains both weak and strong sustainability and describes bridging and bonding social capital. Concepts include the tragedy of the commons, environmental and social impacts, and the triple bottom line.

Chapter 3 begins by acknowledging the importance of managing the authenticity of the food tourism product. It then describes specific types of food tourism, including agritourism, culinary tourism and food trails, food and drink events and attractions, food souvenirs, and local sourcing. It highlights managerial responsibilities to ensure successful food tourism implementation for each type of food tourism operation and recognizes that many food tourism ventures fall into multiple categories. Concepts include culture, authenticity, commodification, voluntourism, and value-added products.

Chapter 4 explains the industrialization of agriculture over the past 200 years and highlights growing concerns for consumer safety. Specifically, it reviews agricultural innovations and structural changes and how they led to specialization and monoculture farming practices. Concepts include competitive advantage, factors of production, and absolute and comparative advantage. It also highlights economic failures and the role of modern agricultural policy, including an overview of multilateral trade negotiations and functions of the World Trade Organization.

Chapter 5 addresses the plight of rural communities and the impact of rural-to-urban migration on the economic and social structure of rural communities. It explains how food tourism can be a successful rural economic development strategy that can improve the quality of life for rural residents and create jobs that slow or reverse rural-to-urban migration. Concepts include clustering, urbanization, self-sufficiency, and brain drain. It explains cost-benefit analysis and illustrates how net present value is determined. It closes with a practical application of cost-benefit analysis to highlight the positive and negative impacts of food tourism development.

Chapter 6 highlights the technological and lifestyle changes that have led to three specific modern food movements, including buy local, foodie, and sustainable consumption. These food movements have spurred food tourism demand and development globally and greatly changed the tourism landscape to include food- and drink-specific travel. The values and characteristics of each movement are discussed in addition to current food-related demand motives and desired product attributes. The rationale behind the rise of these movements—including the historical changes in agricultural production, food processing, and consumption—are detailed. Concepts include industrialization, organic, local, and food miles. The chapter also discusses the importance of food labeling.

Chapter 7 describes how catering to tourists' needs and expectations is vital to the success of any food tourism operation. It explains a variety of tourist types and highlights the need to assess tourism typologies in order to develop a comprehensive food tourism initiative. Concepts include the connections between expectations, motivations, and satisfaction. This chapter also provides descriptive information about foodies and food tourists, such as age and income profiles, food-related experience and activities, and personal values.

Chapter 8 explains that it is imperative to design activities, products, or events that appeal to a specific group of tourists in order to effectively operate a food tourism enterprise or organize a popular destination. This chapter discusses the importance of identifying a target market and explains the various factors by which markets can be segmented. Concepts include geographic, demographic, psychographic, and product-use segmentation. This chapter also provides an overview of tourism data collection and analysis methods, including a detailed description of the advantages and disadvantages of common survey methods. It closes with practical examples of cluster and factor analysis.

Chapter 9 describes the role of destination management and marketing in food tourism. It describes brand development in relation to destinations and explains attributes, benefits, and attitudes as they relate to successful brand awareness. Food has the potential to support or even enhance a destination's image for both domestic and international tourists, as long as food-related messages are consistent with other destination attributes. Concepts include collaboration and networking, differentiation, and sense of place. It concludes with strategies to market destinations and appropriate promotional channels to reach food tourists.

Chapter 10 highlights good governance and the required elements to ensure participation in the policy development process as it relates to food tourism. It explains the policy cycle, including top-down and bottom-up policy approaches. Concepts include laws and regulations, regressive and progressive taxes, and zoning. International, national, and regional policies and policy organizations are described and the role that policy plays in the development of food tourism destinations, enterprises, and programs is explored.

Chapter 11 introduces food safety to ensure that visitor health and safety are at the forefront of any food tourism program, product, or business. It includes aspects of food preparation for on-site consumption and food processing for specialty and souvenir products as well as the potential for visitor illness resulting from contact with animals. Concepts include contaminants, pathogens, sanitation, viruses, and bacteria. It provides valuable information about facility design for food processing accessible to tourists and highlights the importance of food safety plans.

Chapter 12 provides tools for proper food tourism operation planning, including creating a financial feasibility assessment or business plan to ensure success. It highlights business and marketing plans and explains when each should be used. It offers an overview of the components of a business plan, including a SWOT (Strength, Weaknesses, Opportunities, and Threats) analysis and a detailed description of each section's contents. Concepts include the 4 Ps of marketing (the marketing mix); various pricing strategies; fixed, variable, and total costs; and break-even analysis. The chapter introduces income statements and balance sheets and the uses of each.

This textbook has been designed to provide valuable insight into food tourism, agritourism, culinary tourism, and other forms of farm- or food-related activities that support the tourism industry, the tourist experience, rural development strategies, and economic growth. Food tourism requires a new management and marketing approach that is distinctly different from traditional agriculture or tourism diversification strategies. Before investing in this unique and exciting market niche, it is important to understand the tourism industry, the agricultural industry, rural development strategies, consumer demand, food service expectations, and the challenges of collaborative efforts between tourism and food industries.

Furthermore, accessing tourists, understanding their travel patterns, and effective marketing can be taxing for small-scale farms, food producers, chefs, market managers, and destination-marketing organizations. Food tourism can be a rewarding and profitable endeavor, but determining how food tourism plays into existing activities and amenities, the infrastructure needed to support food tourism development, and how visitors affect the use of local resources need to be considered before investing time and energy into food tourism.

Susan L. Slocum   Kynda R. Curtis

References

Di Giovine, M.A., and Brulotte, R.L. (2014). Introduction. In R.L. Brulotte and M.A. Di Giovine (Eds.), *Edible identities: Food as cultural heritage* (pp. 1–23), Burlington, VT: Ashgate.

Everett, S., and Aitchison, C. (2008). The role of food tourism in sustaining regional identity: A case study of Cornwall, South West England. *Journal of Sustainable Tourism, 16*(2), 150–167.

Everett, S., and Slocum, S.L. (2013). Food and tourism: An effective partnership? A UK-based review. *Journal of Sustainable Tourism, 21*(7), 789–809.

Hall, C.M., Sharples, L., Mitchell, R., Cambourne, B., and Macionis, N. (Eds.). (2003). *Food tourism around the world: Development, management and markets.* Oxford: Butterworth-Heinemann.

Acknowledgements

Writing a textbook requires extensive research. The authors acknowledge that without past scholars bringing attention to the exciting fields of food, agriculture, rural development, and tourism, this book could not have been written.

We owe our appreciation to the numerous contributors who provided valuable case studies, which explain complex food tourism concepts through easily digestible applications.

- Karin Allen—Associate Professor & Extension Food Quality & Entrepreneurship Specialist, Department of Nutrition, Dietetics, and Food Sciences, Utah State University, Utah, USA
- Sierra Allen—Extension Intern, Department of Applied Economics, Utah State University, Utah, USA.
- Luísa Augusto—Associate Professor at the School of Education, Polytechnic Institute of Viseu, Portugal
- Lurdes Martins—Lecturer at the School of Technology and Management, Polytechnic Institute of Viseu, Portugal
- Azizul Hassan—Ph.D. candidate, Cardiff Metropolitan University, Wales, UK
- Barry Ballard—Technical Trainer, Amazon Web Services, Washington, USA
- Cristina Barroco—Associate Professor at the School of Technology and Management, Polytechnic Institute of Viseu, Portugal
- Tracy Berno—Associate Professor, School of Hospitality & Tourism, Auckland University of Technology, New Zealand
- Vivina Almeida Carreira—Associate Professor, Higher School of Agriculture, Polytechnic Institute of Coimbra, Portugal
- Paul Cleave—Independent Research Professional, The Business School, University of Exeter, England
- Montserrat Crespi-Vallbona—Assistant Professor, Faculty of Economics and Business, University of Barcelona, Spain
- Darko Dimitrovski—Assistant Professor, Faculty of Hotel Management and Tourism, University of Kragujevac, Serbia
- Savannah Gleim—Research Associate, College of Agriculture and Bioresources, University of Saskatchewan, Canada
- Laxmi Gurung—Secretariat, Local Peace Committee, Ministry of Peace and Reconciliation, Nepal

Acknowledgements

- Fidel Martínez-Roget—Professor, Faculty of Economics, University of Santiago de Compostela, Spain
- Lurdes Martins—Representative, ISCTE – University Institute of Lisbon, Portugal
- Kelly McMahon—Senior Manager, Dell EMC Education Services, Washington, USA
- Eric T. Micheels—Assistant Professor, Bioresource Policy, Business and Economics, Department of Agricultural and Resource Economics, University of Saskatchewan, Canada
- José Alberto Moutela—Ph.D. Candidate in Economics, Faculty of Economics, University of Santiago de Compostela, Spain
- Anukrati Sharma—Associate Professor, Department of Commerce and Management, University of Kota, India
- David G. Simmons—Professor, Department of Social Science, Parks, Recreation, Tourism, and Sport, Lincoln University, New Zealand
- Izaak Wierman—Music Educator, Mountain West String Academy, Utah, USA

We would like to thank our families, friends, and colleagues for their patience and willingness to pick up the slack while we focused on this project. Specifically, we must thank Kynda's husband Izaak, who's considerable efforts in keeping their household functioning and kids healthy while she travelled extensively for this project, were essential to completing the project.

Lastly, we owe a great debt to Amy Bekkerman and Karin Allen for their dedicated support on this project. Specifically, to Amy Bekkerman for her skillful technical editing, without which this project may have never come to fruition, and to Karin Allen for her contribution on food safety issues and the supporting case study. Thank you, ladies.

Part I

Food tourism and sustainable rural development

Image I.1 Lancaster outdoor tasting room, Swan Valley, Australia
Source: Kynda R. Curtis

Chapter 1

Tourism, agriculture, and rural economic development

Overview

Agriculture and tourism represent two of the world's largest industries. This chapter explains the unique attributes of agriculture and tourism, including common economic development strategies and how they support rural development. These industries have direct, indirect, and induced effects as well as economic leakages associated with imports and exports of goods and services. This chapter also explains how these economic impacts are measured and concludes with an understanding of how food tourism can support a region's economic growth.

Learning Objectives

This chapter will enable students to:

1 Understand the scope and nature of tourism.
2 Understand the scope and nature of agriculture.
3 Explain the direct, indirect, and induced effects of tourism and agriculture, multipliers, and leakages.
4 Assess the challenges facing rural development.
5 Compare and contrast input/output modeling and tourism satellite accounts.
6 Explain how tourism and agriculture can be combined to enhance the visitor experience and economic impact on a region.

Understanding tourism

Humans have always traveled. In the earliest civilizations, people journeyed to secure vital resources, such as food and water, and to trade with other civilizations. Travel as a form of recreation or for cultural experiences was also a pursuit of early individuals. The first known travel guide was written by Pausanias in 170 AD for Roman visitors traveling in his home country of Greece. Yet it is only recently that travel has become a world-wide phenomenon. Ease of travel is directly related to technology; as different modes of transportation developed, so too did the ability to tour. Wind-powered boats were replaced by horse-drawn stagecoaches, which in turn have been superseded by motorized vehicles such as automobiles, cruise liners, and airplanes. As travel times shortened and travel became less costly, tourism became a reality for more than just the upper classes. Today, travel is fairly efficient and most of the world—even Antarctica—is accessible to large numbers of people.

Tourism has a variety of definitions, but in its simplest form, tourism is an economic endeavor. Therefore, the most common definition of **tourism** is "the temporary movement of people to destinations outside their normal places of work and residence, the activities undertaken during their stay in those destinations, and the facilities created to cater to their needs" (Mathieson & Wall, 1982, p. 1). As an economic venture, tourism consists of a number of industries that develop and promote the travel experience, such as airlines and hotels. Tourism involves numerous types of service activities and physical commodities (see Figure 1.1).

Tourism can also be defined from the tourist's perspective, emphasizing the experiential nature of visiting foreign or exotic places. The United Nations World Tourism Organization (UNWTO) (2014) defines tourism as "a social, cultural, and economic phenomenon" (p. 1) that begins long before any actual travel occurs and extends long after the trip has been completed. Excitement builds as travelers plan their trip, usually focused around a particular interest or activity, such as skiing, sunbathing, or exploring a natural area or a specific culture. Travelers frequently choose their destination based on many factors, such as recommendations from family and friends, marketing materials available on the Internet, or guidebooks. Most tourism purchases occur before the trip even starts,

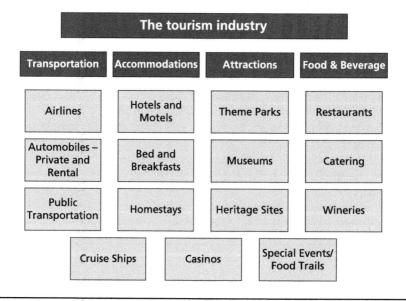

Figure 1.1 The tourism industry

including transportation, tour packages, and accommodations. Tourists also purchase many items while they are traveling, including food, souvenirs, and gasoline. After the trip is complete, tourists often share their experiences through stories, photos, and mementos. The pre- and post-travel experiences are as much a part of tourism as is the actual trip.

There is still much debate about the difference between tourism and leisure activities. Some definitions of tourism require visitors to be a certain distance away from home (usually more than 150 miles or 240 kilometers) or require them to spend the night away from home in order to be strictly classified as tourists. Other definitions recognize day trippers, or excursionists, as tourists. **Excursionists** are generally classified as visitors who use tourism services but live in close proximity to the destination and only stay for a short period of time (a few hours to a single day). Regardless of the type of traveler included in the definition, the experience is often the same. For example, a farm-based enterprise, such as a farm shop, may have customers who are local residents, people from nearby communities, and travelers from far-away countries. For the purposes of this book, both nearby and distant visitors can be classified as tourists. Much of the practical information in this book can be used regardless of whether tourists are local, domestic, or international.

Tourism is often classified as the world's largest industry, with an estimated 1 billion travelers generating US$1.4 trillion in direct spending worldwide in 2013 (UNWTO, 2014). This translates to US$2.3 trillion in economic impact and 292 million jobs, which accounts for 1 in 10 jobs in the global workforce (World Travel and Tourism Council, 2017). However, tourism is not a standalone economic industry but is made up of numerous economic sectors such as accommodations, transportation, food and beverage, and attractions, just to name a few. These economic components of tourism are explained later in this chapter.

Understanding agriculture

Agriculture is the world's oldest industry, and humans began domesticating flora and fauna for human consumption approximately 15,000 years ago. Evidence of trade networks among pre-agricultural ancient civilizations is even older. As particular foods thrive in different climates, trade in food quickly spanned the globe. The most extensive trade route in historical times was the Silk Road, over which exotic spices, among other goods, traveled from China, India, and the Far East to the tables of Northern Africa and Europe.

Agriculture is defined as the science or practice of farming and ranching, including cultivating the soil for growing crops and the rearing of animals to provide food and other products. Agriculture is practiced in every country in the world. Trade in agricultural merchandise represented US$8.0 trillion in 2014 worldwide, representing 10% of the world's gross domestic product (Food and Agriculture Organization of the United Nations, 2016). China is currently the world's largest agricultural producer, followed by India and the United States.

The global food trade is still a vital component of regional economies. Even today, certain areas—particularly those with lower wages or higher crop yields—specialize in agricultural production, which is often traded with other countries. Globalized food chains are discussed in more detail in Chapter 4. For example, California generated US$54 billion in agricultural production in 2014 and exported almost US$22 billion of that (California Assembly Committee on Jobs, Economic Development, and the Economy, 2014). These food items—including milk, fruits and tree nuts (almonds), and livestock—were sent

Image 1.1 Agriculture as viewed from an airplane outside Sacramento, California, USA
Source: Susan L. Slocum

mainly to the European Union, Canada, China, Hong Kong, Japan, and Mexico (California Department of Food and Agriculture, 2014). In the same year, California imported US$10.8 billion worth of agricultural products from Mexico, China, Vietnam, and Chile including coffee, tropical fruits (bananas), and preserved meats (California Assembly Committee on Jobs, Economic Development, and the Economy, 2014).

However, globalized food chains have created challenges for both consumers and producers. Food that travels long distances must be picked before it is ripe to prevent spoilage in transport, so it is treated with preservatives and ripening agents. One such ripening agent, calcium carbide, has been associated with mood disturbances, mental confusion, seizures, and hypoxia in humans (Asif, 2012). Additionally, outbreaks of food-borne illnesses—such as salmonella, listeria, and E. coli—have increased consumers' interest in knowing the geographic origins of their food. Food safety is covered in detail in Chapter 11.

Agricultural producers also face numerous challenges such as decreasing commodity prices, increasing operational costs, and fluctuating consumer demand in a global food market. Furthermore, increased regulation associated with food safety and crop insurance have created additional burdens on the profitability of small farms. Consider where the money goes when a cereal grain (such as rice, wheat, or corn) is purchased (see Figure 1.2). A majority of the revenue generated by the sale goes to retail profit, food processing, and wholesale; only 7.4% of the retail price goes to the farmer. For a loaf of bread that costs $5, farmers receive only $0.37. At the same time, farmers are experiencing rising costs for production inputs such as fuel, wages, water, and fertilizer. If the cost of seeds or fertilizer increases, the price a consumer pays for bread will increase, which may result in less bread being sold. With such a small profit margin for farmers, increased costs may mean bankruptcy.

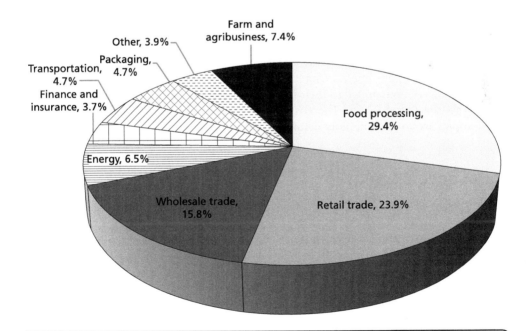

Figure 1.2 Breakdown of retail food distribution costs
Source: Adapted from U.S. Department of Agriculture, Economic Research Service (2007)

The Australian Bureau of Statistics (2012) reports that there were 19,700 fewer farmers in Australia in 2011 than in 2006, an 11% drop over 5 years; just over half (55%) of remaining farmers had agricultural operations with an estimated value of less than AUS$100,000. Many farms are forced to sell out to corporations that realize economies of scale not available to small farms. **Economies of scale** are the cost savings gained by increasing levels of production. For example, if you buy a single orange, you may pay $1.00. However, if you buy twenty oranges, you may pay only $15.00, or $0.75 per orange. This is because it is often cheaper to buy in bulk. Small farms generally buy inputs in smaller quantities, meaning that they may pay more for them per unit than larger farms would. Economies of scale are discussed further in Chapter 4.

Demand for local food

New strategies to increase the profitability of small farms take advantage of consumer demand for local food through **direct market sales,** which allow farmers to sell their products directly to consumers (as opposed to wholesalers and other middlemen). Direct market sales have increased steadily since the early 1990s as a result of a growing "buy local" movement. Venues for direct market sales include farmers' markets, farm stands, and community supported agriculture (CSA) as well as sales to local restaurants and grocery stores.

It seems the world cannot get enough of farm-fresh foods. In 2015, 167,000 farms in the United States sold US$8.7 billion in food directly to customers; 33% of those sales took place in California (USDA-NASS, 2016). Denmark, Switzerland, and Austria report the highest per capita consumption of farmers' market produce (Willer et al., 2010), and the European Union has required all fresh food to be labeled with its place of origin since 2011. Other countries are quickly following suit. There is also evidence that consumer demand for local food is growing faster than small farms can accommodate it, especially in the Unites States (Day-Farnsworth et al., 2009). Local food has gained popularity because consumers are interested in knowing where their food comes from and what inputs have been added to their food (chemicals and antibiotics), and they want to ensure that their food is safe. There is also increasing interest is supporting local farms. These topics are covered in more detail in Chapter 6.

Rural development

The majority of agricultural production occurs in rural areas, which face numerous challenges related to economic growth and opportunity. Traditionally, rural development has focused on extracting or exploiting natural resources (for example, forestry and mining) or intensive land use, as in agriculture. With the decline in the number of small farms globally, rural areas are losing their economic base. Moreover, global industrial development in urban areas has drastically changed the nature of rural areas over the past 200 years. In particular, an increase in the number of urban jobs available has increased rural-to-urban migration. As younger generations are moving to cities for employment and education, rural areas are left with aging populations. Rural areas also suffer from a lack of investment—such as roads, hospitals, and schools—primarily because as their economy shrinks, so too does their tax base. Many governments are addressing the decline of rural areas through the process of rural development.

Rural development is the process of improving the quality of life and economic well-being of people living in relatively isolated and sparsely populated areas (Moseley, 2003). Traditionally, rural areas have specialized in certain economic sectors or industries. Detroit, Michigan, was a hub for automobile production, in part because of the ease of transporting steel from Pittsburgh, Pennsylvania. Pittsburgh produced steel because of its close proximity to coal deposits in Pennsylvania and West Virginia, which were necessary to smelt iron. The same development pattern occurred in England, where southern regions specialized in agricultural resources (due to fertile land and relatively warmer climates) and the north developed manufacturing as its economic base during the Industrial Revolution. However, **sectorial development**—leaning on a single economic sector as the primary economic driver—leads to overdependence and can result in regional job losses if that sector fails.

Modern rural development is aimed at diversifying the economic base, and sectorial development has been replaced by territorial development. **Territorial development** integrates the development of multiple sectors or industries across a region using all of the available resources to encourage economic growth. Many regions now have clusters of manufacturing, service industries (such as banking, insurance, or tourism), and traditional agriculture. Additionally, many of these industries are linked because one sector purchases from the others. For example, farms require crop insurance, so agricultural businesses purchase services from insurance providers. Territorial development encourages local businesses to sell insurance as a means to support nearby farms.

Diversifying an economy and using territorial development practices reduces the impact of national and international economic downturns on a regional economy. Recent emphasis on economic development in rural areas has involved a strategy of **diversification**, which involves the reallocation of resources—such as land, capital, infrastructure, and labor—into new activities as a means of avoiding risk (UK Department for Environment, Food and Rural Affairs, 2012). Areas dependent on only one industry face numerous financial challenges if the market price of that product drops. Basing an economy on a variety of industries shields regions from the threat of unemployment, reduced tax revenue, and decreasing infrastructure investment when a recession occurs. Rural areas have therefore begun investing in less extractive industries, including recreation, niche manufacturing, and tourism. Rural areas have also emphasized locally produced economic development strategies. Rural economic development is covered in more detail in Chapter 5.

Understanding an industry's economic impact

Revenue from any industry is broken down into three different types of economic impacts as a tool for assessing the industry's economic contribution. Both tourism and agriculture provide economic returns.

The **direct effects** of tourism and agriculture are changes in local economic activity resulting from sales, such as businesses selling directly to tourists (that is, the actual money that tourists spend on their trip) or farmers selling to local customers. For tourism, these expenditures include travel arrangements—usually made while at home—and any in-country or local spending on tours, food, souvenirs, or other activities.

To serve visiting tourists, businesses need to secure inputs to operate. For example, restaurants need to purchase food and beverages in order to supply meals, and accommodations may need to purchase linens or towels for their guests. The changes in sales

Image 1.2 Rice fields near Sapa, Vietnam, a main tourist attraction
Source: Kynda R. Curtis

within a region in industries supplying goods and services to tourism businesses are called **indirect effects**. Without the direct input of tourism and the money that tourists bring, things like food and linens would be purchased in much smaller quantities. Indirect effects in agriculture include a farm's purchase of seeds, fertilizer, machinery, or packaging supplies.

Finally, tourism and agricultural businesses must hire staff. The money earned by that staff is spent in the local economy on housing, groceries, or school fees. These contributions to the local economy as a result of household spending of the income earned in tourism, agriculture, and supporting industries are called **induced effects**. Tourism introduces new currency that would otherwise not have entered the local economy; many of the jobs supporting the production of tourist goods and services would not exist otherwise. Exporting agricultural products also brings new money into an economy.

The sum of the direct, indirect, and induced effects is the total **economic impact** of an industry on an area. **Multipliers** capture the size of the indirect and induced (collectively referred to as secondary effects) in a given region, usually as a ratio of total effects to direct effects. For example, for every $1.00 spent on tourism in British Columbia, Canada, $1.50 is generated in indirect and induced effects, resulting in an economic contribution of $2.50 (see Table 1.1). If the tourist had not visited British Columbia and spent their $1.00, the additional $1.50 would not have been earned in the province.

Table 1.1 Tourism multipliers by country

Region	Tourism multiplier
British Columbia, Canada	1.50
British Virgin Islands	1.98
Cyprus	2.0
Hong Kong	0.98
Gwynedd, Wales	1.16
Puerto Rico	2.08
Washington, DC, USA	1.63

Source: Adapted from Horváth & Frechtling (1999)

Different destinations and industries have unique multipliers because of variations in the levels of economic **leakages**, which are the revenue lost to an area when inputs are purchased outside the local economy or newly acquired foreign currency is spent on buying foreign (as opposed to local) goods for resale. For example, hotels might import food from outside the region because they trust certain vendors or there may be fears related to food safety in the region where they do business. Another example is a farm buying commercial fertilizer rather than buying manure waste from the neighboring chicken farm. This money does not impact the region's economy and is lost as an indirect effect. Hotels may also hire senior executive staff from outside the region, who send large parts of their salary back to banks in their home region, reducing the induced effects of tourism in the region. Farmers may hire migrant laborers who send remittances to family members back in their home country. Using a tourism example, the regions in Table 1.1 with higher multipliers are better at keeping tourism money in the local economy and generate fewer leakages.

The majority of an international tourist's expenditures stay in their home country because the most expensive components of a trip are often purchased before the trip occurs. A large portion of expenditures on airline tickets, tour packages, or hotel accommodations may never reach the destination's local economy. Much of the money spent on accommodation may be transferred to the hotel's corporate headquarters, which may not be where the hotel room is actually located. Excursionists generally provide a larger economic impact in relation to gasoline, food, and other local items (Oh & Schuett, 2010). However, excursionists may not purchase hotel rooms or eat as many meals locally. Lastly, excursionists are more inclined to be repeat visitors, primarily because the distance of travel is much less. Often businesses and destinations promote their tourism services to local, regional, and long-distance travelers.

Measuring an industry's economic impact

Understanding the economic impact of any industry is important to measuring its contributions to society in relation to job creation and generating wealth. It is also important to understand the interrelationships between industries to ensure that the economic impacts remain in a region and leakages are reduced. For example, agriculture

Table 1.2 Direct requirements matrix

	Agriculture	Mining	Manufacturing	Construction
Agriculture	0.09	0.00	0.07	0.00
Mining	0.01	0.08	0.05	0.01
Manufacturing	0.13	0.08	0.25	0.28
Construction	0.01	0.01	0.00	0.00
Transportation	0.07	0.07	0.09	0.09
Service Industries	0.07	0.08	0.07	0.06
Public Administration	0.00	0.00	0.01	0.01
Intermediate usage	**0.38**	**0.32**	**0.54**	**0.45**
Wages, Salaries, Supplements	0.12	0.15	0.17	0.22
Gross Operating Surplus	0.42	0.45	0.16	0.21
Commodity Taxes	0.02	0.01	0.02	0.01
Indirect Taxes	0.02	0.01	0.01	0.01
Competing Imports	0.03	0.05	0.10	0.10
Duty on Complementary Imports	0.01	0.01	0.00	0.00
Complementary Imports	0.00	0.00	0.00	0.00
Duty of Complementary Imports	0.00	0.00	0.00	0.00
Total Production	**1.00**	**1.00**	**1.00**	**1.00**

relies on certain inputs, such as seeds, animal feed, water, fertilizer, and machinery. If the agriculture industry faces economic hardships, all of the industries that rely on agricultural production to purchase their products—such as seeds, animal feed, water, fertilizer, and machinery—will also be affected.

Input/output modeling (IO) is a quantitative process that is commonly used to measure these reciprocal relationships. In simple terms, IO quantifies the goods and services an industry purchases, the number of jobs (and jobs in connected industries) it generates, and the interconnections between industries (Leontief, 1986). Using Table 1.2, we see that in order to produce one more dollar of agriculture (say 1 kilogram of carrots), $0.09 of another agricultural product is needed (perhaps fertilizer) and $0.07 of transportation is needed (to get the carrots to market). Agriculture does not require inputs from mining or construction. Additionally, 1 kilogram of carrots provides $0.12 of labor and generates approximately $0.40 in taxes. These interconnections represent the indirect and induced effects of an industry. Notice that all of the multipliers add up to $1.00 (total production), meaning that the cost to produce a kilogram of carrots ($1.00) is made up of all the costs listed in column 2 (including $0.38 in intermediary usage costs and other costs). If those carrots were not produced, these sales would not occur, implying that not only would the agriculture industry lose potential sales, but that loss would also affect other agricultural producers, transportation businesses, employee wages, and regional taxes.

IO modeling works for established industries where input costs are well understood and relatively constant. However, tourism is not, in itself, an industry but rather a conglomeration of interrelated industries, including airlines, hotels, restaurants, and transportation. Input amounts for different destinations or travel types are not consistent and can be difficult to estimate. For example, what a tourist spends on a beach holiday in Jamaica will impact different industries than what a tourist spends on a driving trip along the Amalfi Coast of Italy.

To quantify the impacts of economic sectors that are not defined as industries in their own right and where the interconnection to other industries is not easily understood, we use **satellite accounting**. A **tourism satellite account** (TSA) is a detailed analysis of all the aspects of demand for goods and services associated with the activity of visitors, to observe the operational connections with the supply of such goods and services within the economy, and to describe how this supply interacts with other economic activities. The United Nations Statistics Division (2008) recognizes that conducting TSAs has numerous benefits for tourism destinations, including:

- providing credible data on the impact of tourism and associated employment;
- creating a standard framework for organizing statistical data on tourism;
- designing economic policies related to tourism development;
- providing data on tourism's impact on a nation's economy; and
- providing information on employment and wealth creation through tourism.

Tourists buy both tourism services, such as hotel accommodations, and non-tourism services, such as gasoline and groceries; TSAs measure tourism's economic impact better than IO. In order to understand the economic linkages within tourism, tourists must be surveyed on their spending patterns using established industries where the interrelationship is well documented. For example, tourists may be asked how much they paid for accommodations, gasoline, car repairs, restaurant expenditures, and souvenirs (retail). Table 1.3 highlights the common tourism expenditures and the industries associated with each.

By way of example, Table 1.4 shows the economic impact of tourism to Las Vegas, Nevada, USA, using the common industries associated with tourism spending (Table 1.3). For every $1.00 spent by tourists in Las Vegas, eating and drinking establishments earned $0.07 directly (maybe from a tourist's meal in a restaurant) and $0.05 indirectly (maybe from a tour company that bought boxed lunches from a restaurant). Additionally, the restaurant meal and the box lunch created 0.13 full-time jobs. According to this table,

---

Table 1.3 Tourism satellite account categories

Hotels
- Hotels and motels, including casino hotels
- Other accommodations
- New multifamily housing structures, non-farm
- Real estate

Other recreation including gambling
- All other amusement and recreation Industries excluding gaming
- Gaming excluded in hotel casinos
- Travel arrangement and reservation services
- Performing arts companies
- Spectator sports

Retail
- Motor vehicle and parts dealers
- Furniture and home furnishings stores
- Electronics and appliance stores
- Building material and garden supply stores
- Food and beverage stores
- Health and personal care stores
- Gasoline stations
- Clothing and clothing accessories stores
- Sporting goods, hobby, book, and music stores
- General and consumer goods rental except video

Table 1.3 continued

Independent artists, writers, and performers	**Eating and drinking establishments**
Promoters of performing arts and sports	Bread and bakery products
Museums, historical sites, zoos, and parks	Food services and drinking places
Fitness and recreational sports centers	General merchandise stores
Bowling centers	Wineries and breweries
Transportation	**State and local non-education**
Air transportation	Entertainment tax
Water transportation	Retail sales tax
Transit and ground passenger	Transportation airport fees
Scenic and sightseeing transportation	Gasoline tax
Highway, street, bridge, and tunnel construction	Hunting and fishing licenses
Maintenance and repair of highways, streets	Timeshare property tax
Automotive equipment rental and leasing	State and local non-education
	Other state and local government enterprises

Source: Slocum (2006)

tourism spending was US$20 billion (direct impact), with an additional US$13 billion spent by tourism businesses (indirect impact), creating 236,000 full-time equivalent jobs for the city of Las Vegas. It is easy to see how tourism revenue can be spread across a destination, providing economic returns to other businesses not normally associated with tourism.

Food tourism for economic development

From an economic development perspective, it is important to enhance and support interconnections between a region's traditional industries and emerging industries. Food tourism is increasingly being used to support rural development because it generates more indirect and induced economic impacts. Rather than importing food from outside a destination, businesses promote local food and increase the interrelationship between local agriculture and tourism.

Food has become a central part of the tourist experience, sparking an interest in promoting food as an enhancement of a particular destination or as a main attraction to a region. From an economic standpoint, tourists tend to be insensitive toward the price of food, which makes up one-third of tourism expenditures (Hall & Sharples, 2003). This topic is covered in more detail in Chapter 2. Food tourism offers two unique advantages for a region: it provides new experiences for tourists and encourages increased visitation, and it enhances economic impacts—such as higher farm income and job creation—to the community where tourists visit.

Table 1.4 Economic impact of tourism to Las Vegas, Nevada, USA

Commodity	Direct impact	Direct requirements	Indirect impact	Indirect requirements	Fulltime job equivalents	Induced requirements
Eating and Drinking Establishments	$1,369,866,414	0.07	$677,642,889	0.05	30,540.90	0.13
Retail	$385,473,916	0.02	$291,444,869	0.02	6,195.40	0.03
Accommodation including Hotel Casinos	$10,780,436,588	0.54	$9,010,439,648	0.64	111,156.60	0.47
Other Recreation including Gambling	$3,741,076,881	0.19	$2,118,066,307	0.15	54,116.30	0.23
Transportation	$3,099,961,872	0.15	$1,133,463,044	0.08	21,765.30	0.09
State & Local Non-Education	$746,056,000	0.04	$746,056,000	0.05	12,930.50	0.05
Total	**$20,122,871,671**	**1.00**	**$13,977,112,757**	**1.00**	**236,705.00**	**1.00**

Source: Slocum (2006)

Image 1.3 Local sourcing at Whole Foods in Las Vegas, Nevada, USA
Source: Kynda R. Curtis

Food tourism has the potential to increase economic multipliers, decrease leakages to a destination, and diversify rural areas with a strong agricultural economic base. It is easy to see why interest in accessing this lucrative market is on the rise. **Food tourism** is generally defined as a tourist's "desire to experience a particular type of food or the produce of a specific region" (Hall & Sharples, 2003, p. 10). Tourists must, of course, eat during their travels, but food also provides opportunities to "taste" the culture and experience a society or community. Food is recognized as an expression of heritage based on historical landscapes, traditional farming heritage, and social celebrations. Local recipes, often promoted through tourism, reflect traditional herbs and spices and traditional cooking techniques. It makes sense that consumers interested in local food at home would consider those interests when they travel. Consumers embrace the freshness and quality of local foods, support local economies, and establish personal relationships with farmers (Everett & Aitchison, 2008; Gumirakiza, et al., 2014). An increasing number of tourists wish to support local food regardless of where in the world they find themselves. This traveling public offers new and unique opportunities to support economies for local farms and other small businesses near tourism destinations or on routes between tourist attractions. This topic is addressed in more detail in Chapter 3.

Summary

This chapter provided an overview of the tourism and agricultural industries and the challenges facing rural economic development. Both tourism and agriculture are primary economic sectors. Measuring the impact of these industries on the economy is important in determining the economic impacts to an area, including the connections between industries and job creation. Estimating the direct effects of an industry and understanding the indirect and induced effects shows the size of the economic impact and the leakage of revenue from an economy. Using input/output modeling and tourism satellite accounts, multipliers can illustrate this impact.

This chapter also defined food tourism and demonstrated how food and agricultural partnerships can support local sourcing, which in turn creates a larger economic impact for a region through secondary effects. Combining food production, processing, and local recipes with tourism allows rural areas to diversify their economies, reduce risk, and decrease rural-to-urban migration through job creation. Food tourism also allows for increased economic impacts to a region.

Study Questions

1. How did a food experience impact a recent holiday taken?
2. Would you consider visiting a farm on vacation? Why or why not?
3. Which of the following expenditures would be a direct, indirect, or induced effect?
   a. One night at a bed and breakfast
   b. A wooden doll dressed in traditional clothing
   c. A flower arrangement used to decorate a restaurant's table
   d. The bus fare paid by a hotel worker on their way to work
   e. A tip to a local guide
   f. Complementary bottled water provided by a tour company
   g. Income tax paid by a craft vendor
   h. A donation made by a tourist to support a local orphanage
4. Would $100 spent in Cancún, Mexico, have the same economic impact as $100 spent in Puerto Plata, Dominican Republic? Why or why not? Which would you expect to be greater? Why?
5. Make a list of industries impacted by agriculture. Now make a list of industries impacted by tourism. What industries would gain the most from uniting food and tourism into a new tourist activity?

Definitions

Agriculture—the science or practice of farming and ranching, including cultivating the soil for growing crops and rearing animals to provide food and other products.

Direct effects—changes in local economic activity resulting from businesses selling directly to tourists.

Direct market sales—sale of farm products to consumers at farmers' markets, farm stands, and through community supported agriculture (CSA) and sales to local restaurants and grocery stores (as opposed to sales to wholesalers and other middlemen).

Diversification—the reallocation of resources—such as land, capital, infrastructure, and labor—into new activities as a means of avoiding risk.

Economic impact—the sum of direct, indirect, and induced effects.

Economies of scale—the cost savings gained by increasing levels of production.

Excursionists—visitors who use tourism services but live in close proximity to the destination and who only stay for a short period of time (a few hours to a single day).

Food tourism—a tourist's desire to experience a particular type of food or the produce of a specific region.

Indirect effects—changes in sales, income, or employment within a region in industries supplying goods and services to tourism businesses.

Induced effects—changes in expenditures within a region as a result of household spending of the income earned in tourism and supporting industries.

Input/output modeling—a quantitative economic technique that represents the interdependencies between different branches of a national economy or different regional economies.

Leakages—the revenue lost to an area when inputs are purchased outside the local economy or newly acquired currency is spent on buying foreign (as opposed to local) goods for resale to tourists.

Multipliers—a ratio of total effects to direct effects that captures the size of secondary effects.

Rural development—the process of improving the quality of life and economic well-being of people living in relatively isolated and sparsely populated areas.

Satellite accounting—a quantitative economic technique that estimates the interdependencies between economic activities that are not defined as industries in their own right.

Sectorial development—development that depends on a single economic sector or industry as the primary economic driver.

Territorial development—development that integrates multiple sectors or industries in a specific region.

Tourism—the temporary movement of people to destinations outside their normal places of work and residence, the activities undertaken during their stay in those destinations, and the facilities created to cater to their needs.

Tourism satellite account—a detailed analysis of all the aspects of demand for goods and services associated with the activity of visitors undertaken to observe the operational interface with the supply of such goods and services within the economy and to describe how this supply interacts with other economic activities.

CASE STUDY 1.1

The economic impact of food tourism in England

Susan L. Slocum and Kynda R. Curtis

The United Kingdom's Department for Environment, Food and Rural Affairs (DEFRA) tasked independent consulting firm ICF International (ICF) with measuring the economic impact of food tourism on the rural economy of England. The challenges were, first, defining local food in contrast to non-local food; second, defining a rural area; and, third, determining who qualifies as a tourist. Not an easy task!

Due to the lack of statistical data, ICF developed six case studies across eight rural areas in England to generate qualitative data. These areas represent very different agricultural structures and tourist types. For example, southwest England is known for its dairy production, particularly cream that is naturally sweetened by the variety of lush grasses on which the cows feed. Northern England is famous for Northumberland sausage and other processed meats. Exmoor and Tebay are located near national parks and see many outdoor enthusiasts as visitors, while Dersingham and Hunstanton are located close to the historic port of King's Lynn. IFC's goal was to assess a variety of food tourism destinations to establish a basis for generalizing spending patterns of rural tourists and establish a tourism satellite account that could be used to calculate the economic impact (direct, indirect, and induced) of food tourism in rural England.

The size of the economic impacts was determined not only by the scale of visitor expenditures but also by how much money was retained in the local economy (the multiplier effect) through:

- tourist expenditures on local food (direct effects);
- local purchases of food and drink and other goods and services from local suppliers (indirect effects); and
- wages and profits paid to local residents and the extent to which that income is also re-spent in the local economy (induced effects).

The process of defining food tourism was complex. ICF found that even establishing a definition of local food and drink was difficult, as each rural area defined *local* differently. Based on the common theme of distance that food traveled to reach the consumer. ICF chose to define local food and drink as "that produced within 30 miles from where it is purchased" (ICF International, 2016, p. 10). "Rural" areas, consisting of villages and towns with a population of 10,000 or fewer residents, had previously been defined by the government. In order to measure tourists' expenditures on local food, ICF used data from the local food and drink sector, which included a range of activities including farming, processing, food service, and food retail activities (supermarkets, specialty food shops, food festivals, and farmers' markets). Because the data available did not separate tourist and local receipts, standard multipliers were used.

The scale of food tourism was very different at each research site. For example, Padstow and Bude attract different types of visitors and have different levels of food tourism development, even though they are both located on the north Cornwall coast. Because Bude is just establishing food and drink tourism activities, the contribution of food tourism to the economy was less than half of the impact of food tourism in Padstow, even though Bude is a larger community and attracts more tourists overall. The degree of economic benefits accrued by area were based on four conditions:

- a strong and varied supply chain that is willing and able to source produce locally;
- high levels of awareness and a good reputation for local food and drink amongst visitors;
- a high-quality tourism offer to attract and support high-value visitors; and
- strong support from public sector decision-makers and delivery bodies (p. 2).

DEFRA also wanted ICF to establish a set of best practices to encourage successful food tourism development for rural communities exploring food tourism opportunities. Many of the barriers to successful food tourism were also identified. Local food was perceived to be more expensive, which was problematic in areas where tourists were more price sensitive. In some areas, the seasonality of local agriculture did not coincide with the tourist season, limiting the availability of local food

Image 1.4 Local farm shop in central England, UK
Source: Kynda R. Curtis

Image 1.5 Agritourism with tea shop in England, UK
Source: Kynda R. Curtis

for purchase. In addition, many local food establishments (farm shops, farmers' markets) were hard to access or were poorly advertised to tourists. Many retail establishments did not know how to access local food as supply chains were sporadic or underdeveloped. Lastly, some areas showed a lack of cohesion between public sector decision-makers and tourism businesses.

The study estimated that sales of local food and drink totaled almost UK£10 billion across England, of which almost UK£3 billion was sold in rural areas. Total tourism expenditures on local food and drink were estimated to be UK£2.6 billion across England, of which approximately UK£1.4 billion was spent in rural areas. This study suggested that tourists account for almost 50% of local food and drink sales in rural areas, supporting an estimated 81,000 jobs and adding UK£1.5 billion of additional value across rural tourism economies in England.

Questions

1 What are some of the problems associated with the way ICF measured food tourism? Can you suggest a different approach? What might be some of the weaknesses associated with your new approach?
2 Do you think the estimated economic impact is accurate? If not, is it too high or too low? Why?
3 What are simpler and more cost-effective ways for a small community to measure the success of their food tourism industry?

References

ICF International. (2016). Rural tourism and local food and drink: Final report to the Department for Environment, Food and Rural Affairs. Retrieved from randd.defra.gov.uk/Default.aspx?Menu=Menu&Module=More&Location=None&Completed=0&ProjectID=19114

References

Asif, M. (2012). Physico-chemical properties and toxic effect of fruit-ripening agent calcium carbide. *Tropical Medicine and Public Health*, 5(3), 150–156.

Australian Bureau of Statistics. (2012). Australian farming and farmers. Retrieved from www.abs.gov.au/AUSSTATS/abs@.nsf/Lookup/4102.0Main+Features10Dec+2012

California Assembly Committee on Jobs, Economic Development, and the Economy. (2014). Fast facts on California's agricultural economy. Retrieved from ajed.assembly.ca.gov/sites/ajed.assembly.ca.gov/files/Fast%20Facts%20on%20California's%20Agricultural%20Economy.pdf

California Department of Food and Agriculture. (2014). California agricultural production statistics. Retrieved from www.cdfa.ca.gov/statistics/

Day-Farnsworth, L., McCown, B., Miller, M., and Pfeiffer, A. (2009). Scaling up: Meeting the demand for local food. Madison, WI: UW-Extension Ag Innovation Center and UW-Madison Center for Integrated Agricultural Systems. Retrieved from www.cias.wisc.edu/wp-content/uploads/2010/01/baldwin_web_final.pdf

Everett, S. and Aitchison, C. (2008). The role of food tourism in sustaining regional identity: A cast study of Cornwall, South West England. *Journal of Sustainable Tourism*, 16(2), 150–167.

Food and Agriculture Organization of the United Nations. (2016). The state of agricultural commodity markets—Trade and food security: Achieving a better balance between national priorities and the collective good. Retrieved from www.fao.org/3/a-i5090e.pdf

Gumirakiza, J.D., Curtis, K., and Bosworth, R. (2014). Who attends farmers' markets and why? Understanding consumers and their motivations. *International Food and Agribusiness Management Review*, 17(2), 65–82.

Hall, C.M., and Sharples, L. (2003). The consumption of experience or the experience of consumption? An introduction to the tourism of taste. In C.M. Hall, L. Sharples, R. Mitchell, B. Cambourne, and N. Macionis (Eds.), *Food tourism around the world: Development, management and markets* (pp. 1–24). Oxford: Butterworth-Heinemann.

Horváth, E., and Frechtling, D.C. (1999). Estimating the multiplier effects of tourism expenditures on a local economy through a regional input–output model. *Journal of Travel Research*, 37(4), 324–332.

Leontief, W. (1986). *Input–output economics* (2nd ed.). New York: Oxford University Press.

Mathieson, A., and Wall, G. (1982). *Tourism: Economic, physical and social impacts*. Harlow, UK: Longman.

Moseley, M.J. (2003). *Rural development: Principles and practice*. London: SAGE.

Oh, J.Y., and Schuett, M.A. (2010). Exploring expenditure-based segmentation for rural tourism: Overnight stay visitors versus excursionists to fee-fishing sites. *Journal of Travel & Tourism Marketing*, 27(1), 31–50.

Slocum, S.L. (2006). The impact of tourism on the economy of Nevada: A tourism satellite account and computable general equilibrium model (Master's thesis). University of Nevada, Reno.

U.S. Department of Agriculture, Economic Research Service. (2007). Food dollar series. Retrieved from www.ers.usda.gov/data-products/food-dollar-series

U.S. Department of Agriculture, National Agricultural Statistics Service. (2016). Direct farm sales of food: Results from the 2015 local food marketing practices survey (ACH12-35/). Retrieved from www.agcensus.usda.gov/Publications/2012/Online_Resources/Highlights/Local_Food/LocalFoodsMarketingPractices_Highlights.pdf

UK Department for Environment, Food & Rural Affairs. (2012). How farmers can add business activities to traditional farming to develop new sources of income. Retrieved from www.gov.uk/guidance/diversifying-farming-businesses

United Nations Statistics Division. (2008). Tourism satellite account: Recommended methodological framework (ST/ESA/STAT/SER.F/80/Rev.1). Luxembourg: United Nations. Retrieved from https://unstats.un.org/unsd/tradeserv/tourism/manual.html

United Nations World Tourism Organization. (2014). *World tourism barometer and statistical annex*, *12*(5), Madrid: World Tourism Organization.

Willer, H., Yussefi, M., and Sorensen, N. (2010). *The world of organic agriculture: Statistics and emerging trends 2008*. London: Earthscan.

World Travel and Tourism Council. (2017). Travel & tourism global economic impact & issues 2017. Retrieved from www.wttc.org/-/media/files/reports/economic-impact-research/2017-documents/global-economic-impact-and-issues-2017.pdf

Chapter 2

Food tourism and sustainable communities

Overview

This chapter explores both the positive and negative impacts of tourism and agriculture on the economy, environment, and society. It describes sustainable development and sustainable tourism as avenues to support food tourism development that attempts to mitigate the negative impacts of food tourism and defines both weak and strong sustainability. It shows how food tourism can be used to protect the environment and traditional societies. A description of the tragedy of the commons demonstrates how people make independent decisions without realizing the far-reaching consequences of everyone making the same choices. It concludes with a discussion on bridging and bonding social capital.

Learning Objectives

This chapter will enable students to:

1   Analyze the benefits of food tourism to local communities.
2   Understand the impacts and externalities of food tourism growth.
3   Describe globalization and its impacts on societies and culture.
4   Define sustainable development and sustainable tourism.
5   Evaluate weak and strong sustainability.
6   Understand food tourism as environmental protection and an expression of culture.

Impacts of food tourism

Chapter 1 described the macroeconomic effects of tourism, but tourism creates other impacts, both positive and negative. Tourism can impact the environmental health of a destination and the social fabric and culture of a region. Local residents may be affected by these impacts even if they are not directly involved in the tourism industry. **Externalities** are costs or benefits that affect individuals who did not choose to incur them. One common example is pollution. Rural areas often lack public transportation opportunities, so tourists may have to rent cars, increasing air pollution. Tourists also produce a lot of waste, which can increase the need for landfills. When hotels or shopping districts are developed to support tourism, parking spaces may become scarce or traffic may increase. Agriculture can result in the seepage of chemicals into groundwater or entice biting insects that feed on cattle as well as human populations. Residents did not choose to incur these costs; they are all negative externalities associated with tourism or agricultural growth.

Estimating the costs and benefits of a development project can be tricky. One problem occurs when an impact is not easily measurable. For example, tourism tax revenue can support schools (a benefit), but how should improvements in a local school district based on tourism tax revenue be measured? "Quality" in education can be measured by school budgets, students' grades, the number of students finishing high school, or the qualifications of teachers hired (more qualified teachers require higher pay). Of course, in many poorer areas, students may drop out of school in order to work in tourism jobs, such as driving a taxi or selling souvenirs on the street. This would be considered a cost to increased tourism.

Understanding the costs and benefits of food tourism is also more difficult than it sounds. Increased revenue for farmers is a positive impact of food tourism, but many businesses involved in food distribution may lose out by direct sales to consumers. If tourists shop at local farmers' markets, grocery stores may lose revenue, which might mean that grocery stores hire fewer people. Most studies have shown that increases to local food purchases result in higher prices and more indirect and induced impacts to a community, but these increased prices are passed along to local residents. In general, food tourism results overall in more positive benefits than negative costs to communities (Telfer & Wall, 1996).

Determining whether the positive benefits of tourism growth outweigh the negative costs can be accomplished through a cost-benefit analysis. A **cost-benefit analysis** estimates and totals the equivalent monetary value of project benefits and costs within a community to establish whether those projects are worthwhile. Cost-benefit analysis is covered in detail in Chapter 5.

Benefits of food tourism

Tourism can provide small business opportunities and create jobs, which often require low levels of human capital. **Human capital** is defined as the knowledge (education), habits, and social and personality attributes (including creativity or entrepreneurship) held by members of society and the ability to perform labor to produce economic value (O'Sullivan & Sheffrin, 2003). In areas that lack quality educational opportunities, such as developing countries or rural communities, tourism jobs provide employment to people who may not otherwise have the opportunity to work. However, because tourism supports the relatively uneducated members of society, tourism jobs are often low paying and seasonal. The availability of tourism jobs may lead to inward migration, which can cause overcrowding when infrastructure (electricity, clean water, transportation, or housing) is not developed at the same pace. This influx of new people can also affect the social and cultural relationships of a community, bringing cultural conflict and changing values to the region.

Food tourism provides many positive impacts for local communities, such as creating opportunities to market and develop regions without traditional tourism resources (e.g., natural attractions) or enhancing destinations that already offer typical vacation

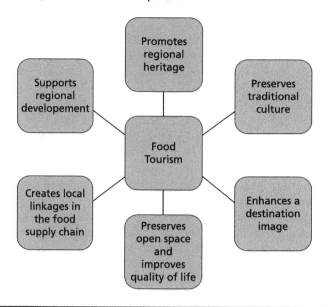

Figure 2.1 Benefits of food tourism

experiences. Food tourism allows communities to turn their food traditions into market-able attractions and can create new business opportunities for local farmers and food producers. Food can be promoted through food-specific events (e.g., food festivals, farmers' markets) that enhance the appeal of tourist attractions and foster the develop-ment of sustainable community economies. Food and food-related traditions, events, and products can be valuable assets to enhance or develop local communities involved in tourism. Figure 2.1 shows many advantages of developing food tourism.

Sustainable tourism

Globalization—the process of international integration as a result of the exchange of worldviews, products, and ideas—is encouraged by the ease and affordability of travel, increased communication channels, and the internationalization of corporations bringing Western products and services to the world. Globalization has created enormous oppor-tunities for fast access to international tourism destinations, but this access has come with a cost: environmental degradation and cultural assimilation. The loss of traditional dress in favor of blue jeans and T-shirts, conservation practices that remove traditional societies from nature reserves, and the increasing use of a cash economy (rather than bartering and trade) are other results of globalization. Some authors argue that tourism itself is a result of globalization, while others view tourism as a cause of globalization. Regardless of whether tourism is a cause or an effect of globalization, the two phenomena are closely linked. Fayos-Solà (2002) recognizes that:

- demand for tourism and travel—including intra- and inter-regional travel—has increased worldwide, although many people still travel only locally or are strangers to tourism;

- tourism demands are globally similar; consumer preferences, tastes, and lifestyles have converged, although the type of travel is segmented; and
- tourism supply has become concentrated and homogenized; distribution systems and business mergers have expanded, although new specialist agents have appeared on the scene.

The effects of globalization on agriculture are covered in more detail in Chapter 4.

Despite the known benefits of food tourism, the tourism industry has traditionally encouraged international food chains, a product of globalization that provide tourists with welcome brand consistency regardless of location (Slocum & Everett, 2010). A **brand** is a name, term, design, or other feature that distinguishes one seller's product from those of

Image 2.1 Kona Coffee, Kona, Hawai'i, USA
Source: Kynda R. Curtis

others and is very important in tourism marketing. Marriott, Hilton, Jin Jiang International, and Accor Hotels are well-known hospitality brands. Sourcing local food for tourism can build a destination brand that supports other local tourism businesses, such as museums, festivals, and bed-and-breakfast establishments. For example, the district of Kona on Hawai'i is well known for its coffee, and the Kona brand is internationally recognized. Kona coffee has also become a major draw for tourists who visit local coffee farms. Branding is covered in more detail in Chapter 9.

The concept of sustainable development has grown since the 1980s as a response to increased globalization, which has resulted in the destruction of natural habitats and traditional cultures. **Sustainable development** is development that meets the needs of the present without compromising the ability of future generations to meet their own needs (World Commission on Environment and Development, 1987). Sustainable development emphasizes the **triple bottom line**—the economy, the environment, and the society. The goal is to grow the economic opportunities of a region while at the same time maintaining natural and social resources so that future generations have an opportunity to experience them. For example, sustainable development around food can preserve agricultural lands by providing income for small farms, discouraging the sale of land to developers, and ensuring open space preservation into the future. The World Commission on Environment and Development (1987) provides four components of sustainable development:

- holistic planning and strategy making;
- preservation of ecological processes;
- protection of heritage and biodiversity; and
- development that can be sustained into the future.

Tourism depends on natural and cultural resources that offer travelers a unique experience and differentiate destinations from one another. **Sustainable tourism**—tourism development that meets the needs of present tourists and host regions while protecting and enhancing opportunities for the future—is a natural offshoot of the sustainable development movement (United Nations World Tourism Organization, 2005). Sustainable tourism development can assist in the improvement of the triple bottom line to ensure a vibrant tourism industry.

Weak sustainability, a concept derived from environmental economics, is the philosophy that man-made capital is more important than natural capital (Neumayer, 2003). In other words, humans will develop technologies to replace dependency on natural resources. In tourism, weak sustainability places equal emphasis on the economy, environment, and society and is often viewed as "greening" the tourism value chain to support a more ethical approach to tourism consumption.

Strong sustainability assumes that "human capital" and "natural capital" are complementary but not interchangeable, so that the existing stock of natural capital must be maintained and enhanced because the functions it performs cannot be duplicated by manufactured capital (Dobson, 1998). Strong sustainability prioritizes the environment for protection, followed by societies and, lastly, finding economic opportunities only after developing the environment and society. Figure 2.2 shows the differences between weak and strong sustainability. Strong sustainability is often associated with ecotourism or community-based tourism, where conservation or poverty reduction efforts are supported through tourism-generated revenue.

Foodways are the cultural, social, and economic practices relating to producing and consuming food (Darnton, 2013) and are closely tied to the triple bottom line of

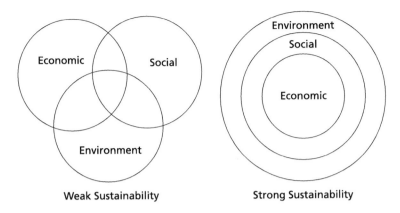

Figure 2.2 Weak versus strong sustainability

sustainability. By using traditional food items and preparing them in traditional ways, foodways preserve both the environmental and social components of food production. Foodways also offer an opportunity to enhance the tourism experience and sustain local economies. Foodways imply a strong form of sustainability because emphasis is placed on ensuring that traditional components of food production, cultural expression, and consumption maintain priority over economic opportunities.

Food tourism as environmental protection

One reason that local food sourcing is increasing in popularity has to do with concerns about the potential impacts of globalized food chains on the environment (Gössling & Hall, 2013). There is ample evidence that intensive agriculture increases the need for chemical inputs into the production process (e.g., chemical fertilizers, ripening agents). Additionally, long-distance hauling of agricultural goods contributes to greenhouse gas emissions (Delind, 2006). Local agriculture, especially in the form of small farms, reduces these environmental impacts by offering a more seasonally varied and shorter supply chain. Because of the close interaction between farmers and customers, many local farms support free range or pasture grazing practices that reduce the need for chemical additives, hormones, or antibiotics in food. There is also evidence that local farms encourage waste reduction by recycling byproducts into the farm's production process in order to reduce input costs (Gössling & Hall, 2013), such as using animal waste as fertilizer. Farmland protection also preserves open space, which increases quality of life for community members (Gimmi et al., 2011).

We know that human population growth creates increased strain on limited resources, which jeopardizes sustainability (Hardin, 1968). Environmental problems are often an externality associated with economic growth. All goods produced in an economy come from a natural resource. For example, plastic water bottles are made from petroleum, and cardboard packaging is made from trees. Most companies do not intend to create negative environmental consequences. Instead, each company uses resources without considering that all other companies are also using resources, an example of the **tragedy of the commons**. Individuals, acting independently and rationally according to their individual self-interest, behave contrary to the best interests of the whole group by depleting some common resources.

An example in agriculture might be ranchers grazing their cattle on publicly owned land. Each rancher may know that the pasture can only feed so many head of cattle without depleting the grass. If one rancher believes he can make additional money by adding one more cow to the field, which will cause very little damage, then it is in his best interest to do so. Of course, all the other ranchers are thinking the same thing. As each rancher adds another cow, the population becomes too large and no grass returns the next season. The most viable solution to the tragedy of the commons is to assign property rights to the pasture so that only one rancher has access to it. In the long run, it is in the rancher's best interest to ensure the health of the pasture. Since he owns the land, he has control over how many cattle graze on the land.

Tourism is also prone to the tragedy of the commons. Food tourism provides a viable way to encourage more positive environmental changes to agricultural systems. Urban populations, who often become tourists in rural areas, can be well-versed in the local food movement and are inclined to support organic, free-range, and cage-free food options (Renko et al., 2010). Furthermore, foodways ensure that elements of traditional production and consumption remain a part of the food tourism experience, reducing the impacts of globalization.

Urban tourists often envision pristine rural environments and idyllic lifestyles as opportunities for rest and relaxation (Croce & Perri, 2010). Rural areas must preserve tranquil places in order to remain competitive in tourism markets over the long run. Urban travelers also view rural populations as friendly and welcoming, creating a sense of hospitality, making them natural partners in tourism development. Farming communities can support additional preservation of their environments and reduce pressures to develop their valuable landscapes by capitalizing financially on these beliefs. In other words, the effects of the tragedy of the commons can threaten the environment and the perceptions of visitors can negatively impact the sustainability of a region's triple bottom line.

The social value of food

Food plays a role in strengthening local economies by encouraging the use of local products, which have a larger economic impact on a region than using products imported from elsewhere. Food is essential for tourist consumption, constituting up to one-third of tourism expenditures (Hall & Sharples, 2003). The fact that food is a basic need for tourists empowers regional development agencies to use agriculture and traditional recipes as an economic development tool, creating employment and small business opportunities for local residents. Economic growth comes not only from gastronomic establishments (e.g., restaurants, hotels) but also from farmers and other local producers. Research suggests that consumers prefer food that is labeled (or branded) as locally grown and are willing to pay a premium for it over food of unknown or other origin (Bosworth et al., 2015; Curtis, 2014). Labeling is covered in Chapter 6.

When traveling either to local destinations or to another country, people want to experience local gastronomy. Food in Latin American countries is a great example of such tendencies. For instance, countries in Mesoamerica (which includes Mexico and Central America) are historically, culturally, and economically related and have similar but distinct food traditions. Dishes such as tamales, while common throughout Mesoamerica, are not cooked the same way everywhere. Travelers can discern noticeable regional differences within the framework of a national cuisine, such as Mexican food, if they take enough

Image 2.2 The restaurant at Montgrony Monastery, Catalonia, Spain, serves local specialties and has preserved ancient architecture
Source: Susan L. Slocum

time to travel throughout the whole country. Every community has idiosyncratic food and drink traditions that are central to their folklore.

Promoting local foods and local food traditions allows communities to develop pride in their heritage and culture, which can lead to the development of **social capital**, the links, shared values, and understandings that enable individuals and groups in a society to trust one another and so work together (Keeley, 2007, p. 102). Social capital consists of two primary elements: social networks (who people know) and the inclinations that arise from these networks to do things for one another (norms of reciprocity). Figure 2.3 shows the conditions that support social capital. Social networking and cooperation provide avenues for working together to develop forms of economic growth. For example, say that a community wants to build a park. If the local government has a piece of land but no money to build the park, the community may need to utilize their networks to complete the project. A church group may clear the land on weekends. A local contractor may donate supplies. Other small businesses may donate funding, and students at a local college may design the park. The community can build its park by working together.

There are generally two types of social capital. **Bonding social capital** are social networks made up of homogeneous groups of people. Examples of these networks include college fraternities and sororities, church youth groups, and street gangs. Industry

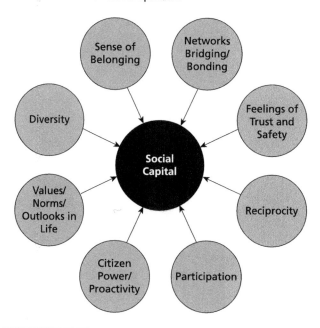

Figure 2.3 Elements of social capital

associations, such as networks of local growers or members of a local convention and visitors' center, would also constitute bonding social capital. These are groups of people with common values and beliefs. **Bridging social capital** refers to social networks made up of socially heterogeneous groups that include people with different backgrounds, such as famers who may work with tourism companies to create a food-based destination.

A combination of bridging social capital and government or industry leadership provides the most effective form of social capital building and "is where sound development, management, and promotion of rural tourism initiatives, such as food tourism, can best be implemented" (Everett & Slocum, 2013, p. 796). Food tourism can help unite farmers in one area or restaurants in another area (bonding social capital) or it may bring together both farmers and restaurants (bridging social capital) to promote a local food destination.

Summary

Sustainability is vital to the long-term success of food tourism destinations because it allows communities to maintain the unique attributes (environments and culture) that encourage tourism visitation. This chapter explained the triple bottom line of sustainability and discussed weak and strong sustainability models.

Globalization can potentially impact the sustainability of communities. In a positive light, globalization can offer opportunities to increase human capital, but it can also cause negative externalities such as the overuse of resources. The importance of doing cost-benefit analyses to ensure that changes in a community caused by tourism provide net benefits overall cannot be overstated.

Food tourism has the potential to provide positive influences for sustainable development by decreasing negative environmental impacts and developing social capital. In particular, food tourism can bring together different groups within the community (bridging social capital) to mediate both environmental and social changes. Food tourism can preserve open space and traditional cultures, promote regional heritage, and enhance a destination's image. It can also provide tourism opportunities for regions that do not possess traditional tourism attributes such as outdoor activities and heritage resources.

Study Questions

1 How has globalization affected the choice of restaurants in your town? How authentic do you think these restaurants are?
2 Which of the following are examples of weak sustainability and which are examples of strong sustainability? Why?
   a Staying for a week at a working cattle ranch working with cows and learning about cowboy culture
   b Spending two hours at a pick-your-own farm collecting raspberries to take home
   c Spending a weekend in Italy at a cooking school learning authentic recipes
   d Picking and crushing grapes in Chile to make your own signature wine
   e Visiting a spice market in Morocco to see, touch, and taste a variety of authentic traditional flavorings
3 What are the positive and negative impacts of tourism in your area? How could food tourism increase positive impacts and reduce negative impacts? What potential side effects do you predict?
4 Explain a situation on your university campus that exemplifies the tragedy of the commons. How has that area been degraded? What can be done to encourage more responsible use of that area?
5 Think of your personal networks. Where do you find bonding social capital? Where do you find bridging social capital? What can each of these different networks accomplish? What are some of the challenges each of these networks face?

Definitions

Bonding social capital—social networks of homogeneous groups of people with common values and beliefs.

Brand—a name, term, design, or other feature that distinguishes one seller's product from others'.

Bridging social capital—social networks of socially heterogeneous groups that include people with different backgrounds.

Cost-benefit analysis—a method for estimating and totaling the equivalent monetary value of a project's benefits and costs within a community to establish whether the project is worthwhile.

Externalities—costs or benefits that affect a party who did not choose to incur them.

Foodways—cultural, social, and economic practices relating to the production and consumption of food.

Globalization—the process of international integration as a result of the exchange of worldviews, products, and ideas.

Human capital—the stock of knowledge, habits, social, and personality attributes, including creativity, embodied in the ability to perform labor to produce economic value.

Social capital—the links, shared values, and understandings that enable individuals and groups in a society to trust each other and so work together.

Strong sustainability—the belief that the existing stock of natural capital must be maintained and enhanced because the functions it performs cannot be duplicated by manufactured capital.

Sustainable development—development that meets the needs of the present without compromising the ability of future generations to meet their own needs.

Sustainable tourism—tourism development that meets the needs of the present tourists and host regions while protecting and enhancing opportunities for the future.

Tragedy of the commons—a situation where individuals, acting independently and rationally according to their individual self-interest, behave contrary to the best interests of the whole group by depleting a resource.

Triple bottom line—the economic, natural, and social resources that must be protected in sustainable development.

Weak sustainability—the philosophy that man-made capital is more important than natural capital.

CASE STUDY 2.1

Tourism and agricultural development: A sixty-year waltz to a sustainability tune (Kagbeni, Mustang, Nepal)

David G. Simmons and Laxmi Gurung

Foreign tourism only began in Nepal in 1950. The remote Himalayan village of Kagbeni provides unique insights across a sustained period of the coevolution of the tourism and agriculture sectors. Gurung (2012) identified five distinct periods of development.

Isolated and independent (1950–1962)

Early foreign trekkers who traveled through Kagbeni mainly did so in commercial tour groups. All supplies, including fresh fruit and vegetables, were provided by the tour organizers, and tourists stayed in nearby camping sites provided by the trekking companies. Visitors rarely ventured into local villages or interacted with residents. From the outset, tourism presented cash opportunities for local workers, and it soon competed with local food producers for labor. As a result, many locals abandoned farming during these times, and rural-to-urban migration occurred as farmers moved south to Pokhara City or India for better employment opportunities, resulting in their lands remaining uncultivated.

Increasing connectivity, increasing demand (1962–1976)

The opening of a basic airport at Jomsom in 1962 (a three-hour trek to the south) led to an increasing number of more independent tourists. The Nepalese government made investments in tourism training opportunities (human capital) for residents, including the development of a national language (versus the numerous ethnic languages that had previously been in use). However, basic education and English proficiency set the foundations for future tourism growth. The government also made available new agricultural crops that supported tourists' taste preferences, but most locals did not see the value in growing them.

Development (1976–1992)

As the regional Annapurna Conservation Area became known to the outside world, the flow of tourists increased dramatically. By 1993, over 14,000 tourists arrived in Jomsom annually, with many trekking through Kagbeni on their way to Upper Mustang. Small groups of trekkers began staying in local teahouses and small lodges. Some trekkers began eating local foods and liking some of them.

Adventurous and socially engaged tourists provided Western-style recipes for the locals to prepare and sell (e.g., omelets, potatoes, pizza, various meats). In response, farmers began growing different types of food not previously known in the area (e.g., vegetables and fruit) to sell directly to tourists and lodge owners. The first real linkages between tourism and agriculture began through the increasing use of local foods to feed foreign tourists.

Integrated management (1993–2006)

The relationship between tourism and agriculture became much stronger as the economic benefits became recognized. Increasing use of fresh, locally produced foods decreased costs to lodge owners, generated revenue for farmers, and reduced costs for visitors. Farmers were not only encouraged to grow different foods but also to raise and sell livestock to meet tourists' increasing demands for meat. Slowly, locals and returning migrants started to re-cultivate land that had been left fallow for many years. This period is seen as the turning point for villagers in understanding the importance of linking local agriculture with tourism to make both profitable.

Contemporary times (2007–present)

The start of this period is marked by the completion of the 4-wheel-drive road access to Kagbeni, which caused additional growth in visitor arrivals and the diversification of tourist attractions (especially to a sacred Hindu Shrine, Muktinath, 10.5 kilometers further up the valley from the village). Today, 30,000 predominantly independent visitors visit this remote village annually. Among the 216 households in Kagbeni, 22 have a small hotel or lodge, while 10 have shops and 10 operate small teahouses. Gurung (2012) reports that about 60 households benefit directly from tourism, while many of the others benefit indirectly through various activities.

Discussion

Tourism and agriculture links in the remote Himalayan village of Kagbeni can be seen as mutually beneficial to both sectors. This has not been instantaneous but a consequence of trial and error over 65 years. At the core of today's integration is the fact that both sectors are labor intensive and seasonal but peak at different times (i.e., agriculture in the summer and winter while the tourist season is in the spring and autumn). As tourism has increased, so too has the need for local agricultural products and workers. Positive economic growth has encouraged villagers who had previously emigrated to return to Kagbeni. Positive interaction between early independent trekking tourists and local villagers has been identified as a key initiator of integration between the tourism and agricultural sectors. Development has also been assisted by slow, but constant, attention to "market links," particularly infrastructure development, such as the airport (1962) and road links (2006). A final supporting element has been the central government's nation-building program focusing on a common language (Nepali), human resource development, and regional attraction

Image 2.3 A local farmer and his son in Mustang District, Nepal
Source: Laxmi Gurung

development initiatives such as the creation of the regional Annapurna Conservation Area. Furthermore, the introduction of better varietal seeds to assist agricultural diversity has supported economic growth. Today, agriculture and tourism are the cornerstones of sustainable livelihoods in the area.

Questions

1 Why didn't early tourists make direct community links with the community?
2 What are the key physical elements required in opening remote areas to tourism and agriculture development?
3 What impact did globalization have on Kagbeni? What were the positive and negative impacts of globalization on the economy, the environment, and the society? Did globalization result in net benefits or net costs?

References

Gurung, L. (2012). *Exploring the links between tourism and agriculture in sustainable development: A case study of Kagbeni VDC, Nepal*, (master's thesis). Lincoln University, Lincoln, New Zealand.

Food tourism, agriculture, and cultural heritage in the South Pacific

Tracy Berno

Take a moment and imagine tourism in the South Pacific. What did you picture? Palm trees, white sand beaches, and beautiful blue water? Other than some coconuts or tropical fruits, not many people imagine the rich cuisines of the South Pacific. It is fair to say that tourists do not travel to the South Pacific for the food.

Socio-cultural influences such as urbanization, migration, and globalization have contributed to changes in cuisine and food consumption patterns in the South Pacific. As a result, countries such as Fiji and Samoa are losing their traditional foodways. This places them at risk of losing both their unique food heritage and the diversity of crops that support it. As a result of these changes, the authentic food of the South Pacific is not only at risk but the region's cuisine now has a very poor reputation. Victor Bergeron, who founded the famous Polynesian-themed Trader Vic's restaurant chain, once said in an interview, "The real, native South Seas food is lousy. You can't eat it" (OChef, nd) Mr. Bergeron's observations about South Pacific food, however, are not entirely accurate. Although the food that visitors to the islands experience may be somewhat lacking, the countries of the South Pacific all have cuisines rich in history and heritage.

Unfortunately, rather than reinforcing the cultural integrity and heritage value of traditional South Pacific cuisine, tourism has often had the opposite effect. Much of the food served in the tourism industry fails to deliver an authentic South Pacific experience. Some menus do offer "Pacific food," but for the most part this cuisine is a parody of authentic Pacific foods, inauthentic and reflecting what has come to be expected as Pacific Island "tourism food" at themed, island-night events. As Pacific chef Robert Oliver stated in response to the absence of authentic Pacific foods in the tourism industry, "Consider the consequences of telling a whole region that their food isn't good enough. Food is core to who we are ... it is what nurtures us, it is our culture and sense of self ... it is us" (Oliver, 2013a, p. 16).

For us as researchers, this raised an interesting question: Could tourism be "flipped" and used to rejuvenate and preserve authentic South Pacific cuisines? We decided to explore this further by looking at links between agriculture and tourism in Samoa and Fiji to identify ways that would encourage Pacific Islanders to celebrate their traditional cuisine and food heritage and promote it as a unique, valued attribute of an authentic Pacific tourism experience. Our approach was different from more traditional value-chain approaches in that it focused on activities to both stimulate demand and to build capacity for providing local cuisine in the tourism industry. We worked in partnership with farmers, chefs, restaurateurs, government agencies, non-governmental organizations, national tourism organizations, and a range of other stakeholders to identify barriers and facilitators along the value chain linking agriculture to cuisine in tourism.

Another unique aspect to the work we undertook was discovering that local chefs are in a powerful position as gatekeepers, leaders, and influencers in relation to what is offered on tourist menus. As Chef Oliver has pointed out, "In tourism-led economies [like those in the South Pacific], the menus are the business plan of the nation" (Oliver, 2013b). We therefore placed particular emphasis on chefs as gatekeepers and on the power of cuisine to facilitate positive social, cultural, and economic change. In order to support these chefs and help make the connections

Image 2.4 Me'a Kai: How a cookbook can empower rural economies
Source: Penguin Random House

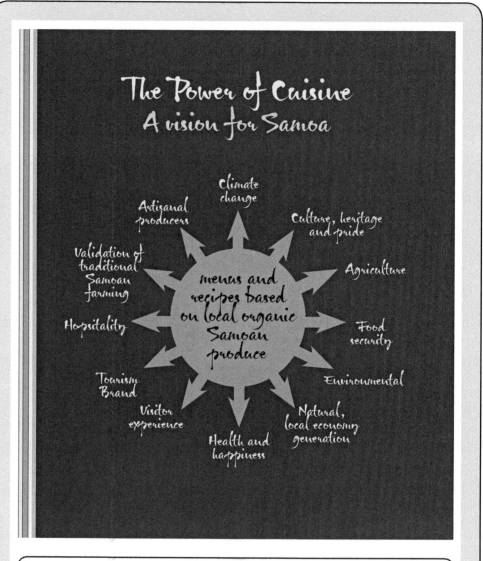

Image 2.5 The power of cuisine: A vision for Samoa
Source: Penguin Random House

with the farmers who supply them, we developed two types of tools: two Pacific cuisine cookbooks focusing on the farm-to-table approach and an accompanying television series highlighting the successes of Pacific chefs in their efforts to champion Pacific cuisine in tourism.

Over the course of our research we found that incorporating authentic South Pacific foods into the tourism experience can be a powerful means for sustaining and reinforcing a destination's cultural identity and cultural capital. An important element of this is working along the entire farm-to-table value chain and harnessing the influence that chefs can have in promoting cultural heritage through cuisine/menu choices. This type of approach can also contribute to outcomes as diverse as climate change mitigation, enhanced visitor experiences, economic development for rural communities, a stronger and more differentiated tourism brand, and reinforcement of traditional agricultural products and practices (which in the South Pacific are primarily organic).

Questions

1 With particular reference to the relationship between cuisine and cultural heritage, in what ways can agriculture-tourism linkages (farm-to-table) create opportunities for both producers (host nationals) and consumers (tourists)?
2 What are the benefits of taking a multi-stakeholder approach to considering the role that traditional foods and cuisine play in tourism?
3 What consequence may result from emphasizing restaurants and chefs in defining or promoting ethnic food?

References

OChef (nd). The hunt for Polynesian recipes. Retrieved from www.ochef.com/95.htm.

Oliver, R. (2013a). The power of pacific cuisine. *Spasifik*, *58*, 14–18.

Oliver, R. (2013b). Recipes for development. [Presentation at Tedx Auckland 5 August 2013.] Retrieved from https://www.youtube.com/watch?v=orfB1UkoKdQ

References

Bosworth, R., Bailey, D., and Curtis, K. (2015). Consumer willingness to pay for local designations: Brand effects and heterogeneity at the retail level. *Journal of Food Products Marketing*, *21*(3), 274–292.

Croce, E., and Perri, G. (2010). *Food and wine tourism: Integrating food, travel and territory*. Wallingford, UK: CAB International.

Curtis, K.R. (2014). Premium potential for geographically labeled, differentiated meat products. *Journal of Agriculture, Food Systems, and Community Development*, *4*(2), 97–111.

Darnton, J. (2013). Foodways: When food meets culture and history. East Lansing, MI: Michigan State University Extension. Retrieved from msue.anr.msu.edu/news/foodways_when_food_meets_culture_and_history

Delind, L. (2006). Of bodies, places, and culture: Re-situating local food. *Journal of Agricultural and Environmental Ethics*, *19*(2), 121–146.

Dobson, A. (1998). *Justice and the environment: Conceptions of environmental sustainability and dimensions of social justice*. Oxford: Oxford University Press.

Everett, S., and Slocum, S.L. (2013). Food and tourism: An effective partnership? A UK-based review. *Journal of Sustainable Tourism*, *21*(7), 789–809.

Fayos-Solà, E. (2002). Globalization, tourism policy and tourism education. *Acta Turistica*, *14*(1), 5–12.

Gimmi, U., Schmidt, S.L., Hawbaker, T.J., Alcántara, C., Gafvert, U., and Radeloff, V.C. (2011). Increasing development in the surroundings of U.S. National Park Service holdings jeopardizes park effectiveness. *Journal of Environmental Management, 92*(1), 229–239.

Gössling, S. and Hall, C.M. (2013). Sustainable culinary systems: An introduction. In C.M. Hall and S. Gössling (Eds.), *Sustainable culinary systems: Local food, innovation, tourism, and hospitality* (pp. 3–44). London: Routledge.

Hall, C.M., and Sharples, L. (2003). The consumption of experience or the experience of consumption? An introduction to the tourism of taste. In C.M. Hall, L. Sharples, R. Mitchell, B. Cambourne, and N. Macionis (Eds.), *Food tourism around the world: Development, management and markets* (pp. 1–24). Oxford: Butterworth-Heinemann.

Hardin, G. (1968). The tragedy of the commons. *Science, 162*(3859), 1243–1249.

Keeley, B. (2007). *Human capital: How what you know shapes your life.* Paris: OECD Publishing.

Neumayer, E. (2003). *Weak versus strong sustainability: Exploring the limits of two opposing paradigms.* London: Elgar.

O'Sullivan, A., and Sheffrin, M.S. (2003). *Economics: Principles in action.* New Jersey: Pearson Prentice Hall.

Renko, S., Renko, N., and Polonijo, T. (2010). Understanding the role of food in rural tourism development in a recovering economy. *Journal of Food Products Marketing, 16*(3), 309–324.

Slocum, S.L., and Everett, S. (2010). Food tourism initiatives: Resistance on the ground. In C.A. Brebbia (Ed.), *The sustainable world (WIT transactions on ecology and the environment 142)* (pp. 745–757). England: WIT Press.

Telfer, D. and Wall, G. (1996). Linkages between tourism and food production. *Annals of Tourism Research, 23*(3), 635–653.

United Nations World Tourism Organization. (2005). Making tourism more sustainable: A guide for policy makers. Retrieved from www.unep.fr/shared/publications/pdf/DTIx 0592xPA-TourismPolicyEN.pdf

World Commission on Environment and Development. (1987). *Our common future.* Oxford: Oxford University Press.

Chapter 3

Food tourism offerings

Overview

Food tourism is an umbrella concept comprising a number of viable food-based tourism opportunities and on-farm enterprises. This chapter defines and discusses a variety of food tourism activities and products, including agritourism, culinary tourism and food trails, food and drink events and attractions, food souvenirs, and local sourcing. Each aspect of food tourism has advantages and disadvantages depending on community or destination attributes and the businesses and facilities available. The roles of authenticity and commodification in food tourism offerings are also covered.

Learning Objectives

This chapter will enable students to:

1 Define authenticity and commodification as they apply to food tourism offerings.
2 Understand and explain the differences between the various types of food tourism offerings.
3 Evaluate and explain the challenges and opportunities facing different food tourism strategies.
4 Explain how competition and cooperation can exist simultaneously to vet coopetition.

Authenticity and commodification in food tourism offerings

As mentioned in Chapter 1, food tourism is "the desire to experience a particular type of food or the produce of a specific region" (Hall & Sharples, 2003, p.10). Food tourism implies cultural distinctiveness, a quality, experience, or product unique to a specific region. These experiences can be exotic, like eating ostrich at the Carnivore Restaurant in Nairobi, Kenya, or they involve attending an event centered on a regional specialty, such as garlic ice cream at the Garlic Festival in Gilroy, California, USA.

Food tourism should promote the **authenticity** of food, meaning that food should be true to place, based on historically accurate understandings of periods and cultures, and uncontaminated by market forces (Scarpato & Daniele, 2003). In other words, authenticity is the idea that something is true, accurate, or real. But authenticity is much more complicated than this simple definition implies.

For example, tourists expect people in rural areas to be hospitable. They also believe the pace of life is much slower than in urban areas and feel that visiting rural areas offers an opportunity to go back in time (McGehee & Kim, 2004). Obviously, this idyllic perspective of rural life does not address many of the economic hardships associated with rural communities, such as low pay, limited job opportunities, and an aging population. Managing the tourists' expectations and the authenticity of rural lifestyles can be difficult.

From a production standpoint, authenticity can incorporate traditional materials, traditional production processes, or traditional modes of delivery. An example might be delivering a traditional meal accompanied by dancing and art. The ingredients may be traditional, although they may be prepared or cooked in a microwave. The cooking techniques may be traditional (roasting over an open fire), but the variety of food may be a recent import (maybe a new breed of pig). Or maybe the process of sitting on the

Image 3.1 Open food market in Bangkok, Thailand
Source: Kynda R. Curtis

floor and eating communally without utensils is traditional, regardless of how the food is prepared.

From a consumer perspective, tourists may often have preconceived ideas about what is authentic; variations from those ideals may feel inauthentic. In other words, culture is often perceived as static (never changing), and authenticity implies that there is only one "real" way to do something. Reality and the forces of globalization as discussed in Chapter 2 means that culture is actually ever-changing and authenticity (like beauty) is in the eye of the beholder.

The very process of producing and selling food to tourists commodifies culture. **Commodification** refers to the process of transforming goods, services, ideas, and people into commodities or objects of trade in an effort to support economic growth or profit (Mitchell & Hall, 2003). Commodification naturally alters the authenticity of a cultural good. Take for example a local Chinese restaurant. Most likely, the flavor of the food has been altered to accommodate local tastes and preferences and is different from food found in China. If local residents do not like the food, the restaurant will go out of business. The process of adjusting to customer preferences alters the food and makes it inauthentic.

Tourism often results in adjustments to local culture. First, local culture changes to meet the expectations of the tourist and match what the tourist believes to be authentic. Second, tourism defines authenticity through basic supply and demand interactions. What is "good" or authentic will sell better, and what is "bad" or inauthentic will be unprofitable. Managing authenticity and commodification is an important part of developing food tourism because the long-term sustainability of any tourism product or destination depends on economic success. At the same time, making sure that locals feel that the tourism product is authentic, is vital if tourism is to be used to preserve cultural traditions, and develops community pride (as in sustainable tourism). Chapter 9 discusses collaboration in more detail, but stakeholders should come to a common understanding of authenticity when developing a tourism destination.

Types of food tourism

As tourism destinations become increasingly competitive, it is vital to find ways to differentiate them through authenticity. Food tourism comprises a variety of different types of food and tourism business opportunities and tourism experiences, each with their own necessary resources, management challenges, and clientele. While the number of potential food tourism activities is extensive, this chapter looks at five specific types:

- agritourism;
- culinary tourism (including drink tourism);
- food and drink events and attractions (including food and drink trails);
- food-based souvenirs; and
- local sourcing and value-added products.

Although these types share many similarities (and some offerings may fall into multiple categories), the overall goal is to understand each sector's unique traits and be able to evaluate which food-related opportunities best fit local tourism development goals.

Figure 3.1 provides an overview of different types of facilities, events, activities, and products that fall under the umbrella of "food tourism." Keep in mind that many types of food tourism opportunities can fit into multiple categories. For example, a winery is a

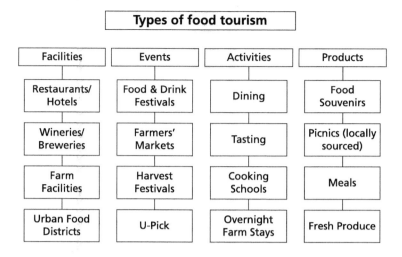

Figure 3.1 Types of food tourism
Source: Adapted from Everett & Slocum (2013)

type of facility, but it is also a culinary activity that allows tourists to experience wine tastings and pairings; wine is also a product that tourists may want to buy as a souvenir. Each of the following sections highlights the needs and considerations unique to businesses and destinations in each sector. Local populations may also be potential food tourists, and many of the tools provided apply to local customers, excursionists, and tourists visiting from farther away.

Agritourism

As students in a food tourism class, it is reasonable to assume that many of your grandparents lived or worked on a farm when they were young. It is also safe to say that many of your fellow students have never lived on a farm. If you are an agriculture student, you may be the exception, or perhaps you have worked on a farm or visited farms owned by family members. If you are a tourism student, odds are that you have never even visited a farm. You are not alone. The industrial development of farming (covered in Chapter 4) and rural-to-urban migration that has dominated development since the end of World War II has isolated recent generations from food production (Sims, 2009). Farm-based activities provide a way for urban and suburban dwellers to reconnect with the land, nature, and rural people (Petty, 2002).

From an agricultural perspective, **agritourism** is "rural tourism conducted on working farms where the working environment forms part of the product from the perspective of the consumer" (Clarke, 1999, p.27). More broadly, agritourism incorporates farming activities into the tourism experience. Other parts of the world may have different definitions, some referring specifically to farm stays, as in Italy, or a wide variety of other activities, such as buying produce directly from a farm stand, navigating a corn maze, picking fruit, feeding animals, farm tours, related farm-based special events, or staying at a bed-and-breakfast on a farm. Other terms associated with agritourism are "agritainment," "value-added products," "farm direct marketing," and "sustainable agriculture."

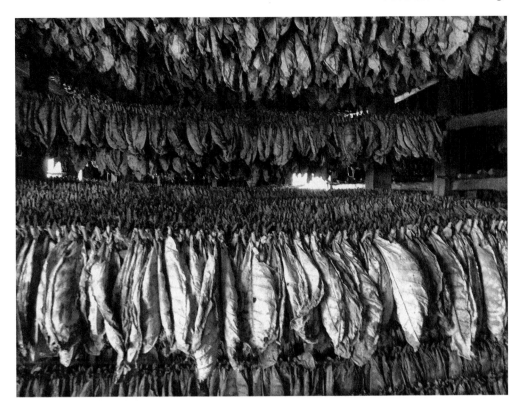

Image 3.2 A tobacco farm open for tourism in Cuba
Source: Kynda R. Curtis

Agritourism most commonly occurs in rural areas with working farms. These areas may have limited opportunities to participate in tourism (due to a lack of "traditional" tourist attractions), and the primary draw to tourists is open space and idyllic communities.

Often visitors want to participate in farm-based activities, whether harvesting vegetables and fruit (pick your own), interacting with farm animals (petting zoos or cattle ranching), or hiking through the open space surrounding agricultural communities. Agritourism also offers an opportunity for visitors to engage in **voluntourism** (often called volunteer tourism), which is a holiday that involves working alongside local residents, usually in an effort to give back to communities or help alleviate poverty (Wearing, 2004). Since rural areas face a number of economic challenges (see Chapter 5), voluntourism on working farms can be beneficial to rural communities where labor is scarce and can offer authentic opportunities for tourists.

Planning is one of the most important steps when starting a new farm-based venture or a rural agritourism destination. It is important to assess the properties on which agritourism will occur and ensure that tourists will be able to find the properties offering farm-based activities. Participant safety must be a primary concern (see Chapter 11). It is also necessary for the farm enterprise to offer something unique and fun, as tourists desire activities, not just tours. They expect to learn something new, so educational or interpretive programs are helpful. Table 3.1 provides a list of important consideration for any agritourism enterprise.

Table 3.1 Planning an agritourism enterprise

The plan	The activities
Determine what will be offered	Identified some activities that seem doable, that fit with the goals and resources of the farm. List all the tasks or steps to get started. Once done, have someone else review it.
Protect the investors and the visitors	Make sure to understand the regulatory and legal aspects of any new enterprise. Develop a risk assessment plan.
Make sure the ideas are good ones	Call the agricultural or tourism office for input, or enlist the help of a business counselor or event planner. What may sound good to one person may not sound good to others.
Start small	Develop a launch date for the activity, then work backwards and list all the resources needed and the tasks that need to be performed to be ready for the launch.
Get the word out	Make sure publicity figures prominently into all plans as it takes a lot of promotion to get the attention needed to launch a new enterprise. Advertising and promotion costs may outpace returns initially. Remember that word of mouth is a key way to build business, so if it is done right the first time, the next visitors will not be so hard to attract.
The soft opening	A way to get started without a big launch is to plan a small activity targeted at a select group to test the ideas. The use of local customers can provide valuable insight.
Take it slow	Take time to get feedback from visitors about what else they might like to see, do, learn or buy at the farm. Then each year, add in another attraction. Don't forget to plan with the big picture in mind.

Source: Adapted from Ochterski & Roth (2008)

Culinary tourism

As discussed in Chapter 2, food can be an expression of **culture**, which is defined as learned knowledge based on material and non-material elements such as beliefs, art, morals, customs, laws, behaviors, values, traditions, and folklore (Timothy & Ron, 2013). Food traditions are often based on sociocultural traditions, climate, migration patterns, local varieties of ingredients, and history (Timothy, 2011). However, the flavor of our food is changing. Not only has industrialization created the "McDonaldization" of recipes (fast, greasy, and always the same), but the globalized food chain requires fruits and vegetables to be harvested prior to ripening (and chemically ripened during transport) and ethnic food to be altered to support the tastes of mainstream consumers (Delind, 2006). The globalization of food has given rise to the revitalization of tasting traditional foodways.

Another type of food tourism—**culinary tourism**—is "the pursuit of unique and memorable eating and drinking experiences" (Long, 2004). Tourists believe that experiencing a region or country's food is essential to understanding its culture (Boyne & Hall, 2003). Culinary tourism is more than just trying new and exotic foods; it unites anthropology, folklore, and history and can comprise ethnic recipes, international cookbooks, folk and food festivals, cooking shows, cooking schools, specialty food stores, food tours, breweries, wineries, and historical attractions. Many related businesses across the globe have capitalized on their regions' culturally unique cuisines.

Image 3.3 Culinary tourism event highlighting specialty meats in Australia
Source: Kynda R. Curtis

Culinary tourism requires a destination approach to tourism that involves numerous businesses and community organizations working together. While local residents may have a clear understanding of local cuisine, tourists may not understand specific cultural or historical cooking recipes or techniques. It is not only important to establish a destination image that ties into culinary heritage but also to communicate these characteristics to visitors who may have little or no experience in the area. By partnering with other food and cooking establishments, tourists find common cultural threads that encourage experimentation with new foods or recipes. Other examples of culinary tourism include visiting restaurants specializing in local foods or attending cooking schools. Table 3.2 highlights a few tourism destinations and their culinary specialties.

Table 3.2 Culinary destinations and food specialties

Destination	Specialties	Environment
Louisiana Cajun	Gumbo Jambalaya Dirty rice Boudin sausage Po'boy sandwiches	French and Caribbean influences with local ingredients (shrimp, pork sausage, celery, cayenne pepper).
Mediterranean	Greece – Moussaka, pita breads, feta Turkey – Baklava, pilaf, couscous Italy – Ribollita, parmigiano reggiano, antipasto Spain – Tapas, paella, gazpacho	Common climate results in similar ingredients, such as fresh vegetables (tomatoes, onions, cucumbers), olive oil, sundried tomatoes, dates, lamb/goat, mild cheeses, and yogurt.
Scandinavian	Fish Berries Venison	Harsh climate without fruits or vegetables for 9 months of the year. Food consists of tubers (turnips, parsnips), dried berries (bilberries, lingonberries), wild game (reindeer, moose), and fish (salmon, pike, herring).
Brazilian	Feijoada Caruru Caipirinha (sugar, lime and distilled Cachaça)	Native ingredients influenced by European and African cooking techniques. Staples include cassava, guaraná, açaí, cumaru and tacacá, and tropical fruits such as mango, papaya, and guava.
Vietnamese	Stir fried fish, meat, tofu Dipping sauces – garlic, ginger, soy sauce Canh or Pho type soups	Comprises a combination of five fundamental tastes: spices, organs, colors, senses, and nutrients. Contrasting texture and flavors are an important part of Yin Yang balance.

Drink tourism

Drink tourism focuses on beverages rather than food as the key element of the tourism experience. Drink tourism is most commonly associated with alcoholic beverages—

examples include visiting a winery, exploring a whiskey trail, or watching craft beers being made—but other types of drink experiences are gaining popularity. It is now possible to visit tea or coffee plantations in Costa Rica or Sri Lanka or experience afternoon cream tea (and accompanying scones) in Devonshire, England. Coffee houses, such as those in Europe or the Middle East, have also gained popularity. Understanding the subtle difference between Greek coffee and Turkish coffee is as rewarding as tasting the difference between a Petite Sirah and a Cabernet Franc or learning which rice wines of Japan, Korea, and China should be consumed warmed versus iced.

Food-based events and attractions

Historically, food choices were often dictated by social status or environmental landscapes reflecting lifestyles. Celebrating these unique lifestyles and the annual cycle of food production gave rise to special events and later, event tourism (Getz et al., 2014). Food and drink have always been a part of cultural celebrations and religious holidays, such as Thanksgiving in the United States, or Eid al-Fitr (the end of Ramadan) in Muslim communities.

Modern events or attractions are generally more commercial in nature, although they are still useful in showcasing local distinctiveness. **Food-based events**, which are closely related to culinary tourism, are special events focusing on food or drink and can include food festivals, farmers' markets, wine regions, and food trails. **Food-based attractions** include museums (such as the Lindt Chocolate Museum in Cologne, Germany), famous markets (such as Pike's Place Market in downtown Seattle, Washington, USA), or food-processing plants (such as the Dole Pineapple factory in Hawaii, USA). Food-based attractions are generally permanent structures that operate all year, whereas special events are temporary gatherings offered cyclically (weekly, monthly, yearly, etc.).

It is important to ensure that events do not compete with other fairs in the same region; establishing a distinct theme or targeting a specific audience can help avoid duplication. While food events may start out small, long-term growth planning is important. Food events are rarely profitable on their own, but they offer new avenues for sponsorship and marketing outlets for local businesses, so managing sponsorship is an important consideration. Communities may start non-profit or charity groups to run special events and hire event managers with specialized skills. A regional board of directors can support further community collaboration and inclusion to ensure that the festival remains true to the heritage it was designed to support rather than excluding local attendees. Event managers are responsible for planning and executing the festival or fair, specifically overseeing site preparation, staging and production, event support, sponsorship, and security. Figure 3.2 provides additional considerations for food and drink festivals.

Marketing a food event starts months before the festival and may continue right through to the following year's event. Tourists usually plan ahead and want to know what activities to expect in their intended destination months before they arrive. Media partners and sponsors can help reduce advertising expenses and can support early marketing when cash flow is tight. They can incorporate festivals into existing advertising, public relations, and marketing campaigns and around major nearby tourism destinations. A well-planned event brochure print-production schedule helps drive festival planning deadlines, and the creation of individual press releases ensures that visitors keep the festival on their travel itineraries.

Starting a food and drink festival
Establish a theme that enhances your destination image
If a similar program already exists, avoid duplication
Gain buy-in where you want to hold the event
Vary the programming for a general audience
Make sure the space can accommodate the crowds
Make sure vendors can handle attendee volumes
Create a budget and get bids from reputable companies
If this is your first time planning the event, hire an outside festival vendor
Market through traditional tourism channels, partnering with tourism area businesses

Figure 3.2 Starting a food and drink festival

Food and drink trails

A **food or drink trail** is a linear route primarily intended for recreational and educational travel involving the consumption of local food or drink (Marsh, 2004). Related local businesses may establish trails or other joint products in order to market them together. Even if one brewery competes with another brewery, it is to both brewers' advantage to work together to enhance the visitor experience when forming a drink trail, a phenomenon referred to as "coopetition" (Larsen & Hutton, 2011). **Coopetition** allows stakeholders in a particular industry to simultaneously cooperate and compete in order to support joint community-building projects. By differentiating their products (one offering tours, the other offering brewing classes), tourists can visit both breweries and have unique opportunities to learn more about brewing. Table 3.3 shows some well-known food and drink trails.

Another option is to think about offering special, focused, low-cost events, such as guided tastings, to bring people in, or offering large-scale events that highlight regional varieties and provide an opportunity for coopetition behavior. All tourism stakeholders must be invited to participate in order to ensure community buy-in and that the event accurately represents community heritage. Chapter 9 includes further discussion on collaboration and networking, but it is important to note that food and drink trails require especially cooperative attitudes.

Food-based souvenirs

Souvenirs—"commercial objects usually purchased during travel that remind people of past experiences and places visited" (Collins-Kreiner & Zins, 2013, p.30)—offer opportunities for small businesses to make additional sales. Most food-based souvenirs are value-added items produced by local businesses and sold at tourist attractions, local retail outlets, farms, or special events. Examples include homemade jams and salsas,

Table 3.3 Unique food and drink trails

Location	Name	Specialty	Website description
Ireland	Irish Food Trail	Urban restaurant trail	On the Irish Food Trail you will experience the best Irish food, restaurants and pubs in Ireland. This is an exciting walking food tour of Irish cities, in which 'craic agus ceol' is the main course.
Louisiana, USA	The Cajun Boudin Trail	Traditional cooking	The Cajun Boudin Trail puts you on the path to discovering Louisiana's best boudin and other regional specialty items, be they pork chop sandwiches, beef jerky, cheesy boudin balls, specialty sausages, cracklin, smoked meats, plate lunches, stuffed chickens, or chili dogs.
Singapore	Food Safari	Urban restaurant and market tour	Little India, Chinatown, Geylang Serai, and Katong each offer distinctive, delicious cuisines. Penetrate them with local experts from Makansutra, who organize "mainstream" and "off the beaten track" food safaris, plus a fascinating midnight tour.
Bregenzerwald, Austria	The Cheese Road	Dairy tours and special events	The Bregenzerwald area is famed for its ski routes, its mountain walks, and its cheese trail. The Cheese Trail comprises 69 alpine cheesemakers, innkeepers, and grocers, each marked with a large K.
Tasmania, Australia	Cradle to Coast Tasting Trail	Regional self-drive tours	By using interactive maps and itineraries you'll unfold the delights of the Cradle to Coast Tasting Trail. With rolling green hills and stunning coastal vistas as a backdrop you will be welcomed into a world of berry-sweet possibilities, paddock to plate dairy, dark fudge desires, and malty cheer.
Coorg, India	Coffee Trails	Farm stays and tours	When you visit a plantation, you can join hands with expert coffee pickers. They entertain you with never-heard-before information on the techniques of coffee picking.

honey, cheese, or handcrafts made from farm scraps (baskets made from corn stalks or mats made from coconut leaves).

Traditional souvenirs provide opportunities for visitors to support artisan products, such as value-added food items. Healy (1994) suggests that souvenirs offer a number of advantages for rural business development. Residents do not need to leave the local area to make money from souvenir production; they offer opportunities for women, the elderly, and the infirm in areas where these individuals may be marginalized; producing souvenirs requires low levels of capital investment; and locally-made souvenirs have low levels of economic leakage. Furthermore, food-based souvenirs can be produced during the growing season but stored and sold throughout the year. The food safety aspects of producing value-added foods are covered in more detail in Chapter 11, but businesses that engage in value-added food production should pay close attention to local regulations, as food safety is of critical concern in such endeavors.

Food offers unique opportunities as souvenirs because it allows tourists to relive a particular memory through the re-consumption of culture. Tourists can also take food souvenirs home to share with loved ones who may not have traveled. Purchasing souvenirs falls within the activity of shopping, one of the most common tourist activities, and food-based souvenirs are gaining in popularity.

Local sourcing

The food service industry is highly competitive, and businesses attempt to differentiate themselves from their competition in a variety of ways. Some use price as a distinguishing feature (family-style versus high-end) and may not be receptive to more expensive food offerings. Others, however, may use local food as a distinctive feature; they may be willing to cook using local and seasonal products, which may cost more than other options. **Local sourcing**—selling local agricultural products to tourism establishments, such as restaurants, hotels, and conference centers—is often considered a component of culinary tourism. Local sourcing requires food establishments to buy produce that is in season, requiring menu options to change throughout the year. Restaurants that cater to tourists may be more flexible with seasonal varieties, although sometimes patrons may expect their favorite menu item to be available year-round.

Local includes **value-added products**, which "have experienced some type of post-harvest processing" (Curtis et al., 2015, p.50). Examples include turning raspberries into jam or drying beef for jerky. Value-added could also refer to specialty items such as regional labels that promote local products or organic vegetables. In general, anything that adds value to basic food supplies is considered value-added. These products generally cost more than unprocessed food items. Value-added can also refer to cooking of regional food items using specific regional recipes. Local sourcing may include raw goods (fruits, meats, cheeses)—to which a restaurant adds value through preparation—or locally produced hot sauces that restaurants buy directly and make available to their patrons.

Restaurants

Consistency and reliability are important to food service establishments, which require fresh food, especially fruits and vegetables, to be delivered several times each week. Farmers may have difficulty competing with large-scale producers with large-scale marketing budgets. Dealing with multiple farmers requires considerable time, something that chefs lack. If a farm is unable to source enough food to meet demand, one solution may be to partner with neighboring farms.

Another option is using drop-off points, such as **food hubs**—centrally located facilities with business management structures that aggregate and distribute local foods—which can consolidate and transport agricultural products in bulk to food service establishments. Food hubs provide logistical support, marketing savvy, and food safety expertise, and they deliver a steady supply of "locally grown" products that can be channeled into the large-scale purchasing systems that restaurants, hotels, and institutions already use to source their ingredients. Food hubs also help match supply with demand so that if a temporary surplus exists in one location, the hub can make that excess available to dealers in other market areas through reciprocal purchasing agreements. The result is stable prices and predictable income for farmers.

Hotels and conference centers

Many hotels or conference facilities may be limited in their ability to purchase directly from farmers. These venues—often multinational corporations—may be expensive or bureaucratic to work with, requiring extensive certifications, paperwork, and rigorous safety standards. Partnering with a major distributor, such as Cisco or Avendra, can mitigate some of these issues. Major distributors have recognized the value in sourcing locally and have programs to provide local food. These companies have a wide reach and often hold contracts with hotels or conference facilities.

Hotels and conference centers may operate jointly but have different requirements for their unique sets of customers. Hotel operations require larger supplies of food during the peak seasons, usually summer, when people are traveling recreationally and farmers are at their busiest. Conference centers need larger supplies in the off-season when people travel for business and when farms are idle (often without produce). Hotels and conference centers usually know in advance the number of guests they expect and, therefore, the quantity of food they need. Hotels require a more consistent supply while conferences may be more randomly scheduled.

Remember that many hotels and conference centers are owned by multi-national corporations, which means that supply chains are complex. These companies partner with suppliers across multiple countries for purchasing food and beverages, heavy equipment, linens and pillows, and personal toiletries. Additionally, sourcing options for most hotels and conference centers are constrained by national sourcing contracts with major distributors.

Summary

In order for food tourism to be successful, tourists and locals must perceive experiences to be authentic. As food becomes commodified, maintaining authenticity becomes more difficult. While tourists have expectations about what is authentic, destinations need to incorporate educational opportunities to ensure that tourists learn about cultural practices and ensure that food opportunities remain authentic for local residents as well.

A variety of food tourism types can highlight regional distinctiveness and provide economic opportunities for both rural and urban areas. This chapter described five primary types of food tourism, although there are many others. Food tourism provides business development opportunities, whether they occur on a farm (agritourism) or in urban restaurant districts (culinary tourism). Businesses may, at first, consider other food tourism enterprises to be competition, but food tourism destinations must find ways to develop cooperation, or coopetition, to compete against other food-based destinations.

Study Questions

1 Which types of food tourism enterprises complement one another? Which ones would be difficult to combine? Why?
2 Consider your hometown. How would you define authentic food from your area? What types of food tourism would complement your town's image? Why?
3 Categorize the following types of food tourism experiences (there may be more than one good choice):
   a Visiting a farmers' market
   b Attending a wedding in an elaborate barn
   c Visiting a winery for a tour and tasting
   d Driving along Scotland's Malt Whiskey trail
   e Watching a cooking demonstration at a county fair
   f Having a romantic dinner at a five-star restaurant
   g Watching chocolate being made at a Swiss chocolate factory
4 Go to wwoof.net, the site for World Wide Opportunities on Organic Farms. Find a specific volunteer opportunity. What attracted you to this opportunity? What aspects do not appeal to you? How could it be improved?

Definitions

Agritourism—rural tourism conducted on working farms where the working environment forms part of the product from the perspective of the consumer.
Authenticity—the idea that something is true, accurate, or real.
Commodification—the process of transforming goods, services, ideas, and people into objects of trade in an effort to support economic growth or profit.
Coopetition—simultaneously cooperating and competing in order to support joint community-building projects.
Culinary tourism—the pursuit of unique and memorable eating and drinking experiences.
Culture—learned knowledge based on material and non-material elements such as beliefs, art, morals, customs, laws, behaviors, values, traditions, and folklore.
Drink tourism—tourism focused on beverages rather than food as the key element of experience.
Food hub—a centrally located facility with a business management structure that may aggregate, store, process, distribute, and/or market locally or regionally produced food products.
Food or drink trail—a linear route primarily intended for recreational and educational travel involving the consumption of local food or drink.

Food-based attraction—a permanent structure that draws tourists and operates all year.

Food-based events—special events focusing on food or drink that include food festivals, farmers' markets, wine regions, and food trails.

Local sourcing—sale of local agricultural products to tourism establishments such as restaurants, hotels, and conference centers.

Souvenirs—commercial objects usually purchased during travel that remind people of past experiences and places visited.

Value-added products—products that have experienced some type of post-harvest processing that adds value to the basic food item.

Voluntourism—holidays that involve working alongside local residents, usually in an effort to give back to communities or help alleviate poverty.

CASE STUDY 3.1

Building food experiences: The case of food events in small regions

Cristina Barroco, Luísa Augusto, and Lurdes Martins

The Dão Lafões and Alto Paiva Region (DLAPR) of Portugal includes five municipalities: Oliveira de Frades, S. Pedro do Sul, Vila Nova de Paiva, Viseu, and Vouzela. This region has a total area of 1,372,000 km^2 and approximately 142,000 inhabitants.

The DLAPR offers a set of differentiating local products, associated mostly with agricultural and animal production. These are promoted through different strategies, with special emphasis on organizing food events. These events can play a vital role in promoting small regions with fewer tourism opportunities.

Current situation and main goals

In the DLAPR, there are seven traditional products classified as Protected Designation of Origin (PDO) and three products classified as Protected Geographical Indication (PGI). Other local products of excellence can also be found and are widely used in regional dishes. Themed food events—festivals, presentations of new products, innovative food processing methods, developing regional specialties tours, restaurants and famous chefs—can effectively promote these products.

This study aimed to identify all of the food events taking place in the five DLAPR municipalities and analyze their role in communicating the local products and gastronomic identity of the DLAPR.

Research components

Food tourists want contact with local products (methods of production and preparation). They also like to get to know producers, interact with them, and, of course, take part in food events. This type of event is seen as a chance to experience and develop awareness about the region. Food events also play a key role in communicating local products to visitors. To identify and characterize food events in the DLAPR, we interviewed a few stakeholders linked to the organization of these events. We also analyzed the promotional posters of 30 different events.

Food events as an effective communication practice of local products

Thirty gastronomic events are held every year in the DLAPR. The diverse events take place throughout the year and include fairs, festivals, parties, shows, markets, and congresses. Some of the events are based on a single local product (oranges, chicken, lamb, trout, corn bread, beans) or on one typical regional dish (Regedora stew, Lafões veal, Alcofra dry soup, "Rancho" Viseu style). Some of these events promote several products in a single place, usually combining Portuguese smoked sausages ("fumeiro") and sweets, for example, while others take advantage of festive seasons, such as the Easter Flavors Festival. The duration of the events ranges from 1 to 3 days (usually Friday to Sunday).

The Terras do Demo events organized by the municipality of Vila Nova de Paiva should be highlighted, as it is a demonstration showcase for gastronomy and seasonal products. The events take place at different times of the year according to the seasonal products of the region (Regedora stew in February, mutton/lamb in August, Relão (a type of porridge) and pumpkin in October, rabbit in December and January, capretto in April).

Municipalities are the main sponsors of these events. Occasionally they may be sponsored by brotherhoods, cultural and solidarity associations, parishes or unions, professional schools, the DLAPR regional government, or private entities. Several events are held regularly: the Lafões Veal Fair is held annually in Vouzela and is currently in its seventeenth season, the Chestnut and Honey Festival in Macieira de Sul is in its sixteenth season, the Orange Fair in Sejães is in its fourteenth season, and the Corn Bread Festival in S. Pedro do Sul in its eleventh season.

We discovered that of the 30 events listed, posters were the most popular means of promotion. Poster analysis (such as finding common festival topics) allows us to have a better understanding of how events are publicized and whether the theme of the event identifies local products. In general, posters mention the date, location, and main sponsors.

Conclusions and recommendations

Food events in the DLAPR appear as effective communication practices since they represent and promote local products, allow for authentic food experiences, and are seen as extremely important to support the value of local products and the creation of the "regional gastronomy" brand, providing positive economic impacts for the region.

Increasing the duration of these events and diversifying the program could encourage tourists to stay longer at local accommodations, creating a positive economic impact in the local economies. Finding new ways of communicating food events, such as using Internet sites or social media is also very important. Finally, we think that promoting food events in the DLAPR in a more integrated way would be positive for the five municipalities, helping to support a regional gastronomic identity.

Questions

1 How can food events enhance the development of small towns? What economic impacts might they have?
2 What other tools could have been used to promote the DLAPR food events? Would they have communicated the same message?
3 What other types of tourism could complement these festivals? How can different types of food tourism be packaged together?

CASE STUDY 3.2

Connections between agritourism and urban food markets: The case of La Boqueria in Barcelona, Spain

Montserrat Crespi-Vallbona and Darko Dimitrovski

Food markets are interesting tourist resources for those who like culture and gastronomy. In Barcelona, La Boqueria is not only the most popular and frequently visited food market, it is also one of the most famous in the world. Multiple websites, tourist guides, and blogs designate it a highly recommended attraction. It has existed since the twelfth century, when it was an open-air market outside the walls of the medieval town. Today, it is located in a nineteenth-century arcade, recently remodeled, in the Rambles, just inside the historic center and one of the most popular walking areas in the city. Fifteen stalls are located near the arcade at

Image 3.4 Local produce at La Boqueria market, Barcelona, Spain
Source: Monserrat Crespi Vallbona

the Sant Galdric Square. Fifteen additional stalls located along the Rambles' avenue provide plants and bouquets of flowers. These stalls have expanded their business, selling souvenirs for tourists—magnets, ceramic ware, flowerpots, and silk flowers. Inside the venue itself are 257 establishments that mix traditional, international, and delicatessen products. Locals have traditionally purchased their fresh produce, meat, fish, and other wares here as it was considered a good value for the money. Visitors also shop here, and a few of the stalls market their products to these customers. Tourism products include juices, fruits cut into pieces, take-away and ready-prepared meals, sweets, candies, and chocolates. These stalls are heavily photographed due to the colors and the goods displayed, causing serious congestion and disturbing residents' shopping. Other stalls combine local and traditional products and sell to both visitors and residents. These booths use just 5% of the total space and display prepared meals for take-away and food sampling.

A few establishments sell their own locally grown products—mainly fresh produce. At present, these are located at Sant Galdric Square and are called the "Farmers' Market." All the vendors reject tourism because they feel tourists are not real customers. They may buy strawberries, peas, or small broad beans, but only if they are staying in nearby apartments. These vendors also struggle with foreign language skills. Vendors have expressed that they feel like "monkeys in a circus" or decorative elements in a picture. These owners refer to the vegetable patch as an enslaved job without holidays because vegetables grow and must be sold all year long. Most of them will retire in a few years, and no relatives are interested in carrying on the small business as the younger generations place high value on leisure time. In the past, the Sant Galdric market was much larger. It most likely will continue to decline. While farmers will continue to grow vegetables, it will become harder to find shop assistants to work in the market.

The dilemma is clear. Tourists search for authenticity, but the presence of stalls focused on tourism at urban food markets and their relationship with local residents and tourists need to be redefined. Farmers have a chance to promote their activities to tourists, improve cultural understanding, and promote agritourism

Image 3.5 The fish stalls at La Boqueria market, Barcelona, Spain
Source: Monserrat Crespi Vallbona

in the surrounding areas, but there are many barriers to success that could jeopardize the market's existence.

Questions

1 Taking into account some of the issues facing public markets, how can sustainability be achieved to ensure adequate working conditions, farmer profitability, and the future success of the market?
2 How can the markets preserve and promote local heritage to tourists if local producers are neglected?
3 How can tourists be more engaged in supporting local urban markets?

References

Boyne, S., and Hall, D. (2003). Managing food and tourism development: Issues for planning and opportunities to add value. In C.M. Hall, L. Sharples, R. Mitchell, B. Cambourne, and N. Macionis (Eds.), *Food tourism around the world: Development, management and markets* (pp. 285–295). Oxford: Butterworth-Heinemann.

Clarke, J. (1999). Marketing structures for farm tourism: Beyond the individual provider of rural tourism. *Journal of Sustainable Tourism, 7*(1), 26–47.

Collins-Kreiner, N., and Zins, Y. (2013). With the passing of time: The changing meaning of souvenirs. In J. Cave (Ed.), *Tourism and souvenirs on the margins: Global perspectives* (pp. 29–39). London: Routledge.

Curtis, K., Slocum, S.L., and Allen, K. (2015). *Farm and food tourism: Exploring opportunities* (Agribusiness curriculum). Logan, UT: Utah State University Extension. Retrieved from www.westernsare.org/Learning-Center/SARE-Project-Products/Books-Guidebooks-and-Manuals/Farm-and-Food-Tourism

Delind, L. (2006). Of bodies, places, and culture: Re-situating local food. *Journal of Agricultural and Environmental Ethics, 19*(2), 121–146.

Everett, S., and Slocum, S.L. (2013). Food and tourism: An effective partnership? A UK-based review. *Journal of Sustainable Tourism, 21*(7), 789–809.

Getz, D., Robinson, R., Andersson, T., and Vujicic, A. (2014). *Foodies and food tourism*. Oxford: Goodfellows Publishing.

Hall, C.M., and Sharples, L. (2003). The consumption of experience or the experience of consumption? An introduction to the tourism of taste. In C.M. Hall, L. Sharples, R. Mitchell, B. Cambourne, and N. Macionis (Eds.), *Food tourism around the world: Development, Management and Markets* (pp. 1–24). Oxford: Butterworth-Heinemann.

Healy, R.G. (1994). Tourist merchandise as a means of generating local benefits from ecotourism. *Journal of Sustainable Tourism, 2*(3), 137–151.

Larsen, S., and Hutton, C. (2011). Community discourse and the emerging amenity landscapes of the rural American West. *GeoJournal, 77*(5), 1–15.

Long, L.M. (2004). *Culinary tourism*. Lexington, KY: University Press of Kentucky.

Marsh, J. (2004). *Ontario trails council annual conference: Trails and tourism*. Ontario: Travel Manitoba.

McGehee, N., and Kim, K. (2004). Volunteer tourism: Evolution, issues, and futures. *Journal of Sustainable Tourism, 22*(6), 847–854.

Mitchell, R., and Hall, C.M. (2003). Consuming tourists: Food tourism consumer practice. In C.M. Hall, E. Sharples, R. Mitchell, B. Cambourne, and N. Macionis (Eds.), *Food tourism around the world: Development, management and markets* (pp. 60–80). Oxford: Butterworth-Heinemann.

Ochterski, J., and Roth, M. (2008). *Getting started in agritourism* (Working paper). Ithaca, NY: Cornell Cooperative Extension.

Petty, J. (2002). *Agri-culture: Reconnecting people, land, and nature*. London: Earthscan.

Scarpato, R., and Daniele, R. (2003). New global cuisine: Tourism, authenticity and sense of place in postmodern gastronomy. In C.M. Hall, L. Sharples, R. Mitchell, B. Cambourne, and N. Macionis (Eds.), *Food tourism around the world: Development, management and markets* (pp. 296–313). Oxford: Butterworth-Heinemann.

Sims, R. (2009). Food, place and authenticity: Local food and the sustainable tourism experience. *Journal of Sustainable Tourism, 17*(3), 321–336.

Timothy, D.J. (2011). *Cultural heritage and tourism: An introduction*. Bristol: Channel View.

Timothy, D.J., and Ron, A.S. (2013). Heritage cuisine, regional identity, and sustainable tourism. In C.M. Hall & S. Gössling (Eds.), *Sustainable culinary systems local foods, innovation, and tourism & hospitality* (pp. 275–290). London: Routledge.

Wearing, S. (2004). Examining best practice in volunteer tourism. In R.A. Stebbins and M. Graham (Eds.), *Volunteering as leisure/leisure as volunteering: An international assessment* (pp. 209–224). Wallingford, UK: CAB International.

Part II

Evolution of agriculture and importance of food in contemporary culture

Image II.1 Fresh produce stand, Kona, Hawai'i, USA
Source: Kynda R. Curtis

Chapter 4

Globalizing agriculture to feed the world

Overview

The industrialization of agriculture in the nineteenth and twentieth centuries greatly increased agricultural and food production worldwide and ushered in urban expansion and productivity growth in industrial and consumer goods. Increasing international trade and specialization in food production facilitated the growing interdependence among nations and the globalized food system we have today. This chapter examines the agricultural innovations and structural changes that resulted from the industrialization process and how they led to specialization and monoculture farming practices. The technological and political advances that enabled globalization in the food economy in the twentieth century, including the role of multinational corporations, are also discussed. Finally, the role of, and models for, modern agricultural policy are examined, including an overview of multilateral trade negotiations and functions of the World Trade Organization (WTO).

Learning Objectives

This chapter will enable students to:

1 Describe the innovations and structural changes that occurred as a result of industrialization and how each impacted agricultural productivity in the nineteenth and twentieth centuries.
2 Understand the role that economies of scale play in increasing agricultural productivity.
3 Apply the concepts of absolute and comparative advantage to the trade of goods and services.
4 Understand why globalization leads to specialization and consolidation in food production.
5 Describe the three primary functions of modern agricultural policy.
6 Appreciate the role and functions of the WTO.

Industrialization of agriculture

In the early stages of agricultural production and cultivation, farming was very labor intensive, even after the introduction of horses, oxen, and other draft animals. Additionally, the lack of transportation and distribution systems meant that labor was either on-farm or located in nearby villages and towns, and any food harvested was consumed locally, primarily by the farming family itself. This led to low food supplies and occasional famine when crops failed due to drought or other causes. The desire to increase food availability and efficiency stimulated research into labor-saving technology and more sophisticated cropping strategies, eventually leading to the complete industrialization of agriculture in the nineteenth and twentieth centuries. **Industrialization**, which transformed farming globally by introducing scientific and technological innovations and mechanization, resulted in agricultural specialization, drastically transforming farm structures and consolidating global food production and supply chains.

Agricultural **mechanization**, the use of machines or equipment to replace labor requirements in agriculture, began in the nineteenth century. New mechanical devices, tools, and equipment, such as cast-iron plows, seed drills, harvesters, cotton gins, etc., led to massive **productivity** (output per unit of input) gains, which reduced labor force requirements by half, meaning that one worker could now produce double the output. This decline in the

Image 4.1 Traditional irrigation in a Hmong village near Sapa, Vietnam
Source: Kynda R. Curtis

amount of labor needed for agriculture meant that some workers could relocate to urban areas and use their labor in other ways, thus increasing the output of industrial and consumer goods. This rural-to-urban migration allowed for the growth of large cities removed from food production areas. The vast amounts of land available and limited labor force in the United States, Australia, Canada, and Argentina led to rapid adoption of mechanized agricultural techniques. Productivity growth in these countries created a surplus of food that was made available to urban areas and exported to other regions, such as Europe and Latin America (Barkley & Barkley, 2015).

The transformation in farm structures—from small, diversified farms to large-scale monoculture farms in the twentieth century—took advantage of economies of scale, which spread the high fixed costs of farming (such as purchasing land, machinery, and livestock) across many acres or number of livestock, lowering the cost of producing a single unit. Economies of scale and **monoculture** (the agricultural practice of producing or growing a single crop, plant, or livestock species, variety, or breed in a field or farming system at a time) improved farming efficiency considerably in terms of the cost of production and productivity.

While monoculture farming took hold in the twentieth century, crop rotation and fallowing strategies had been used on larger tracts of land by the Egyptians and early Europeans (Barkley & Barkley, 2015) to manage soil fertility and pest issues. **Crop rotation** is the practice of planting a succession of different crops in a field from year to year. For example, three fields are planted with three separate crops, which are then rotated among the fields the following year. **Fallowing** a field, or leaving it unused for one season, was also common.

Scientific and technological advances greatly increased agricultural productivity after World War II. In the United States alone, agricultural production expanded by 90% between 1950 and 1990. Advances in plant breeding led to the creation of new crop varieties. The purpose of these innovations was to increase **yields**, the output or amount harvested, to produce more food. The new varieties were less vulnerable to drought, heat, diseases, and other stresses, and thus had higher and more reliable annual yields. As a result, one farmer in 1930 could grow enough to feed just four people, but by 2010 a single farmer could produce enough to feed 155 people (U.S. Department of Agriculture, National Agricultural Statistics Service, 2014).

The 1940s saw the identification of plant genetic material and the adoption of genetic modification, which was typically achieved by applying chemicals or radiation to DNA to create plants with advantageous characteristics. All plant breeding techniques in use since the mid-nineteenth century manipulate plant DNA in some way (Hamilton, 2009). These modifications can take the form of mistakes or mutations that occur during natural cell division, the natural but random movement of DNA sequences from one part of a plant's genome to another, or as a result of genetic changes induced by plant breeders. These types of modifications led to the green revolution of the 1960s and 1970s, during which global wheat yields tripled (Hamilton, 2009).

The green revolution created high-yielding seed varieties of grains such as wheat, rice, corn, and soybeans and enhanced agricultural productivity in Asia and Latin America enormously. India, which had experienced food shortages for decades, became self-sufficient in wheat and rice production. Rice production in India increased by 300%, and prices decreased by over half from 1970 to 2001 (Barta, 2007). However, these new varieties required more water than traditional varieties, as well as the use of agricultural chemicals, such as fertilizers and pesticides. Additionally, they required homogeneous or monoculture farming systems, which was a change from the diverse production systems focusing on ecological principles that had been traditional to India (Barkley & Barkley, 2015).

In the 1960s, the use of chemical inputs in agricultural production, such as fertilizers and pesticides, expanded greatly and became an integral part of modern farming. Early research into commercial chemical inputs began in the early nineteenth century. German chemist Justus van Liebig identified the factors required for plant growth and found that nitrogen was the most effective at increasing plant yields. While plant nutrients—such as nitrogen, phosphorous, and potassium—are found in nature, yields increase dramatically when additional quantities are applied to crops. Commercial chemical applications are available in liquid or powder form and are applied often, either in combination with one another or one at a time, depending on crop needs (Barkley & Barkley, 2015).

Chemical pesticide and herbicide applications are used to eliminate pests, insects, weeds, and other crop diseases. Commercial chemical inputs can be dangerous to humans and the environment and are therefore highly controlled in terms of their availability and the crops on which they can be applied. Usage is strictly monitored, and many countries require growers and farmers to have permits to use chemical inputs on their crops.

Agricultural biotechnology, often referred to as genetic engineering, was developed in the last quarter of the twentieth century. The first plant genome was fully sequenced in 2004; the number of plant genomes sequenced has doubled every two years since then

Image 4.2 Beef cattle in Oklahoma, USA
Source: Susan L. Slocum

(Hamilton, 2009). Genetic engineering allows plant breeders to introduce specific genes into crop DNA by directly manipulating an organism's genome using biotechnology, including transferring of genes both within and across species to produce an improved or unique organism. This process changes the genetic makeup of cells to introduce a new trait that does not occur naturally in the plant, usually to increase agricultural yields while decreasing the need for fertilizer, water, fossil fuels, and other negative environmental inputs (Hamilton, 2009). Examples include a crop's resistance to certain pests, diseases, or environmental conditions; reducing spoilage (extended shelf life); resistance to chemical treatments, such as herbicide; or improved nutrient levels. One example is rice strains that have been modified to increase levels of Vitamin A and reduce vision loss; these have been effective at reducing the incidence of blindness in children in Africa and Asia. Other benefits include improvements in the health of farm workers due to the reduced need for chemical applications to crops.

Globalizing the food economy

One component of globalization is the process of expanding interdependence among countries through increased integration of product and resource markets. A country is endowed with resources that can be used in the production of goods and services, called **factors of production**, which include land, labor, and **capital** (assets that can be invested or used to produce goods or services). These resources can be enhanced through technological advances or the creation of human capital—skill, education, and training—that enhance a worker's productivity. Through trade, immigration, and foreign investment, nations can exchange their resources to become more efficient at producing goods and services (Carbaugh, 2007). Nations with optimal land endowments might specialize in cattle production, for example, which is land-intensive due to grazing requirements; hence, the reason the United States and Argentina are large producers of beef. Nations with optimal labor endowments, such as Vietnam and China, might specialize in vegetable production, which is labor-intensive. **Specialization**, the production of one specific product, takes advantage of economies of scale and leads to increased efficiency or reduced costs of production.

According to the **principle of absolute advantage**, a nation should **import** (bring in from abroad) goods in which it has an absolute disadvantage and **export** (sell abroad) those goods in which it has an absolute cost advantage. But what happens when one nation has an absolute cost advantage in producing all goods? In this case, David Ricardo developed the **principle of comparative advantage**, in which mutually beneficial trade can occur even when one nation is absolutely more efficient in the production of all goods (Carbaugh, 2007). The less efficient nation specializes in and exports the good in which it is relatively less inefficient and the more efficient nation specializes in and exports the good in which it is relatively more efficient. For example, as shown in Figure 4.1, if France has an absolute cost advantage over Holland in cheese and wine production but its advantage is smaller for cheese production, than France should produce and export wine and Holland should produce and export cheese.

Globalization has been driven by a number of factors, the first of which is technological change. Advances in transportation, steam ships, railways, air travel, and pipelines, for example, have greatly reduced transportation costs and allowed the timely movement of goods worldwide. In addition, rapid development in communications and computing technology—the telephone, facsimile, email, and cloud sharing—has decreased the influence

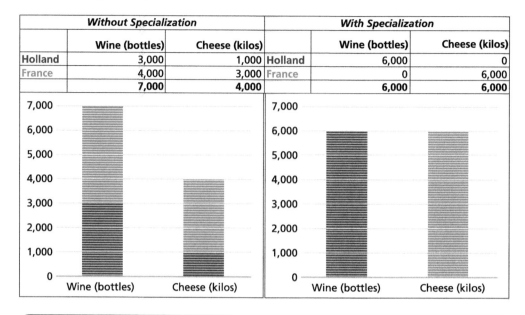

Without Specialization			With Specialization		
	Wine (bottles)	Cheese (kilos)		Wine (bottles)	Cheese (kilos)
Holland	3,000	1,000	Holland	6,000	0
France	4,000	3,000	France	0	6,000
	7,000	4,000		6,000	6,000

Figure 4.1 Productivity gains through specialization and trade

of time and distance between countries and their respective industries. For example, the information and communication flow now afforded by computer technology allows companies to purchase inputs or have parts made in several countries and then have them shipped to one location for product assembly.

Second, technological advancements in the banking industry have allowed for the transfer of money and investment funds and led to the development of international financial markets. These changes have made conducting business across borders and oceans much more efficient. Even for travelers, accessing money in foreign countries is much easier today, through use of ATMs and credit cards, than it was in the twentieth century when traveler's checks and cash were required, and money could only be exchanged during banking hours.

Finally, continued liberalization of trade and investment, as a result of bilateral and multilateral trade negotiations, have allowed for the creation of multinational corporations—companies that operate in several countries. A **multinational corporation** (MNC) is usually incorporated in one country, the home country, and produces or sells goods or services in at least one additional country. The MNC's worldwide activities are centrally controlled by the parent company in the home country. Activities may include importing and exporting goods and services, making significant investments in a foreign country, buying and selling licenses in foreign markets, engaging in contract manufacturing or permitting a local manufacturer in a foreign country to produce their products, or opening manufacturing facilities or assembly operations in foreign countries.

MNCs benefit from their global presence in a variety of ways. First, MNCs may benefit from economies of scale by spreading research and development (R&D) expenditures and distributional and promotional costs over their global sales, using global purchasing power to reduce supply costs, and utilizing their technological and managerial skills globally at minimal additional costs. Additionally, MNCs can use their global operations to take advantage of lower-priced labor available in certain countries and gain access to special R&D capabilities and skilled labor available in other countries.

MNCs serving worldwide markets have led to **consolidation** (merging) in global food processing and distribution. For example, the foreign acquisition of local grocery chains has now placed 40%–75% of the retail grocery market share by region into the hands of large multinational companies such as Ahold (Netherlands), Walmart (US), and Carrefour (France). The top five chains (by market share) comprise 65% of the super-market sector in Latin America and 40% in the United States (Reardon et al., 2003; Statista, 2016).

Consolidation can lead to oligopoly power in retail markets and oligopsony power in input markets. An **oligopoly** occurs when a small number of firms control the majority of the market share. Since only a few firms sell a given product or service, they may set prices higher than they would be in a competitive market, i.e. a market with many sellers. An **oligopsony** occurs in a market when numerous suppliers are competing to sell their product to a small number of large buyers. Thus, the buyers may ask for lower prices than they could ask for in a competitive market. For example, consolidation in the livestock processing industry has resulted in an oligopsony, where four firms process 64% of all hogs and 84% of all cattle in the United States (Johnson & Becker, 2009). The market power of these processors may drive down pricing for animal inputs and negatively impact ranchers.

Agricultural and food policy development

Agricultural and food-related policy is enacted through legislative processes in which laws are enacted for programs affecting agriculture products, conservation of natural resources, directing food and nutrition programs, and supporting economic development and health in rural communities. Agricultural policy has been a primary concern of society and its governing bodies throughout history. Mention of agricultural and food policy is found in the Book of Genesis in the Old Testament, in Assyrian codes of law, and ancient Chinese texts. Roman law included agricultural subsidies and nutrition programs and Chinese dynasties governed grain storage programs (Novak et al., 2015). The rationale for these early policies was primarily the redistribution of food to the poor, managing food availability during times of drought or war, setting up laws concerning land use and the handling of ownership disputes, regulating landlord-tenant relationships, and outlining punishment for financial misdealing. Importantly, these policies were used to set up taxation schemes to generate revenue for government activities, often in the form of grain taxes paid by landowners.

For example, the English Corn Laws enacted in 1815 restricted wheat imports until domestic prices hit certain levels. Additionally, grain producers were paid subsidies when prices of wheat, rye, and barley fell below certain levels. The laws were supposed to protect domestic food supplies, but were likely to protect landowner profits. The Corn Laws were repealed in 1846 after increases in food prices spurred protests among the urban poor.

Today, agricultural policy primarily focuses on mitigating supply and demand shocks, correcting market failures, and enhancing social **welfare**—the well-being of an economy or country. **Supply** is the amount of a product available for sale at a given price, and **demand** is the quantity of a product or service consumers are willing to purchase at a specific price. The unique aspects of agricultural production, such as weather and pests, create volatility in supplies from year to year; policies to stabilize farm income and insure farmers against crop loss are therefore common.

Market failures occur when resources are not used efficiently, externalities are present, and uneven market power exists. As previously discussed, globalized markets have led to the creation of oligopsonies and oligopolies, where firms have market power at stages along the food supply chain. Anti-trust policy is used to regulate and restrict market power. Policies that enhance social welfare often include environmental protection and conservation, such as clean water and air or the protection of wildlife. They may also include provisions for rural economic development and health, ensuring a safe and adequate food supply, or nutrition programs for unemployed or low-income individuals.

Agricultural policy in the USA and Europe

In the United States, current agricultural policy is regulated through the Farm Bill, which is updated every four years, on average. The first Farm Bill was enacted in 1933 as the Agricultural Adjustment Act. Prior to the Farm Bill, agricultural policy was used primarily to raise federal funds for defense and national security, including taxes on landholdings; taxes on products such as distilled spirits, tobacco, snuff, and sugar; and **tariffs** (taxes or fees) on imports. It was also used to legislate Western land settlement through acts such as the Preemption Act and the Homestead Act. Since 1933, the Farm Bill has included provisions for commodity programs, international trade, farm credit, resource and environmental conservation, agricultural research, and food and nutrition programs. The current Farm Bill, called the Agriculture Act of 2014, allocated almost 80% of its resources to domestic food and nutrition programs and 6% to resource conservation programs (see Figure 4.2).

In the European Union, agricultural policy is governed through the Common Agricultural Policy (CAP). The CAP came into force in 1962, but its principles were established in conjunction with the Common Market, a result of the Treaty of Rome, signed by the six member nations in 1957. Like the Farm Bill in the United States, the CAP has evolved significantly since its inception, moving away from typical production-oriented policy, such as price supports and production quotas. A rural development policy added in 2000 seeks

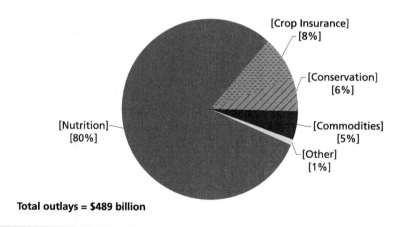

Total outlays = $489 billion

Figure 4.2 2014 United States farm bill allocations
Source: U.S. Department of Agriculture, Economic Research Service (2014)

to increase economic, social, and environmental development in rural areas. The current objectives of the CAP are to increase productivity by promoting technical progress and ensuring optimal use of the factors of production to ensure a fair standard of living for the agricultural community, stabilize markets, secure availability of supplies, and provide consumers with food at reasonable prices (European Commission, 2013).

International agricultural policy

As globalization continues, the need for an international organization to manage international trade and investment policy—including agreements, laws, and regulations—has become self-evident. As the amount of international trade increases, issues such as protectionism, trade barriers, subsidies, violation of intellectual property rights, food safety, and pest management arise due to differences in the laws and production practices of each nation. The WTO serves as the mediator between nations when such problems arise.

The WTO is an intergovernmental organization that regulates international trade. It was officially founded on January 1, 1995, replacing the General Agreement on Tariffs and Trade (GATT) initiated in 1948. As of 2016, the WTO had 164 member nations. The WTO regulates trade between member nations by providing a framework for negotiating

Image 4.3 Local wine production displayed at "Taste of Australia" food festival in Adelaide, Australia
Source: Kynda R. Curtis

trade agreements and a dispute resolution process aimed at enforcing adherence to WTO agreements. Agreements are signed by representatives of member nations and are then ratified by their respective governing bodies. The primary functions of the WTO are to oversee the implementation, administration, and operation of the covered trade agreements and to provide a forum for negotiations and settling disputes. The WTO additionally reviews and disseminates national trade policies and ensures the coherence and transparency of trade policies through observation of economic policies, trade agreements, and laws worldwide. Another priority of the WTO is to assist developing and low-income countries in implementing WTO regulations through technical training. The WTO is also a center for economic research and analysis and provides regular assessments of the global trade situation in its annual publications and research reports (WTO, 2017a).

For many years, WTO trade negotiations did not include agriculture or food. However, trade negotiations under the current round of talks (Doha Round, 2001 to present) have focused on agricultural products. The WTO Agriculture Agreement provides context for the long-term reform of agricultural trade and member domestic policies aimed at increasing competition and reducing trade distortions. The Agreement covers three main issues: market access, or the use of trade restrictions, such as tariffs on imports; domestic supports, or the use of subsidies and other support programs that directly stimulate production and distort trade; and export competition, or the use of export subsidies and other government support programs that subsidize exports (WTO, 2017b).

Under the Agriculture Agreement, WTO members agree to a schedule of commitments that set limits on the tariffs they can apply to individual products and on levels of domestic support and export subsidies. At the 2015 WTO Ministerial Conference in Nairobi, Kenya, WTO member nations committed to abolishing subsidies for farm exports (WTO, 2017b). The WTO Anti-Dumping Agreement and the Sanitary and Phytosanitary (SPS) Agreement also regulate agricultural issues. **Dumping** is selling a product on the open market at a price lower than the price in the home country. The Anti-Dumping Agreement allows member nations to restrict or tax imports of the dumped product if imports may cause injury to a domestic industry. The SPS agreement details when government officials can apply food safety and animal and plant health measures to restrict imports.

Summary

The industrialization of agriculture led to many labor-saving technologies and scientific advancements that made it possible to feed fast-growing populations and allow for the growth of urban areas worldwide. Advances in plant and animal genetics, plant nutrition and pest management, and biotechnology were significant, as were emerging farming techniques such as crop rotation, fallowing, and large-scale production units. Globalization of the food economy, where regions or nations further specialized in products in which they held a comparative advantage and then traded those products for others, further increased efficiency and productivity. So, next time you want an orange in January in Boston or Amsterdam, or fresh flowers on your table in July in Sydney, you can be thankful for globalization.

While the benefits of industrialization and globalization are many, negative impacts also resulted. Both domestic and international agricultural policies focus on decreasing volatility in agricultural markets; correcting market failures, such as externalities and market power; and enhancing social welfare to ensure a healthy population and environment.

Study Questions

1   Using all of its factors of production, Spain can produce 50,000 kilos of table grapes or 10,000 barrels of wine. Italy can produce 60,000 kilos of table grapes or 8,500 barrels of wine. Which product should each country produce and export and why?
2   How do economies of scale impact farm size and the variety of crops grown or livestock raised?
3   What is meant by productivity in agriculture? How might productivity be enhanced?
4   How does globalization lead to specialization in agricultural production?
5   Explain why agricultural output or yields vary from year to year.
6   What three advantages do multinational corporations have that may increase their efficiency?
7   Outline the three primary functions of modern agricultural policy.

Definitions

Capital—assets held that can be invested or used to produce goods or services.

Consolidation—the merging or joining of groups or companies, leading to a reduction in the total number.

Crop rotation—the system of varying successive crops in a definite order on the same ground, especially to avoid depleting the soil and to control weeds and pests.

Demand—the quantity of a product or service that people are willing or able to buy at a specific price.

Dumping—selling a product on the open market at a price lower than the domestic price.

Exports—goods produced domestically and sold abroad.

Factors of production—resources—such as land, labor, and capital—that can be used to produce goods and services.

Fallowing—the practice of leaving a field unused for one season to manage pests or soil fertility.

Genetic engineering—the direct manipulation of an organism's genome using biotechnology.

Imports—goods produced abroad and brought in to sell domestically.

Industrialization—the large-scale introduction of manufacturing, advanced technical enterprises, and other productive economic activity into an area, society, or country.

Mechanization—the use of machines or equipment to replace labor requirements in agriculture.

Monoculture—the agricultural practice of producing or growing a single crop, plant, or livestock species, variety, or breed in a field or farming system at a time.

Multinational corporation—a corporate organization that owns or controls production of goods or services in one or more countries other than the home country.

Oligopoly—a market where there exist few sellers, which as a result can greatly influence price and other market factors.

Oligopsony—a market where there exist few buyers, which as a result can influence the price they pay for products.

Principle of absolute advantage—the ability of a provider of goods or services to produce goods more efficiently than its competitors, such that its total cost per unit of output is lower.

Principle of comparative advantage—the ability of an individual, company, etc., to produce a good or service at a lower cost and more efficiently than another entity.

Productivity—output per unit of input.

Specialization—restricting activity to one specific or unique action.

Supply—the amount of a product available for sale at a given price.

Tariff—the tax or duty imposed by a government on imports or exports.

Welfare—the well-being of an economy, country, etc.

Yield—the quantity or amount of a crop that is produced, harvested, etc.

CASE STUDY 4.1

The British Indian curry industry moves to Bangladesh: Globalization effects

Azizul Hassan and Anukrati Sharma

The number of mainly Bangladeshi-owned Indian restaurants, commonly referred to as "curry houses," in the United Kingdom (UK) has grown tremendously in the last few decades, significantly contributing to its economy. These restaurants are both managed by and serve mainly the expatriate Sylheti people of Bangladesh. There are limited data on the actual number of the Bangladeshis who have moved to the UK because a considerable number of the Bangladeshi immigrant workers employed in the British Indian curry industry are thought to be illegal residents. Many of these immigrants send remittances, called "hundi" (person-to-person money transfers) home to Bangladesh.

The Indian curry industry in the UK originates in the British colonial regime in Southeast Asia during the nineteenth and twentieth century. During their stay in the Indian subcontinent, the British experienced the flavors of the Indian cuisine. When the Indian subcontinent was partitioned in 1947, the British relaxed immigration policies to fill labor gaps in the UK left by World War II, which were partly filled by overseas working-class migrants.

Relying on culinary experiences of native British populations, traditional Indian curry fusions were introduced and blended with English food styles, creating an international cuisine. The spicy dishes soon became popular among multiethnic consumer groups, particularly the English. This industry helped promote the sociocultural well-being of a selected social segment in the UK, while remittances sent home to Sylheti societies in Bangladesh offer socioeconomic freedom for their relatives. The industry is currently expanding to different parts of the world, including back to Bangladesh, where the industry has found a place in the Sylhet region.

Bangladesh has been enjoying favorable tourism policies (Hassan & Burns, 2014) based on economic benefit sharing. The expansion of the British Indian curry industry has created employment opportunities in the Sylhet region in Bangladesh. The region has already seen diverse, world-class facilities resulting from both the direct and indirect impacts of the British Indian curry industry. Standard British food making, processing, and serving procedures have influenced the development of hotels, restaurants, motels, and food shops, another effect of globalization. One of the key social impacts of this movement has been the empowerment of local women by creating more employment opportunities that bring women into the workforce. However, local, authentic Bangladeshi cuisine has been challenged in relation to production and marketing.

The British Indian curry industry in the Sylhet region of Bangladesh is a direct example of globalization and its effects. While the initiators of the British Indian curry industry in the UK are mainly the Sylheti British Bangladeshi community, the expansion of this industry to Sylhet has resulted in economic benefits and has enhanced the tourism product.

Questions

1 What economic and/or social benefits have been generated by the British Indian curry industry? What negative impacts have resulted?
2 Would these impacts have resulted without globalization? Why or why not?
3 Overall, has British curry been a good influence on the global Sylhet community?

References

Hassan, A., and Burns, P. (2014). Tourism policies of Bangladesh—A contextual analysis. *Tourism Planning & Development*, 11(4), 463–466.

Tea in Thailand—globalizing a culture

Kynda R. Curtis and Susan L. Slocum

Before the late twentieth century, tea cultivation and consumption in Thailand was almost nonexistent. Only small indigenous groups were growing tea for their own use. Tea cultivation began thriving in the late twentieth century due to increased numbers of Chinese immigrants and a governmental push to develop more sustainable agricultural crops as well as stricter bans on opium. Opium had been the primary agricultural crop, and while it is still produced today, it is illegal in Thailand.

Tea is now widely consumed in Thailand, both as a warm beverage and the cold Thai iced tea known throughout the world. Thai iced tea is made from strongly brewed black Ceylon tea mixed with spices, sugar, and condensed milk or coconut milk, but Thailand produces several other varieties, including oolong, green, and jasmine teas. Thai-grown tea exports attracted the attention of world markets and gradually tea tourism expanded, with Western tourists, accustomed to drinking tea, infiltrating rural areas and sampling teas at teahouses and touring tea fields. While Thailand is not among the top ten tea-producing nations, it is an important source of high-quality teas. Some of Thailand's teas are among the most expensive and most desired teas and are consumed in countries, such as Taiwan, where there is a strong demand for high-quality tea.

Many of Thailand's tea plantations are located in Doi Mae Salong, Chiang Rai Province, in the northeast corner of Thailand, just six kilometers from the Myanmar border. The area is often referred to as the Golden Triangle, as Thailand, Myanmar, and Laos meet at the banks of the Mekong River, where a large golden statue of Buddha sits above the river on the Thailand side. This mountainous region of Thailand is rugged and scenic, with many opportunities to experience culture. The small Hmong tribal villages in the area, including the Akha, Lisu, and Yao, are nestled high in the mountains. Tourists can explore the villages and meet the local people, although the villagers know very little English, as well as sample teas at many different plantations. There are stunning views of the Mekong River Valley from Doi Mae Salong.

Tea culture in Thailand resonates throughout daily life. It has been said that Bangkok residents rise and fall with green tea in their hands. A plethora of Western coffee shops now line the streets of any city of moderate size, but coffee takes a back seat to tea and fruit drinks in cafés. Starbucks stores are common in larger cities and green tea iced lattes are their most popular drink in Southeast Asia. While Starbucks has expanded considerably in Thailand, both domestic chains and independently owned coffee shops are thriving, as Starbucks is still relatively expensive, especially for locals. Obviously, a large portion of Starbucks business in Asia can be attributed to Western tourists and expatriates living abroad. The author visited a Starbucks in Chiang Mai, Thailand, where 85% of the patrons were of Western descent. A similar experience ensued in Hanoi, Vietnam, a month later.

The "Westernization" of food culture in Asia is not new and is highly visible now that many global food chains, such as Starbucks, have a strong market presence.

Image 4.4 Specialty teas, Kona, Hawai'i, USA
Source: Kynda R. Curtis

Early movers, such as McDonalds and Pizza Hut, established themselves in the 1980s. As Asians altered their diets to include more Western foods, the variety of options has continued to expand. The coffee culture that took off in the Western United States in the late 1980s, including the popularity of coffee shops and cafés as meeting places and points of social interaction, has found a new home in Southeast Asia. While the importance of tea over coffee at cafés is an adaption of the model, both the production of tea and the significant role it plays in Thai culture today are the result of globalization.

Questions

1　Why do tourists seek out food or drink that is common to their home country or region while traveling?
2　From an international trade perspective, why has tea production expanded and flourished in Thailand? Will Thailand always be a producer of quality teas? Why or Why not?
3　How can tea compete against coffee for tourism revenue? What should be done to encourage tourism support for tea production?

References

Barkley, A., and Barkley, P. (2015). *Depolarizing food and agriculture: An economic approach*. New York: Earthscan Food and Agriculture.

Barta, P. (2007, July 28). Feeding billions, a grain at a time. *The Wall Street Journal*, p. A1.

Carbaugh, R. (2007). *International economics*, 11th ed. Mason, OH: Thomson South-Western.

European Commission. (2013). *Overview of CAP reform 2014–2020*. Agricultural Policy Perspectives Brief No. 5. Retrieved from ec.europa.eu/agriculture/sites/agriculture/files/policy-perspectives/policy-briefs/05_en.pdf

Hamilton, R. (2009). Agriculture's sustainable future: Breeding better crops. *Scientific American*, 19(2), 16–17. Retrieved from https://www.scientificamerican.com/article/agricultures-sustainable-future/

Johnson, R., and Becker, G. (2009). *Livestock marketing competition issues*. CRS Report to Congress RL33325. Washington, DC: Congressional Research Service.

Novak, J., Pease, J. and Sanders, L. (2015). *Agricultural policy in the United States: Evolution and economics*. New York: Routledge.

Reardon, T., Timmer, C., Barrett, C., and Berdeque, J. (2003). The rise of supermarkets in Africa, Asia, and Latin America. *American Journal of Applied Economics*, 85(5), 1140–1146.

Statista. 2016. Market share of U.S. food and beverage purchases in 2016, by company. Retrieved from https://www.statista.com/statistics/240481/food-market-share-of-the-leading-food-retailers-of-north-america/

U.S. Department of Agriculture, Economic Research Service. (2014). Agricultural Act of 2014: Highlights and implications. Retrieved from https://www.ers.usda.gov/agricultural-act-of-2014-highlights-and-implications/

U.S. Department of Agriculture, National Agricultural Statistics Service. (2014). 2012 Census of Agriculture - Preliminary report highlights: U.S. farms and farmers. Washington, DC: USDA. Retrieved from www.agcensus.usda.gov/Publications/2012/Preliminary_Report/Highlights.pdf

World Trade Organization. (2017a). The WTO. Retrieved from https://www.wto.org/english/thewto_e/thewto_e.htm

World Trade Organization. (2017b). Agriculture. Retrieved from https://www.wto.org/english/tratop_e/agric_e/agric_e.htmw

Chapter 5

Rural landscapes, heritage, and economic development

Overview

This chapter discusses the history and evolution of rural areas, including how distinct rural heritage and cultural traditions were established. It also covers the impact of advances in communication and transportation systems on rural communities, including the loss of labor due to rural-to-urban migration, the loss of local food production and other manufacturing to urban areas, and the harmonization of culture across regions. Further, current economic development opportunities for rural communities through food tourism are examined, including modern trends in rural relocation and urban residents' desire for rural lifestyles and travel. Finally, the components of successful rural development projects and how food tourism satisfies these components are discussed. The chapter also provides an overview of cost-benefit analysis and how it can be used to evaluate the potential success of new food tourism projects.

Learning Objectives

This chapter will enable students to:

1   Understand how distinct rural cultural traditions and heritage were established.
2   Understand the impact of improved communication and transportation systems on the distinctiveness and production role of rural communities.
3   Identify the impacts of rural-to-urban migration on the economic and social structure of rural communities.
4   Recognize why and how rural communities stand to benefit economically in the modern era.
5   Understand how food tourism can be a successful rural economic development strategy.

6   Recognize the importance of collaboration and partnering to form regional clusters.
7   Apply cost-benefit analysis to assess the potential success of a food tourism project and calculate the net present value of a project investment.

Rural landscapes and heritage

Up until the late nineteenth century, rural landscapes were dotted with small communities. Population growth occurred primarily in areas where available resources could be used to produce needed goods and services. Economic development was primarily in agriculture, fisheries, forestry, and mining or similar resource-based industries. Rural communities were rather isolated as transportation to, and communication with, other communities was slow and unreliable. Hence, **self-sufficiency**—the ability to supply one's own needs without external assistance—was required; all food and household products had to be produced locally. Cultural traditions, language, and customs grew and evolved independently of outside influences or neighboring communities, leading to distinct societies.

Government policy in the nineteenth and early twentieth centuries focused on improving infrastructure—including roads and railroads—and technological developments, such as irrigation projects. These policy priorities reduced isolation and enhanced the production of agriculture and other resources so that large populations could be supported. By the early 1950s, improved communication and diminished isolation had reduced the distinctiveness of rural communities. Rural residents read the same newspapers and magazines and listened to the same radio programs as urban residents. Rural residents could also travel to urban areas in just a few hours rather than a few days. Thus, the distinct cultural traditions of small rural communities began to meld and become more similar. **Urbanization** in the form of rural-to-urban migration multiplied and rural populations plummeted. In 2010, for the first time in world history, more of the world's population lived in cities than in rural areas (United Nations Habitat, 2011). Many rural communities took advantage of their close proximity to transportation routes and urban areas by bringing manufacturing to their area, slowing the pace of rural-to-urban migration. Heavy manufacturing industries brought in raw materials to produce consumer goods for nearby urban markets.

Unfortunately, the communities that remained dependent on agricultural and natural resources experienced heavy economic decline. The loss of skilled labor due to urbanization and reduced local food production were significant contributors to rural economic deterioration. Due to technological and transportation advances, economies of scale could be achieved by shipping basic commodities or raw materials to central urban areas, where final food products were processed and packaged for national or global distribution. Hence, rural areas saw their role in food production reduced to suppliers of raw agricultural commodities, such as wheat, corn, rice, etc. The value of these raw agricultural commodities was much lower than the final food products that had previously been produced for local populations.

Rural-to-urban migration eventually led to a rural **brain drain,** the loss of trained or skilled professionals to another area, as the brightest and most motivated youth from a community moved to urban areas (Albrecht, 2014). Those that stayed tended to be less

Image 5.1 Urbanization in Cabo San Lucas, Mexico
Source: Kynda R. Curtis

skilled and less educated. By 2015, only 19% of rural U.S. residents had a college degree, compared to 33% in urban areas (U.S. Department of Agriculture, Economic Research Service, 2017). Figure 5.1 provides a comparison of educational attainment for urban and rural U.S. residents in 2000 and 2015. Some of the disparity in education may be due to differences in household income, as average rural household income trails urban household income by 25%, making college less affordable for rural families. Geographic distance may create an additional cost to attending college for rural youth. Reduced education levels in rural communities led to lower average incomes and higher levels of poverty and unemployment, which resulted in increased occurrences of substance abuse and the deterioration of traditional family structures (Albrecht, 2014). Low incomes mean lower tax revenues, reducing the availability of public services such as public schools, and residents have less money to support local businesses. These deficiencies make it hard for communities to attract outside businesses or industries when skilled labor is unavailable.

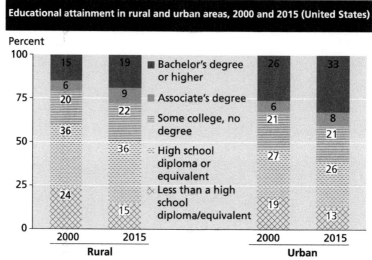

Note: Educational attainment for adults ages 25 and older; urban/rural status is determined by 2015 metropolitan area definitions from the Office of Management and Budget.
Source: USDA, Economic Research Service using data from the U.S. Census Bureau, Census 2000 and 2015 American Community Survey.

Figure 5.1 Educational attainment in rural and urban areas, 2000 and 2015 (United States)
Source: U.S. Department of Agriculture, Economic Research Service (2015)

Rural economies in the modern era

The potential for economic growth in rural communities is perhaps better in the modern era than it has ever been before. Three primary factors contribute to an optimistic view of the future of rural economic development:

1   The decreased relevance of location to access markets and supplies;
2   A growing population seeking the rural lifestyle or way of life; and
3   The high interest among populations, especially those with families, to experience rural customs and culture, local foods, and agricultural open space or natural amenities.

The existence of higher-paying jobs in urban areas has traditionally placed rural communities at an economic disadvantage. However, the introduction of advanced communication and information technology means that many high-paying, quality jobs are no longer geographically constrained. Individuals and their families, and businesses and their owners, can be located just about anywhere and still be connected to markets and consumers through computers, the Internet, and cellular phones. For example, in the United States today, 37% of all workers telecommute, or work remotely (Gallup, 2015). Telecommuting is much more common among upper-income, white-collar professionals with a formal education.

For those who may not find the urban lifestyle appealing, perhaps due to the high stress or congestion in urban areas, the decreased relevance of location offers the option of relocating to enjoy the many benefits of rural living. The isolation created by growing affluence in developed countries has led to an increased desire to build a home, establish personal relationships, and be actively involved in community (McKibben, 2007). Today, a significant proportion of the population aspires to live closer to natural amenities and in rural areas with less crime, smog, and reduced travel time to the workplace (Albrecht, 2014). For example, in Italy, the number of young urban dwellers who have moved to rural areas to take up small-scale farming and food production increased by 9% in just one year, 2015–2016 (Eckhardt, 2017). The "death of location" and rural-movement trends both lend themselves to increasing educational levels and income in rural areas, which raises tax revenues and gives local business access to creative and talented labor.

Finally, the interest among the population to experience rural customs, culture, food, and open space on vacation or on weekend excursions has rapidly grown over the past three decades. The USDA Forest Service's *National Survey on Recreation and the Environment* found that almost 30% of the population visited farms one or more times in 2000 (Barry & Hellerstein, 2004). Additionally, the agritourism industry has been growing at a rate of around 6% annually in Europe and North America (Tchetchik et al., 2008). This rising interest is fueled by the growing separation between the population and food production and the lack of natural landscapes and open space in most urban areas. Spending the weekend at farm stays, picking pumpkins, and riding bicycles through wine country, for example, are the types of experiences sought by urban residents. These rural vacations provide a getaway from the hectic lifestyle and stress of urban living through peace, relaxation, and rest. Rural tourism lends itself to job creation and increased spending at local businesses and hospitality operations and is in most cases a positive economic and social development for communities.

Tourism as a rural economic development strategy

Tourism generated US$7.6 trillion (10% of global GDP) and 277 million jobs (1 in 11 jobs) for the global economy in 2014 (World Travel and Tourism Council, 2015). Tourism investment in the United States was US$144.3 billion, or 4.3% of total investment in 2015. In recent years, tourism grew at a faster rate than both the wider economy and other significant sectors, and tourism is among the top three revenue-producing industries in 46 U.S. states.

Tourism development has been a solid rural economic development strategy for several decades and was the leading factor in the success of many rural areas experiencing high growth in the late twentieth century (Galston & Baehler, 1995). It is one of the few industries which, more often than not, provides solid returns to rural areas seeking economic growth. Economic growth in one sector or industry often spurs economic growth in other sectors (due to multiplier effects, discussed in Chapter 1). This is true for tourism, as community investments made for tourists or visitors often lure new residents and improve community amenities for current residents (Galston & Baehler, 1995). But tourism development is more than just a job creation or economic enhancement tool; it creates lasting change in a community's social fabric and way of life.

Walla Walla, Washington, USA, is one example of how tourism development led to the resurgence of one rural community (Walla Walla Community College, 2011). In the 1980s

Image 5.2 Rural Italy
Source: Kelly McMahon

and 1990s, the regional economy around Walla Walla experienced significant economic decline. Walla Walla's traditionally strong agricultural economy suffered from low prices, escalating production costs, and deteriorating markets. The area's primary crops, such as wheat, sold at prices at or below the cost of production, and food processing plants closed due to increased dependence on less expensive, imported fruits and vegetables in the United States. Unemployment rates skyrocketed and the region's tax base decreased significantly. The region had to reinvent itself by diversifying its economy and identifying, producing, and marketing higher-value products. Community leaders realized the need for a new economic driver to create higher-wage jobs and fuel economic growth. A mix of natural resource amenities, creativity, and earning national accolades in wine production put Walla Walla on the map as a world-class wine-producing region. The area's temperate climate, soil conditions, and rolling hills provided ideal conditions for producing premium wines. Although the wine industry in the Walla Walla Valley is comparatively young, especially when compared to wine regions in California or Europe, it has experienced significant growth since the first winery was founded in 1977. Since then, the industry has grown to over 130 wineries and approximately 2,000 acres of wine grape production. Wine industry jobs now amount to 14.4% of total regional employment and are projected to increase to approximately 20% by 2020. The investment and growth in wine production (e.g., wineries and vineyards) drove economic expansion in other sectors as well, including the arts and hospitality.

While the discussion of tourism development so far has focused on the positive, there are negative aspects of tourism development. These include the large up-front investment and ongoing maintenance costs that are primarily paid for by local government. These investments may or may not be fully recovered through additional tax revenues. Also, the jobs created in tourism tend to be low-paying service industry jobs with little or no benefits and little stability or opportunity for advancement. In many regions, these jobs are seasonal. Additionally, not all rural communities can take advantage of tourism as they may not have the natural, cultural, or man-made amenities to support tourism. Finally, as tourism expands, the competition between destinations increases and communities must find new ways to differentiate themselves to remain competitive.

Food tourism and economic development

Rural economic development strategies that significantly impact communities have four primary components: they increase employment opportunities, expand opportunities for entrepreneurial development, enhance local food production, and foster regional collaboration or clusters (Galston & Baehler, 1995; Albrecht, 2014). Food tourism is one rural economic development strategy that can help turn rural communities into tourism destinations through unique branding and image marketing opportunities. Food tourism development has the potential to positively increase the economies of rural communities by bringing in visitors and creating new jobs and local business ventures for rural residents.

Food tourism development meets the four requirements for successful rural development in that it creates additional employment opportunities, especially for community youth who wish to return to rural areas after university graduation, mitigating rural-to-urban migration. Second, food tourism development is primarily a variation on small business development and thus an excellent opportunity to develop a climate of entrepreneurship in a community and expand the local pool of entrepreneurs, increasing human capital.

When, for example, existing farms or ranches add food tourism enterprises to their existing operations, entrepreneurial opportunities are increased, especially for younger family members looking to stay on the farm.

Third, food tourism development can increase local food production, including value-added foods, food souvenirs, expanded farmers' markets, and food and drink festivals. Local sourcing to nearby restaurants and hotels also expands local food production. Rural communities have traditionally been dependent on local or regional food production due to the lack of adequate transportation, storage, and communications systems. Technology and infrastructure improvements moved food production to larger cities, and rural communities produced raw commodities. Increasing the production and consumption of food in rural areas has many financial, health, and environmental benefits. Financial benefits include the higher margins for value-added or processed and packaged products over those of raw materials. Purchasing locally produced goods also means that money stays local; those funds are often used to purchase goods and services from other local businesses, reducing leakages and stimulating business development (see Chapter 1). Local food production can decrease the incidence of food deserts—areas where little or no food is available. Also, local produce and non-processed food consumption leads to dietary improvements, which are needed to reduce the high incidence of diabetes and other diet-related health issues that are common in rural areas (Albrecht, 2014). Treating and managing diet-related disease drains community resources and shrinks economic productivity. Finally, reducing the transportation of foods reduces use of fossil fuels.

Finally, to enhance rural economic development, it is critical for communities to recognize that they will be much better off if they partner with neighboring communities and across industry, governmental, and non-governmental organizations. When communities work together regionally, they greatly increase their opportunities for success by building social capital. One approach to regional development is creating **clusters**, geographically close groups of interconnected companies and associated institutions in an industry that are linked by shared aims and complementary resources (Porter, 2000). A regional clustering approach "would involve a number of firms and would ideally take advantage of the region's culture, history, and local resources to provide comparative advantages, branding, and name recognition" (Albrecht, 2014, p. 150). Such collaboration can create economic, social, and environmental benefits, including enhancing local culture and showcasing rural heritage. This approach is closely related to territorial development.

Shields et al. (2009) discuss three main advantages of regional clustering for operations and the region in which they are located. First, industry clusters provide cost savings in terms of access to specialized input and service providers, a larger pool of trained and specialized workers, and public infrastructure investments and financial markets geared to the needs of the industry. Second, they provide a more conducive environment for change. Establishments have a greater ability to focus on their core activities, production technologies, and organizations. The greater focus on core activities and positive interactions with similar firms increases the chances of innovation. Third, industry clustering facilitates the development of linkages, cooperation, and collaboration among area firms, leading to efficiencies in marketing, brand development, and other cooperative functions.

Successful food tourism requires collaboration and partnership, especially to establish an effective and prosperous destination (see Chapter 9). Figure 5.2 illustrates the earlier example of a regional cluster focused on tourism in the Walla Walla Valley Wine Region. This cluster combines government institutions, non-governmental and non-profit

Image 5.3 Bananas growing in Honduras
Source: Susan L. Slocum

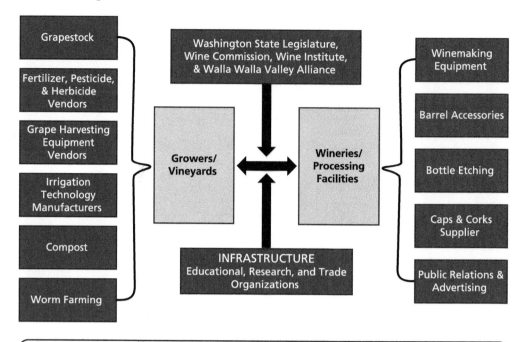

organizations, vineyard owners and grape growers, and wine makers and processors, as well as institutions of higher education and trade organizations, all working together to achieve a common goal with a regional focus. Another example is the Indiana Uplands Wine Trail, which stretches 100 miles throughout central and southern Indiana, USA. The trail was established in 2004 and is a collaboration between seven wineries, six county governments, and numerous local restaurants, bed and breakfasts, and retail locations along the route (Ramsey & Schaumleffel, 2006).

Evaluating the potential for success in food tourism development

Cost-benefit analysis can be used to evaluate the potential for success of a food tourism project. Cost-benefit analysis normally compares options in an effort to choose the best alternative, but it can also be used to evaluate the overall impact of a project after project completion. The analysis assumes a monetary value can be placed on all the costs and benefits of a project, including tangible and intangible returns to others in addition to those immediately impacted. Decisions are made through cost-benefit analysis by comparing the net present value (NPV) of the project's costs with the net present value of its benefits. **Net present value** is a measure of discounted future cash inflows to present cash outflows. Decisions are based on whether there is a net benefit or cost to the project or the total benefits less total costs. Costs and benefits that occur in the future have less weight attached to them in a cost-benefit analysis. Hence, it is necessary to discount or reduce the value of future costs or benefits such that they are equivalent with the project's costs and benefits incurred today. The **discount rate** varies by sector or industry, but the public sector (government) generally uses a discount rate of 5%–6%.

To demonstrate how net present value is calculated, consider the company Multi-Berry Farm. The company is trying to determine whether they should invest in a new line of gourmet jams to sell at their farm store and at a nearby national park. Multi-Berry expects to invest US$500,000 to develop their new products. They estimate first-year revenues of US$200,000, second-year revenues of US$300,000, and third-year revenues of US$200,000. An expected return of 10% is used for the discount rate. The formula used to calculate net present value is

$$NPV = -C_0 + \frac{C_1}{1+r} + \frac{C_2}{(1+r)^2} + \cdots + \frac{C_T}{(1+r)^T},$$

where $-C_0$ = initial investment, C = future revenues, r = discount rate, and T = time. To calculate the net present value of Multi-Berry's new gourmet jam product line, input the projected future revenues into the NPV formula.

$$NPV = -\$500,000 + \frac{\$200,000}{1.10} + \frac{\$300,000}{(1.10)^2} + \frac{\$200,000}{(1.10)^3}$$

Based on this analysis, the net present value of the investment is US$80,015.02. Assuming that their revenue projections for the first three years are correct, the investment will be valuable for Multi-Berry.

A cost-benefit analysis requires a complete and systematic assessment of all potential benefits and costs to a project. This is one of its advantages but also one of its drawbacks. Projecting the long-term impacts of a project is very difficult. For example, tourism development may affect migration patterns; visitors may end up moving to the location in retirement, or the improved community amenities (recreation, historical sites, etc.) may attract outside businesses to the community (Galston & Baehler, 1995). Implications such as these can be difficult to predict and assign monetary values. Additionally, the costs of a project tend to be understated in the analysis. The negative impacts to community roads and additional stress on public services—such as police, fire, health care, and sanitation—are often not considered. Costly public financing of improvement projects, the costs of raising capital and conducting regional promotional campaigns, are also often not included in the analysis.

Cost-benefit analysis: A food tourism example

To illustrate the positive and negative impacts of a food tourism project that must be considered to complete a simple cost-benefit analysis, let us use a farmers' market example. A community starts a farmers' market on Saturdays primarily for local residents and determines that this event could help support tourism growth. Initially, the farmers' market carried both local produce and imported craft goods that appeal to locals, such as imported kitchen items used to cook food, recorded music, and knickknack crafts. As the community begins to market this event to visitors, the number of attendees increases. To perform a cost-benefit analysis, the community must assess the situation based on what happens both before and after tourism occurs and measure the difference between the two scenarios in monetary terms:

- Cost-benefit analysis involves a specific geographical study area.
- Double counting benefits or costs must be avoided.
- Costs and benefits for the future must be discounted using net present values.

Positive impacts

As tourism increases, the sale of goods increases, creating larger economic impacts for vendors. Tourists have more activities to do while visiting, and some may stay an extra night to attend the market, providing more revenue to hotels and restaurants. Tourists begin to ask for locally made artisan goods and want prepared foods that they can eat on-site (assuming they do not have a kitchen in which to cook). The market grows as more vendors attempt to accommodate these preferences. All of these impacts can be measured by the increase in sales at the market and at supporting tourism businesses.

As tourists request more locally made products, small businesses begin to rediscover traditional recipes and artisan skills as an opportunity to meet the needs of the tourists. One person opens a booth selling traditional rugs, as does another who makes local beer. A musician decides to perform at the market and sells CDs. These impacts can also be measured by the amount of sales made at the farmers' market.

However, there are additional impacts. Other residents become interested in learning traditional crafts that they see in the market. The rug maker and the brewer start teaching classes. These activities re-instill a sense of community pride, and the local school starts teaching classes to children about local history and heritage. Social capital develops between the members of the community. These impacts are much harder to measure. You may want to include the revenue generated by these classes or the school's budget to teach heritage classes. New partnerships may develop as restaurants sell the locally made beer, which can also be measured financially. As community members become more united through social capital, crime rates may drop, reducing the local police or jail budgets. Many of these assessments are estimates only, but they offer a good starting point for determining the benefits derived from the farmers' market over time.

Negative impacts

As more tourists arrive, the community may need to grow the market. This might include paving a nearby field to be used for parking. If the field had previously been used to grow hay, the revenue from hay production and the cost of constructing the parking lot need to be included as costs. As new artisan products dominate the market's sales, the loss of revenue from the sale of household goods needs to be included. Furthermore, residents may now need to travel to distant stores to purchase these items, so their gasoline expenses could be part of the cost-benefit calculations. Market prices may increase (inflation) as tourists are willing to pay more for merchandise than locals are. These costs can also be calculated.

Other costs may be harder to determine. If tourism becomes a primary customer base, residents may no longer attend the market. The loss of these sales can be calculated, but the loss of the market experience and social connections resulting from non-attendance must be estimated. Tourism may increase greenhouse gas emissions as tourists drive out of their way to visit the market and may generate more trash that is sent to the local landfill, causing price increases for trash removal. As small businesses cater to incoming tourists, central locations may develop boutique artisan businesses, further pushing residents away. Local traditions and culture can be influenced by the introduction of tourist values, clothing choices, or religious differences. Again, finding ways to quantify these impacts is difficult, but generally a good basis is using changes in purchasing patterns or estimating increased tax expenditures related to social services.

While these impacts may seem excessive for the development of a farmers' market, often all of these costs and benefits occur, even if on a small scale. Using a sustainable tourism approach allows the community to monitor these changes and take actions to find ways to increase benefits while reducing costs. For example, while adding artisan products might be more profitable, maintaining the opportunity for residents to purchase household goods should be preserved, even if it means less revenue is generated at the market. The money saved in gasoline (and greenhouse gas emissions) must be considered in the overall analysis.

Summary

Although many rural areas lost resources and primary production industries to urban areas in the industrial era, the modern era holds many opportunities for rural communities to increase economic development, especially through food and other types of rural tourism. While rural-to-urban migration is still an issue, the desire among a portion of the population to lead a rural lifestyle and the reduced importance of location for business activities are creating business opportunities and bringing highly skilled and educated labor back to rural areas. Tourism, in general, has been a successful rural economic development strategy, but food tourism specifically can perhaps provide even more potential for developing economic activity due to the financial, health, and environmental benefits of expanding local food production as well as its ability to enhance existing agricultural operations through diversification and retention of educated farm youth. Finally, as tourism has been shown to enhance the heritage and culture of an area, food tourism development may aid rural communities in bringing back their distinctive customs and traditions.

Study Questions

1 Explain why rural communities, even those close to each other, had distinct cultures, foods, and even languages up until the nineteenth century.
2 What does the term "brain drain" mean? How did rural-to-urban migration negatively impact rural communities?
3 Describe how food tourism development may increase employment opportunities in rural communities.
4 Why is the economic value of raw commodities lower than that of finished products or goods?
5 What are clusters and how can industry and governmental partnerships increase the probability of success in food tourism development?

6 Calculate the net present value of the following investment. Initial investment of US$200,000 and expected revenues in the first year of US$85,000, second-year revenues of US$120,000, and third-year revenues of US$200,000. Use a discount rate of 5%. Is this investment worth undertaking?

Definitions

Brain drain—a loss of trained or skilled professionals to another area, nation, etc., that offers greater opportunity.

Cluster—geographically close group of interconnected companies and associated institutions in an industry, linked by shared aims and complementary resources.

Discount rate—the interest rate used to discount the value of future earnings or costs.

Net present value—a comparison of discounted future cash inflows to present cash outflows.

Self-sufficiency—the ability to supply one's own needs without external assistance.

Urbanization—a population shift from rural to urban areas.

CASE STUDY 5.1

The culinary landscape—A case study of Devon, UK

Paul Cleave

Devon, a county in southwest England, is well known both as a producer of high-quality food and as a tourist destination. Its two contrasting coastlines, with rugged cliffs on the north coast, and palm trees and lush vegetation on the south, are complemented by the expanse of Dartmoor, a rich, fertile agricultural countryside. The county's farmers and fishermen produce a wide range of meat, fruit, vegetables, and fish. These have evolved and adapted to a changing culinary landscape. New products have appeared, including wines, cheeses, and chilies, whilst retaining and reviving traditions of farming and fishing, regional food distinction, and a unique sense of place.

Image 5.4 Clovelly village and harbor, Devon, UK
Source: Paul Cleave

Evolving food tourism

Devon has attracted tourists for generations. In addition to the climate, scenery, and history, its food heritage adds value to the experience of visiting the county. The popular Devonshire cream tea and souvenirs of clotted cream and clotted cream fudge demonstrate a link between place, agriculture, tourism, and the appeal of local food.

Early guidebooks and visitor journals show that the area's food was regarded as unique and of high quality, specifically its clotted cream and fish (Defoe et al., 1991; Murray, 1851). In an era of food tourism, consumer interests in heritage foods and their provenance is growing, and Devon's food history develops our understanding of contemporary food movements.

Clovelly and the Herring Festival

The connection between food, production, and place today is often showcased through festivals, especially smaller events focused on heritage and local products. The Tavistock Real Cheese Fair, Galmpton Gooseberry Pie Fair and Clovelly Herring Festival are examples of how the attraction of food evolves and uses the legacy of Devon's agricultural traditions. In the context of food tourism, these festivals represent a revival in artisan food and sustainable production. The Herring Festival links food to one place and one community, the historic and picturesque fishing village of Clovelly, nestled on the steeply wooded cliffs of North Devon. It reveals how food stimulates interest and provides opportunities for boosting tourism and revitalizing local industry.

Tourists have long been fascinated by Clovelly's steep cobbled streets, white-washed cottages, and harbor. The money they spend helps support the maintenance of the privately owned village and its local economy. It is a very popular tourist attraction that looks to its past, a history steeped in the fishing industry, around which the village grew. Fishing and the village are diversifying by offering new opportunities for tourism.

The festival, a one-day event, dates from 2007 but presents a longer history and connection with the fishing industry. Held in November, when the herrings, sometimes known as silver darlings, are succulent and of high quality. It is an opportunity for visitors to meet the fishermen and to taste the fish. Stephen Perham, a sixth-generation fisherman, has not missed a season since 1984 and is the last to use the traditional fishing boat, a picaroon.

What are the features of the festival? History, fishing, and the attraction of place, product, and producers. However, sustainability and ethics make this more than a nostalgic re-enactment. The healthy, nutritious herring (rich in omega-3 fatty acids), the fishermen, and the harbor, all provide tangible features for tourists. And an important sense of history provides a human connection, an important food chapter in the story of Devon's tourism.

Image 5.5 Freshly caught Clovelly herrings (silver darlings), Devon, UK
Source: Paul Cleave

Conclusions

Devon has a rich food heritage that can be used in the context of tourism. It is important for supporting and reviving the local economy, providing an edible connection to place and community. The example of herring identifies fashions and trends in food, periods of decline and revival, and shows how, in a competitive market, diversification, culinary uniqueness, and regional differentiation build on the heritage and qualities of food in rural areas. Investigating the connections between food, agriculture, and place shows that the county has much to offer in the framework of food tourism and a sense of place. References to the past and heritage in food and tourism are more than nostalgia; they represent a way of looking to the future and sustainable development. Food captures the spirit of place, linking food to location, culture, and history.

Questions

1 Why does the small-scale, artisan, sustainable local food festival attract tourists? Is this a niche market or does it have a wider appeal?
2 How can food heritage be used to support and revive local economies, especially in rural areas?
3 What role does history play in the development of a food festival? Is it necessary in rural communities to have a history of food production to be successful in food tourism development?

References

Defoe, D., Furbank, P.N., Owens, W. R., and Coulson, A.J. (1991). *A tour through the whole island of Great Britain*. New Haven, CT: Yale University Press.
Murray, J. (1851). *A hand-book for travellers in Devon & Cornwall*. London: John Murray.

Traditional cooking for food tourism in the Shekhawati and Hadoti Regions of Rajasthan, India

Anukrati Sharma and Azizul Hassan

This exploratory case study highlights the role of traditional cooking for food tourism promotion in the Shekhawati and Hadoti regions of the state of Rajasthan, India. In the Shekhawati region, there are three potential food tourism areas including Mandawa, Nawalgarh, and Jhunjhunu. In the Hadoti region there are four, including Kota, Bundi, Jhalawar, and Baran.

Rajasthan is a desert state suffering from water scarcity. The state does not have a suitable season for agriculture, which is one of the key reasons that local people use all vegetable waste, including the outside layers of vegetables—such as potatoes, green peas, or cauliflower stalks—to make pickles, chutneys, and gravies. The cooking stove (chulha), made from mud, is traditional to Rajasthan and uses wood or charcoal, which allows villagers to save money on expensive propane cylinders. This exemplifies how necessity can facilitate environmental friendliness through traditional cooking techniques that can also be used to promote food tourism in rural areas.

Despite unfavorable climatic conditions and a lack of water, money, and education, these regions hold immense scope for food tourism development. Both the central and local governments and the local bodies associated with the food and tourism industries recognize the potential of food tourism and have started working on its promotion. Although the local people of these two areas have limited income, the two regions of Rajasthan possess traditional cooking systems.

Research has documented interconnections between traditional cooking styles and tourism interests in regional identity. As food tourism destinations, Rajasthan requires additional initiatives to address some of the key issues relating to a lack of marketing, promotion, and branding strategies; collaboration with stakeholders; training; education; and research. Key strategies for food tourism promotion should highlight local food through traditional cooking styles and recipes. The opening of new restaurants and food outlets have increased in these areas, and selling regional dishes to visitors/tourists in nearby urban areas is becoming more common. The level of awareness among tourists about these traditional dishes is increasing, so encouraging the enjoyment of these authentic tastes in an authentic setting can further promote these delicacies, which in turn, can further increase rural people's earnings.

The concept of "glocalization"—a combination of globalization and localization—was introduced during the late 1980s (Sharma, 2009). Glocalization can be viewed as the adaptation of global products to the particularities of the regions where they are sold. This study is based on the glocalization concept and highlights how rural areas can develop and promote food tourism within tourism channels. However, to capitalize on the prospects of food tourism, some preliminary steps must be taken in the Rajasthan region, including:

- using innovations in food at the international level with the help of Indian cooking techniques and ingredients;
- starting food festivals that provide an opportunity for participation by local chefs to showcase their cooking skills;
- encouraging governments, the private sector, and educational institutions to collaborate and organize village food festivals;
- encouraging the media to support the initiatives with widespread publicity;
- increasing social media networking, which can be an effective source of marketing; and
- increasing the efforts of regional NGOs, academics, and students to promote local food.

This study suggests that food tourism can be a benefit to rural areas. Traditional food preparation, such as that highlighted here, can become an example for sustainable food tourism.

Questions

1   Do you think food tourism can enhance the standard of living in rural areas?
2   What innovations exist, if any, in the cuisine of the rural Rajasthan region?
3   How can rural areas promote their unique foodways to tourists?

References

Sharma, C.K. (2009). Emerging dimensions of decentralization debate in the age of globalization. *Indian Journal of Federal Studies*, 19(1), 47–65.

References

Albrecht, D. (2014). *Rethinking rural: Global community and economic development in the small town West*. Pullman, WA: Washington State University Press.

Barry, J.J., and Hellerstein, D. (2004). Farm recreation. In H.K. Cordell (principal author), *Outdoor recreation for 21st century America. A report to the nation: The national survey on recreation and the environment* (pp. 149–167). State College, PA: Venture Publishing, Inc.

Eckhardt, R. (2017). When the cows come home. *The Economist*. Retrieved from www.1843magazine.com/features/when-the-cows-come-home

Gallup. (2015). In U.S., telecommuting for work climbs to 37%. Retrieved from www.gallup.com/poll/184649/telecommuting-work-climbs.aspx?version=print

Galston, W., and Baehler, K. (1995). *Rural development in the United States: Connecting theory, practice, and possibilities*. Washington, DC: Island Press.

McKibben, B. (2007). *Deep Economy*. New York: Times Books.

Porter, M.E. (2000). Location, competition, and economic development: Local clusters in a global economy. *Economic Development Quarterly, 14*(1), 15–34.

Ramsey, M., and Schaumleffel, N. (2006). Agritourism and rural economic development. *Indiana Business Review, 84*(3), 6–9. Retrieved from www.ibrc.indiana.edu/ibr/2006/fall/article3.html

Shields, M., Barkley, D., and Emery, M. (2009). Industry clusters and industry targeting. In S. Goetz, S. Deller, and T. Harris (Eds.), *Targeting regional economic development* (pp. 35–46). New York: Routledge.

Tchetchik, A., Fleischer, A., and Finkelshtain, I. (2008). Differentiation and synergies in rural tourism: Estimation and simulation of the Israeli market. *American Journal of Agricultural Economics, 90*(2), 553–570.

United Nations Habitat. (2011). State of the Worlds Cities Report, 2010–2011. Retrieved from https://unhabitat.org/

U.S. Department of Agriculture, Economic Research Service. (2017). Rural Education. Retrieved from https://www.ers.usda.gov/topics/rural-economy-population/employment-education/rural-education.aspx

Walla Walla Community College. (2011). A study of the economic impact of the Walla Walla regional wine cluster as a basis for development of an economic development plan for the Walla Walla IPZ. Retrieved from https://www.wwcc.edu/CMS/fileadmin/wine/DOCS/A_Report_to_the_Department_of_Commerce.pdf

World Travel and Tourism Council. (2015). Travel and tourism: Economic impact 2015 United States of America. Retrieved from https://www.wttc.org/-/media/files/reports/economic%20impact%20research/countries%202015/unitedstatesofamerica2015.pdf

Chapter 6

Modern food movements

Overview

This chapter discusses three modern food movements, including the buy local, foodie, and sustainable consumption movements. The values and characteristics of each are discussed, in addition to the current food-related demand motives and desired product attributes, such as local, grass-fed, fair-trade, and organic. The rationale behind the rise of these movements—including the phases of food-demand development and the historical changes in agricultural production, food processing, and consumption—are detailed. Importantly, these food movements have spurred food tourism demand and development globally and greatly changed the tourism landscape to include food- and drink-specific travel.

Learning Objectives

This chapter will enable students to:

1   Understand the history behind the rise of modern food movements.
2   Define the three primary modern food movements and the values and attributes of each.
3   Recognize the differences among the three phases of food demand and preference development.
4   Discuss current consumer food-related demand motives and product attribute preferences.
5   Describe how modern food movements motivate tourist demand for food-based vacations and foodie destinations.

Rise of modern food movements

In the last decade of the twentieth century and early twenty-first century, a number of consumer food-related concerns emerged, ranging across an array of human, animal, and environmental or ecological dimensions. Examples of these concerns include—but are not limited to—food safety; food origin; natural and sustainable production or growing practices; human health; the treatment of animals in livestock production; the health, treatment, and working conditions of farm workers; maintaining agriculture and farmlands or open space; and supporting local businesses, including farmers. Additional concerns include the loss of plant and animal diversity and "traditional" crops and medicinal plants as well as a loss of culture, including traditional cuisines and recipes.

Four primary factors contributed to the growth of these consumer food concerns. The first has to do with simple long-term changes in consumer food demand and preferences. Worldwide, food-related concerns developed shortly after many developed nations moved to the highest, or third phase, of food demand, referred to as the *high income* phase. The three phases of food demand are food scarcity, growing income, and high income. In the food scarcity phase, food demand is primarily for nutritional needs, and the percentage of family income spent on food is high. Additionally, any change in the price of food or in family income greatly effects consumer demand. In the growing income phase, consumer food demand is less sensitive to price and income changes, and other factors—such as enjoyment, variety, and health—become more important. In the high income phase, product pricing and income are only small factors in consumer demand, and the percentage of family income spent on food is small. In this phase, food safety,

Image 6.1 Ranked 'Best Pizza' in Cuba by the tourist guide book, Guanabo, Cuba
Source: Kynda R. Curtis

environmental and political interests, food events and enjoyment, food availability and variety, and health are primary factors in the decision process. Many characteristics of the modern food movements can be seen in the food demand priorities of the high income phase.

Second, the industrialization of agriculture and the globalization of the food supply in the twentieth century, detailed in Chapter 4, played a large role in cultivating consumer concerns and developing food-related value systems. In developed countries, many farms and ranches transitioned from small, family-owned farms growing a variety of crops into large corporate farms (many family-owned), sometimes referred to as "Big Food." While small farms still make up 89% of all farms in the United States, large-scale farming now accounts for 53% of total agricultural production, up from 33% in 1991 (U.S. Department of Agriculture, Economic Research Service, 2016a). These large corporate farms adopted production systems that allow them to specialize in one or two crops, or monoculture farming.

Similar changes were seen in livestock production, where family farms with a few livestock on hand for their own consumption became large-scale confined animal-feeding operations. In *The Omnivore's Dilemma*, Michael Pollan explains that

> [b]eginning in the fifties and sixties, the flood tide of cheap corn made it profitable to fatten cattle on feedlots instead of on grass, and to raise chickens in giant factories rather than in farmyards. Iowa livestock farmers couldn't compete with the factory-farmed animals their own cheap corn had helped spawn, so the chickens and cattle disappeared from the farm, and with them the pastures and hay fields and fences. In their place the farmers planted more of the one crop they could grow more of than anything else: corn.
>
> (Pollan 2006, p. 39)

Third, agricultural production in the twentieth century experienced significant scientific and technological change that allowed annual world production of cereals, coarse grains, roots and tubers, pulses, and oil crops to grow from 1.8 billion tons to 4.6 billion tons between 1961 and 2009 worldwide (Food and Agriculture Organization of the United Nations, 2011). As scientific advances in agriculture led to the creation of new crop varieties and livestock breeds for the purpose of increasing crops yields or the rate of weight gain (gain rates) in livestock, the use of chemical inputs in farming and ranching also expanded greatly. Unfortunately, many of these new crop varieties rely on numerous input applications, such as fertilizers and pesticides, to succeed, and the proliferation of the new varieties has led to the disappearance of traditional varieties and reduced biodiversity worldwide. For example, in *Slow Food Nation*, Petrini describes the impact of introducing new corn varieties to Mexico: "The spread of the intensive cultivation of corn has threatened other vegetable species, too, such as amaranth. This food, together with beans and corn, was the basis of the Aztec diet" (2005, p. 11).

In the last two decades of the twentieth century, the introduction of genetic engineering and genetically modified organisms (GMOs) also contributed to consumer concerns worldwide. The success of GMOs, or hybrid seed varieties, is well documented, as corn yields in the United States have increased by 500% in recent years, but GMOs have been highly controversial. Public aversion to their use is especially high in regions where there is a general distrust for scientific innovation and a past history of falsehoods in government-provided food safety information. Of primary concern are the potential long-term health effects and environmental impacts of GMOs, including the creation of "super weeds" and

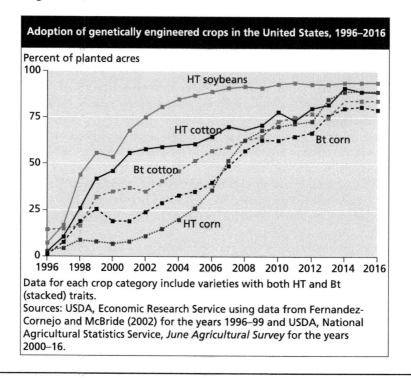

Figure 6.1 Adoption of genetically engineered crops in the United States, 1996–2016
Source: U.S. Department of Agriculture, Economics Research Service (2016b)

cross-pollination of non-GMO and GMO crops. While genetically modified crops—such as corn, rice, soybeans, and tomatoes—have taken hold and now account for a large portion of worldwide production, some crops—such as the genetically modified "BT Potato"—have not fared as well. Media coverage referring to these potatoes as "Frankenfries" led to Monsanto eventually scrapping the technology. Figure 6.1 shows the extent to which biotech crops have been adopted in the United States.

Lastly, changes in global lifestyle and family situations have led to increased demand for fast, convenient food. In the 1970s, many women began earning university degrees and entering the workforce. Average family size shrank considerably and the divorce rate increased. Families with two working spouses experienced increased disposable income. With money at their disposal but constraints on their time (also experienced by single-parent households), individuals began trying to limit the amount of time involved in food production or preparation as much as possible. Food manufacturers moved to fill this demand through increased processing and the creation of ready-to-eat foods and meals. Canned and frozen foods became popular, as did microwaveable meals and ready-to-bake pizzas. The prevalence of processed food is evidenced by the change in the percentage of the consumer food dollar that goes to the farmer, which in 1970 was close to 40% and today is only 15% (U.S. Department of Agriculture, Economic Research Service, 2017a). This means that 85% of money spent on food today goes to processing, packaging, wholesaling, retailing, energy, transportation, etc.

While the variety of products available in grocery stores expanded due to the proliferation of processing, the variety of ingredients used in processing was greatly reduced. Pollan explains,

> There are some forty-five thousand items in the average American supermarket and more than one quarter of them now contain corn. ... Even in produce on a day when there's ostensibly no corn for sale, you'll nevertheless find plenty of corn: in the vegetable wax that gives the cucumbers their sheen, in the pesticide responsible for the produce's perfection, even in the coating on the cardboard box it was shipped in.
>
> (Pollan, 2006, p. 19)

Simultaneously, fast food restaurants and take-out options began to expand. As fewer people prepared their own meals at home, eating food away from home (FAFH) became much more prevalent. Petrini states that

> Children and teenagers in big American cities no longer eat at home; their parents do not cook at all, and the family does not come together for meals. Food is bought either in a form of prepared meals from the supermarket or at the local fast-food restaurant.
>
> (Petrini, 2005, p. 47)

Schlosser in *Fast Food Nation* paints a portrait of the American demand for fast food, stating, "in a given year, Americans will spend over $110 billion on fast food—more than they'll spend on movies, books, magazines, newspapers, videos, and recorded music combined" (Schlosser, 2001, p. 3). In recent years, the average American spent 45% of their food budget on FAFH, up from 25% in 1970 (U.S. Department of Agriculture, Economic Research Service, 2012). Almost half of all meals in the United States are eaten in restaurants, cafés, and cafeterias.

Distance from the food production process both physically (due to urban migration) and structurally (due to increased consumption of processed and prepared foods) has led to a general loss of cooking skills among urban dwellers and created uncertainty and distrust regarding the safety and environmental impacts of farming and food safety in food preparation. This distrust has been further fueled by increased media exposure of food recalls, food safety outbreaks, and government mismanagement of outbreaks of Foot and Mouth Disease and Mad Cow Disease (BSE) in Europe. Published research linking pesticide use to cancer in humans and research clearly connecting the consumption of processed foods and FAFH with increased calorie intake (resulting in a worldwide obesity epidemic) further fueled consumer distrust in food production and the legitimacy of health-food claims.

Modern food movements explained

Three primary food movements emerged in the early twenty-first century, fueled by popular literature—such as *The Omnivore's Dilemma*, *Fast Food Nation*, and *Slow Food Nation*—praising traditional or "old world" food preparation and growing methods and criticized large-scale monoculture farming. The U.S. Department of Agriculture (USDA) further inflated the attention on these movements through its 2009 "Know Your Farmer, Know Your Food" initiative, which focused on increasing local food sales through direct-to-consumer markets in the United States. Similarly, the Department for Environment,

Food and Rural Affairs (DEFRA) in the United Kingdom created the Policy Commission on the Future of Farming and Food in 2001, which aimed to create a sustainable, competitive, and diverse farming and food sector (UK Department for Environment, Food and Rural Affairs, 2002). These food movements have been incorporated into culture globally through buzzwords, including locavore, farm-to-table, farm-to-fork, green, and foodie.

The first of the food movements—the "Buy Local" or "Locavore" movement—emphasizes purchasing food grown and/or processed close to home. A **locavore**, per the Oxford Dictionary (2017), is "a person whose diet consists only or principally of locally grown or produced food." There is no set definition of local, but consumers normally define local as in-state (or province) or within 100 miles (160 kilometers) of their home. Supermarket chains often define local as within 400 miles (643 kilometers) or a one-day drive from the retail location. Locavores use direct markets to purchase fresh produce and processed items such as jams, cheese, honey, etc. as much as possible. Direct markets include farmers' markets, Consumer Supported Agriculture (CSA) programs, farm stands, farm shops, and similar outlets managed or run by a farmer or farming organization. Locavores will shop at grocery stores that source locally and specialty stores if needed and are willing to pay premium prices for locally grown food over those of other or unknown origin (Bosworth et al., 2015; Gumirakiza et al., 2015). Locavores seek fresh, high-quality, safe food and

Image 6.2 Locally made soaps in Las Vegas, Nevada, USA
Source: Kynda R. Curtis

are motivated by a desire to support local farmers, preserve agricultural open space, and develop personal relationships with local farmers or at least know where their food was produced.

Locavores do a lot of cooking at home and, hence, eat out much less compared to the average population (only 10% of the time compared to 55% on average) (Curtis & Cowee, 2011). When they do eat out, they prefer to frequent restaurants that source locally. The National Restaurant Association's 2015 *Restaurant Industry Forecast* reported that seven of ten consumers were more likely to visit a restaurant offering locally sourced items. Finally, locavores often have their own gardens at home.

Evidence of the growing locavore movement in the United States includes a 200% increase in farmers' markets from 2000 to 2016, a 275% increase in CSA programs from 2004 to 2014, and a 288% increase in food hubs from 2007 to 2014. The National Grocers Association 2014 Consumer Panel found that the availability of local foods was a major influence on grocery shopping decisions, as 87.2% of respondents rated local food availability as "very or somewhat important," with 44.2% indicating "very important" (National Grocers Association, 2014). The need for "more locally grown foods" was the second most desired improvement among surveyed grocery shoppers at 36.4%, just under "price/cost savings." Product origin became so important that many countries in the first decade of the twenty-first century instated mandatory county-of-origin labeling (COOL) requirements across a broad range of agricultural and food products. The labeling requirements differ by country, and updates, including added or excluded foods, are made often. Both the United States and the European Union have recently removed country-of-origin labeling requirements for beef to comply with a World Trade Organization ruling against beef country-of-origin labeling (Andrews, 2014).

The second movement is the "foodie" movement, defined by **foodies**, individuals who wish to experience and enjoy food but do not work in the food industry. Foodies consume food not just as nourishment but also as a social and cultural experience. They seek variety and diversity in their food options and are willing to experiment. Foodies have been known to seek prestigious types of food and dining locations, such as gourmet and specialty foods and high-end restaurants. Members of the foodie movement often travel specifically to experience food traditions and ethnic foods as expressions of foreign culture. They are likely to be members of food or wine clubs, such as Slow Food, and have an interest in cooking at home.

Foodies are also heavily interested in drink tourism and often travel specifically to visit wineries or craft breweries and participate in blending and pairing classes. This type of drink-related travel has resulted in substantial economic impacts. For example, in 2011, Napa Valley, California saw wine-related tourism expenditures of US$1.05 billion (Stonebridge Research, 2012) and craft breweries generated US$3 billion in economic impact in California (Richey, 2012). In North Carolina, 1.2 million winery visits led to US$156 million in tourism expenditures (Frank, Rimerman & Co., 2009) and the 2014 Oregon Brewers Festival added US$32.6 million to the economy (Oregon Craft Beer, 2014). Chapter 7 provides additional discussion of foodies as food tourists.

The last of the three modern food movements is the **sustainable consumption** movement, defined by individuals with strong health and environmental concerns that motivate their food choices. They demand natural and environmentally friendly foods as well as sustainable food production processes and practices. They purchase almost exclusively organic foods or, at a minimum, food produced with no synthetic chemicals, and are willing to pay premiums for organics over conventionally grown foods (Curtis & Cowee, 2011; Gumirakiza et al., 2015). **Organic** production uses cultural, biological, and

Image 6.3 Local woman explaining traditional wheat processing in Tanzania
Source: Susan L. Slocum

mechanical practices that support recycling resources, promote ecological balance, and conserve biodiversity. Organic producers are required to avoid the use of synthetic chemicals, antibiotics, genetically modified foods, and hormones in crop and livestock production and rely instead on biological pest management, cover crops, and other ecologically based practices. Research has associated these practices with a variety of benefits, including reduced pesticide residues in food and water, lower energy use, and enhanced biodiversity (U.S. Department of Agriculture, Economic Research Service, 2017b).

As sustainability is very important to this group, they are concerned with reducing food waste and limiting the energy used in food production as well as reducing **food miles**, the distance that food travels from farm to final sale. Due to a lack of trust in conventional food distribution systems, these individuals purchase the majority of their food through direct-to-consumer outlets and specialty stores.

Evidence of the growth in this movement can be seen in the increased demand for organic foods. Organic food purchases in the United States reached US$43 billion in 2016, up from US$10 billion in 2004, and accounted for approximately 5% of total at-home food expenditures in 2015, more than double the share in 2005 (U.S. Department of Agriculture, Economic Research Service, 2017b). There are currently 6 million certified organic farmland acres in the United States. While fresh fruits and vegetables are still the top-selling organic category, organic sales in all other food categories also increased from 2005 to 2015. The organic dairy sector is now the second-largest category of organic sales (see Figure 6.2).

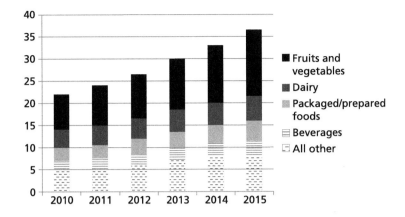

Figure 6.2 Organic food retail sales in the United States, 2010–2015 (US$ billion)
Source: Adapted from U.S. Department of Agriculture, Economic Research Service (2017b)

Need for food labeling

Consumer concerns and uncertainty have made food labeling and certification programs essential. Numerous labeling and certification programs have emerged to reduce consumer uncertainty or distrust in corporate labeling. This stems primarily from the lack of ability to discern labeling designations through visual inspection or by tasting or smelling the product. Only the farmer or the processor knows whether the food was organically grown or sustainable practices were used. Most certification programs center around designating food origin (locally grown), organically grown, natural, fair-trade, grass-fed, humanely raised, free range, non-GMO, sustainable (low water, reduced waste, etc.), environmentally friendly, or antibiotic or growth hormone free.

Communicating the geographic location of food production has been an important labeling strategy in Europe. The European Union has granted legal protection for the names of food products closely identified with where they were produced or methods used in production through the European Union Protected Designation of Origin (PDO) or Protected Geographical Designation (PGI). Examples include Bordeaux PDO (France, wine), Cava PDO (Spain, wine), and Manouri PDO (Greece, cheese). In the United States, state-sponsored designations (SSDs) are commonly used to promote agricultural food products produced in a state. Since 2001, every state has created a promotional program for its agricultural products, such as Utah's Own, Virginia Grown, and Made in Arizona.

Certification programs are commonly run by third-party organizations, such as governmental agencies or non-governmental organizations (NGOs). These recognized and established labeling programs provide consumers with the assurance that products meet the program's standards. Importantly, the third-party does not benefit directly from the sale of the good and thus has no reason to misrepresent it. These programs set standards or specific quality levels that must be met by member companies and defined in consumer-known terminology. Certification programs also conduct testing and inspections, employ objective measures of quality, and set record-keeping requirements. They provide program

Figure 6.3 Third-party food certification labels

members with labels that designate which products have been certified. Finally, they enforce member compliance with program standards by applying fines or penalties for non-compliance. Common third-party food certification labels are shown in Figure 6.3.

Summary

Three modern food movements emerged in the early twenty-first century due to increasing consumer concerns related to food and agricultural production and distribution worldwide. These concerns spanned human, animal, and environmental dimensions but were generally fueled by uncertainty and distrust. While industrial agriculture, scientific and technological innovation in agriculture, globalized food distribution systems, and the immense expansion of food processing and marketing have surely positively impacted society (such as the ability to feed rapidly growing global populations, increased food availability of out-of-season products through transportation and processing, reduced food preparation time, etc.), it is obvious that there are also negative ramifications.

The motivating factors for consumer concerns and the growth of modern food movements should be clear. Purchasing locally grown produce, perhaps even from a farmer you know, could greatly reduce any fears or concerns about where your food comes from and its safety. It also seems plausible that reconnecting with food and how it is grown, prepared, and enjoyed would be more favorable than living off canned soup or fast-food takeout. If you were concerned about your health, you could imagine purchasing organic vegetables and preparing meals at home to reduce extra calories from fats and sugars. If you were concerned about the environment, you might purchase local foods to reduce food miles or buy meats from a local rancher who uses environmentally friendly practices or sells free-range chickens.

While each of the three food movements—buy local, foodie, and sustainable consumption—have specific values and characteristics, together they have fueled increased tourist demand for food-based vacations, visiting wineries and breweries, and the development of foodie destinations. Whether a tourist is a locavore, foodie, or a sustainability enthusiast, they are an eager food tourist. For example, locavores will seek out local-sourcing restaurants, local and ethnic foods, farmers' markets, and food festivals when traveling. Foodies will also seek out locally sourcing restaurants, food and drink festivals, and wineries and breweries when traveling. The sustainable consumer will seek out farmers' markets to buy organic produce and frequent locally sourcing businesses to reduce food miles.

Study Questions

1. What positive impacts could scientific and technological innovation in agriculture have on society?
2. How does the high-income phase of food demand development differ from the food scarcity phase?
3. Do you identify with one of the three modern food movements? Which one and why?
4. How does urban-to-rural migration impact consumer concerns and attitudes toward food?
5. How does third-party certification and labeling reduce consumer uncertainty about the food they purchase?
6. List two food tourism activities, events, or products of interest for individuals in each of the three food movements.

Definitions

Food miles—the distance food is transported from the time of its production until it reaches the consumer.
Foodie—someone with a long-standing passion for eating and learning about food but who is not a food professional.
Locavore—a person whose diet consists principally of locally grown or produced food.
Organic—cultural, biological, and mechanical production practices that support recycling resources, promote ecological balance, and conserve biodiversity.
Sustainable consumption—the purchasing of products and services that support health and environmental well-being.

Mekong Delta, Vietnam—A truly "local" experience

Kynda R. Curtis

The biologically diverse Mekong Delta region of southwestern Vietnam is the country's most productive agricultural and aquaculture area. Most of the local food and drink is made from rice, the primary crop. This section of the Mekong is a group of seven separate forks or "fingers" of the river, with many islands interspersed between each fork. The forks are large rivers in their own right, equal in size to the entire Mekong River in parts of Thailand and Laos. There are several primary towns on the Delta. Among these, Cai Be is accessible from the mainland by roads, but the majority are only accessible by boat. Tourism development here offers a variety of unique experiences, including boat trips, bike tours, wildlife viewing, cooking schools, flower nurseries, and demonstrations of traditional arts and crafts and other handmade goods.

I traveled to the Mekong Delta to experience the local culture, specifically focusing on food and drink. As I had not previously traveled to Vietnam, I signed up for a two-day tour of the Delta. The tour group arrived in Cai Be having traveled by bus from Ho Chi Minh City early that morning. We immediately set off by a small wooden motorboat, typical of the area, to visit the Cai Be floating market, where families—who primarily live on their boats—sell and trade local fruits, vegetables, and other goods. These boats and others that line the corridors of the Mekong are brightly colored and paint the green surroundings in blue, red, and purple. The Cai Be floating market has decreased in size over the years, as rural-to-urban migration in the area has decreased the population of the Delta. Traditional floating markets were used extensively until the mid-1900s, when roads made travel between towns easier. Floating markets are being revived across Southeast Asia to share the history and culture with tourists and the younger generation. We purchased a few fruit items and experienced the local trading traditions that have existed on the Delta for generations.

Our next stop was to a local family business that processes coconut candy, rice paper, crispy rice popcorn, and other rice snacks and rice wine using traditional methods. We were given a demonstration of how each product was made and the techniques that have been passed from generation to generation. This family sells their products through their farm store on-site as well as in local towns. Our next stop nearby was a fruit plantation. There we tasted many unique fruits, many of which were not available in Western markets. While we enjoyed the fruit and local drink, we listened to southern Vietnamese folk music performed by a local music group.

For lunch, we traveled to Tan Phong Island, which the locals call "the green pearl". When we arrived, we bicycled in a long, stretching line around the island

Image 6.4 Cai Be floating market vendor in Vietnam
Source: Kynda R. Curtis

through traditional paths crossing small rivers and canals as we went. This island is a nature preserve and has many homestays and small eco-tourism resorts. When we arrived back at the homestay, we found out that we were going to prepare our own lunch. Through cooking demonstrations, we learned how to prepare three separate traditional Vietnamese dishes, including spring rolls. I was honored to be given a prize for creating the best spring roll among the group.

After our afternoon on Tan Phong Island, I transferred to another island for my homestay for the night. My guide, Miu, was a very energetic and expressive young lady. Before dinner, we strolled the small walkways of the island and then took a short rest before preparing our dinner. Miu and I prepared several traditional dishes, but the primary dish was a rice pancake filled with meat and vegetables. The homestay was a typical Mekong farm home built in the late nineteenth century. That evening as I sat under the netting and experienced the quietness of island living, I felt very much like a local, many, many miles from home.

Homestays are very popular in Vietnam and provide guests with a unique and real cultural experience hard to find elsewhere. Most are in the countryside in small villages. They are especially popular in the Hmong villages in northern Vietnam. Homestays are regulated by the government, and each has a tourism marker with the name of the home and its construction date. The majority have been outfitted with Western-style toilets and showers to accommodate tourists.

The next morning, we traveled to a nearby island to visit a known "ancient" house, which has been preserved to illustrate a combination of Vietnamese and French colonial architectural styles. Out next stop was a rice-husking mill, where rice was processed, loaded into large sacks, and placed on boats for transport. The boats lined up waiting for their loads, similar to the way semitrucks do. It was amusing to watch the boat owners go about their daily chores, such as preparing food and doing laundry, right on the boat.

On our way to lunch at a small, family-run restaurant only accessible by boat, a huge thunderstorm crossed the Delta and we had to pull our boat over to a grouping of trees and lily pads at the river's edge to wait it out. It was raining so hard, it was impossible to see across the river. Sitting on the boat amongst the foliage with Miu and our driver, I again faced what it is like to live on the Delta, a truly local experience.

Questions

1 How would the Mekong Delta experience suit the needs of a locavore, foodie, and sustainable consumer on vacation?
2 While some of the activities discussed here were crafted for tourists, does that take away from their authenticity?
3 How could this type of vacation be replicated in other rural areas? How would locavores', foodies', and sustainable consumers' needs be incorporated?

CASE STUDY 6.2

Campuhan Ridge—Authenticity in the tropics

Izaak A. Wierman

I'm convinced that American culture is obsessed with safety. Hygiene and health, travel and traffic, farming and food, everything is steeped in risk, responsibility, liability, and law. Everything predictable and controlled. Regulated. Indonesian culture was, when I visited, frightening and refreshing in comparison.

Ubud lies in the heart of Bali, the Indonesian island between Java to the west and Lombok to the east. I stayed at a villa behind the Bintang Market, incidentally the same name as the local macro-beer. To reach the villa, one must walk from the roadside up a narrow concrete stair labeled with a handwritten sign reading "to behind Bintang," which, in Ubud, qualifies as a street address, down a narrow, high-walled passage for 50 yards. Then you pass neighboring villas between rice fields, stepping up, stepping down irrigation channels running alongside the small and slippery path, under banana and papaya trees. Beautiful and entirely inaccessible to strollers or wheelchairs or even large roller bags. I'm thankful I packed light for the trip.

Finally, I arrive at the place. It has an outdoor kitchen and bedrooms and bathrooms that are open to the outside. No sterile, glass-windowed, air-conditioned space. But the owner has left a fruit bowl. A fruit bowl that, if I had never been to the tropics, would have been unimaginable. It's piled high with banana, mangosteen, passion fruit, blood oranges, rambutan, mango, salak fruit, and all the papaya one could possibly eat. The only fruit with a sticker on it is a pair of red apples, probably purchased at the Bintang, and definitely out of place in this bowl. The ants arrive at the same time as the fruit, but they don't have fingers and knives and can't really get to the fruit unless you cut it for them. It's a joy to sample these fruits, so ripe they must have been grown and picked within walking distance of the villa.

Image 6.5 Overlooking the Campuhan Ridge in Bali, Indonesia
Source: Kynda R. Curtis

The road from Bintang to the trailhead is busy. Not busy like a U.S. interstate freeway interchange at rush hour, but Indonesia-busy—close, confined, and crowded with motorcycles. Small motorcycles that have creatively balanced loads. You must walk this road back toward town about a mile to reach the trailhead. Varied businesses, shops, and art dealers line uneven narrow walks alongside the road. Each storefront has left an offering to smoke and smolder out front.

The Campuhan Ridge trail begins near the Gunung Lebah Temple, both of which are steeped in tradition. Following along the western wall of the temple, there are views of its particular architecture and of the jungle foliage. It's there that I finally feel enough distance from the main road to breathe freely. It is hot and humid and I have mixed feelings about the climb up the ridge out from under the jungle canopy. The views from the ridge are worth it, though. A young couple is having wedding pictures taken from the ridge, and I wait a while as they try for the perfect shot. As I continue up the trail between the two rivers far below, I follow in the footsteps of generations of Bali residents. The trail finally levels off, eventually meeting the end of a road accessible by vehicles. There's a small community of resident farmers and artists living there. At last, I arrive at the two-story, open-air, thatched-roof Karsa Café, which provides a convenient pause along the trail for refreshments or a quick bite while admiring the view.

Image 6.6 The Karsa Café, Bali, Indonesia
Source: Kynda R. Curtis

A small pickup truck rolls up and workers begin unloading coconuts. I kick off my shoes and take the stairs to the wonderfully shaded second floor, where just a hint of a breeze moves through. The customers are all tourists, but adventurous ones. I order a "Fresh Young Coconut" from the staff because the delivery makes it clear they serve them regularly. Using a large knife, more like a machete, they cut a triangular hole in the coconut, drop in a straw, and it's ready to drink. Perfect after walking up the Campuhan Ridge in the heat. There's no rush, so I'm able to relax and take in the view—rice field after rice field terraced and cultivated, vibrant green, and flourishing in the sun. After a time, they halve the coconut for me and bring a spoon so I can eat the meat from its center. It's the perfect refreshment in a perfect setting. Tropical fruits are best eaten in the tropics.

Questions

1 Which of the three modern food movements does this experience in Bali most likely align with and why?
2 What strategies might be used to reduce consumer uncertainty concerning locally grown foods in Indonesia?
3 How else might rural communities combine fresh produce with tourism economies?

References

Andrews, J. (2014). WTO Rules against country-of-origin labeling on meat in U.S. *Food Safety News*. Retrieved from www.foodsafetynews.com/2014/10/wto-rules-against-country-of-origin-labeling-on-meat-in-us/#.WOJ7hv7ruUk

Bosworth, R., Bailey, D., and Curtis, K. (2015). Consumer willingness to pay for local designations: Brand effects and heterogeneity at the retail level. *Journal of Food Products Marketing*, 21(3), 274–292.

Curtis, K.R., and Cowee, M.W. (2011). Buying local: Diverging consumer motivations and concerns. *Journal of Agribusiness*, 29(1), 1–22.

Food and Agriculture Organization of the United Nations. (2011). *Save and grow: A policymaker's guide to the sustainable intensification of smallholder crop production*. Rome: FAO. Retrieved from www.fao.org/3/a-i2215e.pdf

Frank, Rimerman and Co. (2009). *Full economic impact of wine and wine grapes on the North Carolina Economy – 2009*. Retrieved from www.nccommerce.com/Portals/10/Documents/NorthCarolinaWineEconomicImpactStudy2009.pdf

Greene, C., Ferreira, G., Carlson, A., Cooke, B., and Hitaj, C. (2017). Growing organic demand provides high-value opportunities for many types of producers. *Amber Waves*. Washington, DC: USDA-ERS. Retrieved from www.ers.usda.gov/amber-waves/2017/january february/growing-organic-demand-provides-high-value-opportunities-for-many-types-of-producers/

Gumirakiza, J.D., Curtis, K.R., and Bosworth, R. (2015). Farmers' market consumer preferences for fresh produce attributes: Marketing and policy implications. *Journal of Agribusiness*, 33(1), 63–81.

National Grocers Association. (2014). Supermarketguru consumer survey report. Retrieved from origin.library.constantcontact.com/download/get/file/1102509927195-2152/Consumer SurveyReport2014.pdf

National Restaurant Association. (2015). Restaurant industry forecast. Retrieved from www.restaurant.org/News-Research/Research/Forecast-2015

Oregon Craft Beer. (2014). The economic impact of the Oregon Brewers Fest is $32.6 million. Retrieved from oregoncraftbeer.org/the-economic-impact-of-the-oregon-brewers-fest-is-32-6-million/

Oxford Dictionary. (2017). Locavore. Retrieved from www.oxforddictionaries.com/us

Petrini, C. (2005). *Slow food nation: Why our food should be good, clean, and fair*. New York: Rizzoli Ex Libris.

Pollan, M. (2006). *The omnivore's dilemma: A natural history of four meals*. New York: Penguin Press.

Richey, D. (2012). California craft brewing industry: An economic impact study. Retrieved from www.californiacraftbeer.com/wp-content/uploads/2012/10/Economic-Impact-Study-FINAL.pdf

Schlosser, E. (2001). *Fast food nation: The dark side of the all-American meal*. Boston: Mariner Books.

Stonebridge Research. (2012). The economic impact of Napa County's wine and grapes. Retrieved from https://napavintners.com/downloads/napa_economic_impact_2012.pdf

U.S. Department of Agriculture, Economic Research Service. (2012). Food-away-from-home. Retrieved from https://www.ers.usda.gov/topics/food-choices-health/food-consumption-demand/food-away-from-home.aspx

U.S. Department of Agriculture, Economic Research Service. (2016a). American's diverse family farms. Economic Information Bulletin 164. Washington, DC: USDA-ERS. Retrieved from https://www.ers.usda.gov/webdocs/publications/eib164/eib-164.pdf

U.S. Department of Agriculture, Economic Research Service. (2016b). Recent trends in GE adoption. Retrieved from https://www.ers.usda.gov/data-products/adoption-of-genetically-engineered-crops-in-the-us/recent-trends-in-ge-adoption/

U.S. Department of Agriculture, Economic Research Service. (2017a). Decline in farm share of U.S. food dollar mirrors drop in farm commodity prices. Retrieved from https://www.ers.usda.gov/data-products/chart-gallery/gallery/chart-detail/?chartId=82936

U.S. Department of Agriculture, Economic Research Service. (2017b). Growing organic demand provides high-value opportunities for many types of producers. Retrieved from https://www.ers.usda.gov/amber-waves/2017/januaryfebruary/growing-organic-demand-provides-high-value-opportunities-for-many-types-of-producers/

UK Department for Environment, Food, and Rural Affairs (DEFRA). (2002). *Farming & food: A sustainable future*. Report of the Policy Commission on the Future of Farming and Food. Retrieved from webarchive.nationalarchives.gov.uk/20100807034701/http:/archive.cabinetoffice.gov.uk/farming/pdf/PC%20Report2.pdf

Part III

Food tourism markets and targeted destination design

Image III.1 River transport on the Mekong River, Vietnam
Source: Kynda R. Curtis

Chapter 7

Characterizing the food tourist

Overview

Catering to tourists' needs and expectations is vital to the success of any food tourism operation. This chapter explains a variety of tourist types and highlights the need to assess tourism typologies in order to develop a comprehensive food tourism initiative. In particular, it looks at tourists' expectations and motivation for food-based travel to ensure that the tourists' satisfaction is achieved. This chapter also provides descriptive information about foodies and food tourists, such as age and income profiles, food-related experience and activities, and personal values.

Learning Objectives

This chapter will enable students to:

1 Understand the differences between tourist expectations, motivations, and satisfaction as they relate to food tourism.
2 Explain the difference between neophiles and neophobes as it relates to food consumption.
3 Understand the characteristics and values of a foodie.
4 Describe tourism motivations for food-related travel.
5 Compare and contrast different tourism typologies as they relate to food tourists.
6 Understand the basic characteristics of food tourists.

Understanding the tourist

When developing any tourism destination or attraction, the tourist must be the primary concern in order for the product to be sustainable. Customer satisfaction is the cornerstone of any business's success. Tourists have expectations, and economic success lies in meeting or exceeding those expectations. Purchasing a travel experience represents a number of risks to vacationers; as tourism activities tend to last longer than other leisure activities, they require a larger financial investment, and the quality or suitability of the destination and its associated activities is unknown prior to arrival (Croce & Perri, 2010). The emotional investment tourists have is also high, given that travel experiences become a part of one's life story. Negative experiences may impact the tourists' perceptions of the entire vacation. Therefore, it is important that the tourism experience is very positive.

Tourism provides a number of positive opportunities for people. Primarily, it gives people something exciting to look forward to and frees them from the routine of everyday life as well as exposure to new activities, environments, and cultures. Swarbrooke (1999, p. 71) provides the following list of tourism impacts on tourists themselves:

- the ability to relax and unwind as a remedy to the pressures of modern life;
- an escape from routine or monotonous jobs;
- an escape from everyday living environments (traffic, pollution, household chores);
- an opportunity to see new parts of the world and broaden their worldviews;
- an opportunity to see and experience new sights and sounds (exotic animals, historical sites); and
- the ability to meet and interact with new people.

Most destinations encourage visitation through promotion, which means that tourists are generally invited guests rather than unwanted intruders. They have the right to a quality vacation experience at a fair price; security and safety while they travel; freedom from exploitation; freedom from discrimination on the basis of race, gender, sexual orientation, or religious beliefs; and a clear idea of what a destination offers (or does not offer) through fair marketing. Like any paying customer, tourists expect a certain value for the price they pay. However, how a tourist values travel can vary considerably from person to person.

Tourists also have certain responsibilities when they travel. They must obey local laws and regulations; they should be respectful of local customs, religious practices, and social norms; and they should not deliberately harm the local environment. However, tourists tend to possess a certain level of hedonism (self-involvement) when traveling, as vacation time is something for which they have worked very hard. Tourists sometimes feel that the rules do not apply to them or may be so engrossed in the experience that they forget to practice responsible travel. Examples of inappropriate behavior includes disregard for dress, such as wearing shorts or tank tops in conservative communities; littering or forgetting to recycle; excessive consumption of alcohol; and more critical behaviors such as drug use and sex with minors.

Education is a vital component of any tourism package, ensuring that tourists follow rules and receive the rights mentioned above. It is safe to assume that not all tourists know the specific social norms or regulations associated with every destination in the world. Providing an educational element can support appropriate behavior and ensure a more positive experience for the visitor. A destination's goal is to encourage the "good" tourists—who are the most sustainable form of visitor—and to reduce negative environmental and social impacts to the community.

Tourist motivations

The end goal of any food tourism enterprise is to determine which tourists are best suited to the destination, activity, or product offering. In order to decide the best possible fit, it

Image 7.1 Local fish on skewers so visitors can eat and walk the streets of Stonetown, Zanzibar
Source: Susan L. Slocum

is important to understand visitors' expectations and motivations and what constitutes satisfaction.

Expectations are strong beliefs that something will happen. Expectations are derived from the need to fulfill a goal that has some intrinsic value or attractiveness (Heckhausen, 1989). These expectations lead to **motivation**, the general desire or willingness to do something or go somewhere. Lee et al. (2011) show that when tourists have high expectations, they are more willing to search for tour information and learn about the destination's culture and other travel information. In other words, a tourist must be able to visualize their trip (expectation) before they are willing to invest the time and energy to research the journey (motivation). As a business or destination, the goal is to provide a level of service and an experience that meets or exceeds expectations. This is called **satisfaction** and involves the fulfillment of one's wishes, expectations, or needs and the pleasure derived from having these wishes, expectations, or needs met. Expectations are constantly changing as a person becomes motivated to travel. Travelers may read blogs on potential food tourism packages (say, cooking schools in Naples, Italy), and their expectations may increase. Figure 7.1 shows the relationships between expectation, motivation, and satisfaction.

Expectations and motivations may be influenced by past travel experiences, perhaps a prior visit to Hanoi, Vietnam, where they witnessed a number of cooking schools but did

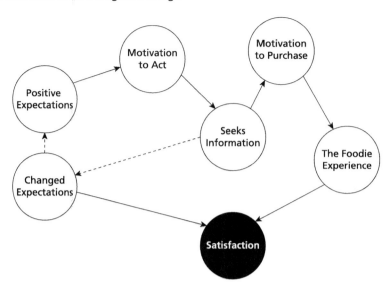

Figure 7.1 Expectation, motivation, and satisfaction

not have enough time to indulge. If a tourist did attend a cooking school in Hanoi, they may expect the cooking school to be the same in Naples or they may expect something completely different. Visitors' expectations are hard to gauge. Motivations, on the other hand, can be more easily influenced through marketing. These motivations, or the process of making travel decisions, are formulated in the information-gathering phase. This is where effective and honest marketing plays a key role. Evidence suggests that food tourists are motivated not only by food but also by learning, cultural emersion, and a sense of adventure. Incorporating these elements into the tourism product is vital to motivating food tourists to choose one business or destination over others.

Evidence also suggests that foodies tend to be less price sensitive due to their higher incomes. They are self-confident and have high expectations. However, tourists who are moderately interested in food may want to attend a food tourism activity because it is convenient. They may be more price sensitive and less inclined for high adventure. Not all destinations can serve all customers. Ultimately, success is derived from differentiating the product from the competition and effectively communicating those differences so that customers have realistic expectations, are motivated to visit, and have their expectations met or exceeded by the product. Market segmentation is discussed in more detail in Chapter 8.

Traveler typologies

Tourism typologies are classifications of tourists by their behavior. Early attempts to distinguish traveler types included Plog's (2001) assessment of psychocentric-allocentric typologies (Figure 7.2). The basic premise is that all tourists are evenly distributed along a continuum between psychocentric (familiarity) and allocentric (exotic). Psychocentric travelers are generally conservative and have little interest in visiting strange places.

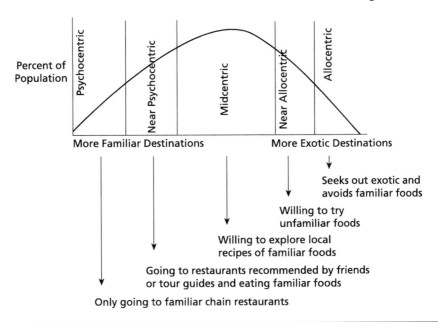

Figure 7.2 Plog's typology applied to food tourists
Source: Adapted from Plog (2001)

They often return to the same destination every vacation and prefer time relaxing. They tend to fear for their safety. Allocentric travelers, on the other hand, seek adventure and new experiences. They are self-confident, enjoy meeting new people, and generally make their own travel arrangements rather than using intermediaries. Plog claims that a majority of tourists lie somewhere between the two extremes. American Express conducted a Global Travel Survey in 1989 and grouped tourists by their perceptions of traveling. They found five basic categories: adventurers, worriers, dreamers, economizers, and indulgers (Table 7.1).

Pliner and Hobden (1992) identified two main types of tourists. **Neophobes**, or individuals with a recognized fear of anything new, and who do not like to experiment

Table 7.1 Tourism types

Adventurers	Worriers	Dreamers	Economizers	Indulgers
Are motivated to seek new experiences	Fear for their own safety	Are fascinated by travel	They travel primarily because they need a break	Like to be pampered
Value diversity and seek new activities, cultures, and people	Suffer considerable anxiety about traveling	Their own travel tends to be more mundane than might be expected	Seek value in travel	Like to go to the hottest new destinations

Table 7.1 continued

Adventurers	Worriers	Dreamers	Economizers	Indulgers
Are independent and in control	Prefer the comforts of what they know	Their trips are oriented more toward relaxation than adventure.	Their experience of travel does not add meaning to their lives	Their travel is not a central or important experience
Travel plays a central role in their lives	Travel is relatively unimportant to them	Lack confidence in their ability to master the details of traveling	Travel is not a central activity for them.	Are generally willing to pay for a higher level of service when they travel
Don't need to be pampered	Are not particularly adventurous	Anxious about the stresses of travel	Their sense of adventure is low	Do not find travel intimidating or stressful

Source: Swarbrook & Horner, 1999

with food; they prefer food that is recognizable and similar to what they would find at home. For example, most Western tourists eat protein derived from animal muscle tissue (steaks, fish, chicken) rather than from insects. Travelers from some Eastern cultures may not be familiar with dairy in their diet. Some American neophobes would not eat grubs while traveling in Namibia and some Korean travelers would not want a French cheese plate for dessert.

On the other side of the scale are **neophiles,** who love to experiment and try new things. In fact, some travelers travel specifically to have new adventures. Neophiles want to try anything new on the menu and may specifically look for something they have never eaten before. Their characteristics include:

- the ability to adapt rapidly to extreme change;
- a distaste or downright loathing of tradition, repetition, and routine;
- a tendency to become bored quickly with old things; and
- a desire, bordering on obsession in some cases, to experience novelty.

Each tourist may fall somewhere on the spectrum between neophobe and neophile, so offering a variety of staple and exotic food items is the best way to please a majority of tourists.

Foodies and food tourists

Foodies are individuals with "a long-standing passion for eating and learning about food but who are not food professionals" (Cairns et al., 2010, p. 592). They are usually considered neophiles (Pliner & Hobden, 1992) and/or adventurers (Swarbrooke & Horner, 1999). They may choose to travel specifically to experience new foods. Foodies may be well educated on food, but often they just have an interest and enthusiasm

Image 7.2 Farm dinner near Girona, Spain
Source: Kynda R. Curtis

for learning about food, regardless of their prior level of knowledge (Cairns et al., 2010). They may have high standards for food quality but may not require expensive or gourmet-style foods (Hermosillo, 2012). For foodies, food interests are a component of social identity; foodies may maintain relationships with other foodies either through organizational membership (Slow Food, culinary, or wine club) or by participating in social cooking with their friends. Numerous websites and television programs cater to foodies. Ultimately, a foodie is someone enthusiastically involved in food-related activities. Barr and Levy (1985) developed a foodie typology that designates seven different foodie types (Table 7.2).

Tourists generally seek experiences that involve the local identities and cultures of the places they visit. Often this can be accomplishing through food-related activities and local cuisine. When a person is keenly interested in travel to explore food, as is the case for many foodies, they become **food tourists**. Food tourists travel to destinations that have established reputations as places to experiment with quality local foods (UNWTO, 2012). In fact, many regions have built reputations as travel destinations around food. As a representation of the increasing value of local food, the United Nations Educational, Scientific, and Cultural Organization (UNESCO) has designated the Mediterranean diet an intangible World Heritage site. This monumental decision brought regional food to the forefront of heritage recognition and made food a global tourism attraction. Other

Table 7.2 Barr and Levy's foodie types

Foodie type	Description
Whole-Foodier Than Thou	Uses only organic methods, grows their own produce and flowers, slaughters their own meat, and uses simple ingredients in their cooking.
Squalor Scholar Cook	Does their research and knows the history of their favorite foods and recipes and values traditional recipes. Academic and historical knowledge of food sets them apart from others.
Made in Paris	Starts off learning basic cooking techniques in small restaurants and manages to move themselves up the ranks through their connections to make a living cooking in Paris, a foodie mecca.
Paris C'est un Dump	The ultimate upscale foodie. Spends much of their time in expensive restaurants, subscribes to important food magazines, and is extremely picky.
Gorgeous East in Me	Drawn to ethnic and foreign foods, constantly wants to try new things and experience new cultures through food.
Foodies on Ice	Regards food as artistic material, aims to impress by creating ice sculptures, elaborately decorated cakes, or butter statues.
All-American	Small-town foodie who searches out local food and ingredients that deserve attention, constantly attempts to improve their products and create new dishes.

Source: Barr & Levy (1985)

food-related attractions and traditions recognized by UNESCO include Turkish coffee traditions, Georgian wine making, Morocco's Cherry Festival, and French gastronomy.

Tourists' food preferences vary based on factors such as destination, seasonality, tourist type, visitor nationality, and other factors. Food tourists are typically open to new experiences, have a desire for lifelong learning, and are educated consumers with high expectations (Croce & Perri, 2010). Of course, the influence of food on tourist experience may vary by degrees. For instance, some tourists treat food consumption as just one part of the travel experience, while others may use food as a basis for their activities, and still others may use food traditions to select their destinations. Food choices can be motivated by cultural experiences, interpersonal relations, sensory appeal, and health concerns (Lee, 2012). For example, Hall and Sharples (2003) define four primary food tourism types by interest level:

1) A high interest in food tourism indicated by traveling to a destination primarily to visit a restaurant, market, or winery; all tourist activities are food-related;
2) Moderate interest including participation in food-related activities as a part of a wider range of activities at the destination;
3) Low interest indicated by participation in food-related activities just out of curiosity or because food-related activities are readily available;
4) No interest in food-related activities or considers food a minor part of the tourist experience.

In order to measure the general size of the food tourism market segments, Sánchez-Cañizares and López-Guzmán (2012) asked visitors about their motivations for visiting Córdoba, Spain. Only 10% chose food as one of the main reasons for visiting the city; 68% considered local cuisine to be an important but not essential aspect of their visit and 22% viewed it as a secondary activity. Overall, income, age, marital status, and education are the most significant predictors of tourists' food consumption. Increases in education, age, and income tend to support higher interest in acquiring knowledge and a higher propensity to travel for food-related experiences (Symons, 1999). A number of researchers have determined that the food tourism market is quite large (Green & Kline, 2013; MacLaurin et al., 2007).

One convenient way to learn about food tourist motivation is through food and drink events, where most participants travel specifically for food experiences. Chang and Yuan (2014) investigated attendees of the Texas Style Wine, Art, and Food Festival and found that older attendees had an increased desire to seek entertainment and escape from their daily routine compared to younger participants. Additionally, more highly educated participants (those with bachelor's degrees or higher) used festivals as an important way to escape from stress. Those with higher incomes ($40,000 per year or more) were motived to attend for escape and novelty, while those with lower incomes valued meeting new people and building relationships as a primary motivation. Additionally, female respondents rated food as more important than men did. At the Lubbock Wine Festival, also in Texas, Sohn and Yuan (2013) measured different lifestyle values (ideals, achievements, and self-expression). This study defined groupings of food tourists with similar values, lifestyles, and motivations (Table 7.3).

Outside of specific food-related travel, there is very little data to provide more than generalizations about tourists and their food-related habits. Shenoy (2005) determined that food tourism comprises five classes of activities, including dining at restaurants known for local cuisines, purchasing local food products, consuming local beverages, dining at high-quality restaurants, and dining at familiar chain restaurants and franchises. Neophobia

Table 7.3 Classification of wine festival attendees

Idealist	• I am a cautious consumer. • I am a conscious consumer. • I am very price sensitive. • I am a penny-pincher. • I consider myself to be a planner. • I see myself as ecology-minded. • I prefer products that I am familiar with and know I can afford. • I am risk-averse. • I am sensitive to the tastes and preferences of people with whom I live and socialize.
Achiever	• I believe brand is an important indicator of quality. • I find brand important. • I am willing to pay more for a brand or a company's reputation. • I am imitative, making purchases similar to those of others whose opinions I value. • I have my favorite brands to purchase or enjoy. • I prefer to buy brands that family and friends use that also meet their social needs.

Table 7.3 continued	

Explorer	• I have a wide range of interests. • I am attached to new and different experiences. • I continue to seek challenges. • I am a practical person who values self-sufficiency but is motivated by self-expression. • I compare to see what new has come out and whether it is any different. • I am concerned with social issues and am open to a change. • I am slow to try new products and ideas.
Belonger	• I enjoy living in the traditional context of family, practical work, and physical recreation. • I see myself a pro-American. • I hold deeply rooted moral codes that I interpret literally. • I respect authority and the status quo.
Innovator	• I spend a lot of time thinking about my appearance and select clothing that reflects my self-image. • I am concerned about functionality, value, style and packaging in a purchase decision. • Image is important as an expression of taste, independence, and character. • I believe money defines success.

Source: Sohn & Yuan (2013)

helped explain a tourist's low participation in certain activities, such as dining at restaurants serving local food, experiencing local beverages, and the preference for eating at fast-food restaurants. However, neophobia did not impact eating at high-end restaurants.

There is ample evidence that food preferences are based on factors such as the destination and visitor nationality. Enright and Newton (2005) found that food was one of the most important factors for visitors to Southeast Asian cities, implying that Asian destinations draw a large number of food tourists. Remmington and Yuskel (1998) showed that food was the fourth-most important variable contributing to the satisfaction of tourists in New Zealand, implying that New Zealand appeals to tourists for reasons other than food. These studies suggest that Asian cities are better situated to market their destinations internationally as food destinations, whereas New Zealand should focus their food tourism opportunities to tourists already visiting the country.

Sims (2010) discovered that domestic visitors to the Lake District of England were most interested in trying foods that were different from the products regularly consumed at home, although many of the food ingredients were similar. Bardhi et al. (2010) found that American tourists in China began the trip with a high level of interest in local food but desired more familiar foods over the travel duration. Both studies imply a need for both exploration and familiarity within food tourism destinations.

Summary

Many theorists consider food tourists similar to cultural tourists because they exhibit educated consumerism, openness to new experiences, desire for lifelong learning, independent travel, and high expectations. This chapter also shows that the food tourism

Image 7.3 Local honey shop in Hawai'i, USA
Source: Kynda R. Curtis

market is sizable and that food tourists may travel specifically to experience new foods. While they may be well educated on food, they often just have an interest and enthusiasm for learning about food. They have high standards for food quality but may not require expensive or gourmet-style foods or frequent food-related festivals and events. Furthermore, food tourists require a certain level of authenticity, and their levels of both formal and food-related education provide a challenge for food tourism destinations.

Study Questions

1 You have been offered $1,000 toward a food tourism trip of your choice. Where would you go? What would you like to do? Why?
2 Would you consider yourself a foodie? Why or why not?
3 You and your family are planning a food-related trip. Think about each member of your family. What type of food tourist are they? What are their expectations for the trip? What type of trip would best satisfy the majority of your family members?

4   Using typical foods or dishes from your hometown, design a menu for a neophobe and a neophile.

5   What are the expectations of the following food tourists? How would you motivate them to consider your product, and what will be required to ensure their satisfaction?

   a   A family of four stopping at a local farm to pick raspberries
   b   A business person taking a client out for a special meal
   c   An independent tourist traveling by train across Belarus
   d   A newlywed couple interested in starting a new hobby together
   e   A neophile who keeps a spreadsheet of all the exotic foods he has eaten
   f   A gap-year student who is just learning to be adventuresome
   g   A group of retired army friends planning an indulgent male-bonding trip

Definitions

Expectation—a strong belief that something will happen.

Food tourist—a person keenly interested in travel to explore food.

Motivation—a general desire or willingness to do something or go somewhere.

Neophile—a person who is more likely to try something new that is either unfamiliar or may not be available at home.

Neophobe—a person who is less likely to be adventurous and prefers familiar experiences and food items.

Satisfaction—deriving pleasure from the fulfillment of one's wishes, expectations, or needs.

Tourist typologies—the classification of tourists by their behavior.

CASE STUDY 7.1

Piedmont Walking Trail

Kelly McMahon and Barry Ballard

Kelly and Barry were looking for an adventure that would combine their loves of wine, food, and physical activity in a region of the world that has a rich cultural connection to the source of their food. They chose a self-guided walking journey in the Piedmont region of northern Italy. Kelly was excited about the trip because each day she would be able to walk off the calories she had consumed the night before. Barry was looking forward to the visual experience—the hills, vineyards, and Old World architecture. They decided to time their trip to coincide with the truffle harvest and the annual Truffle Festival in Alba, Italy.

Kelly was a well-seasoned independent traveler, while Barry traveled primarily for business. This self-guided walking tour was a happy medium, fulfilling their desire for independence while taking care of all the hotel and logistical arrangements and giving them an opportunity to see the back roads of Italy that they might not have found on their own. Prior to departure, the tour company sent a package containing the itinerary, route maps, walking trail route notes, luggage tags, packing suggestions, and local-area information.

Upon arriving in Milan, they opted to take the Malpensa Express to Alba, a 50-minute train ride. They ended up boarding the wrong train, a mistake that cost them several hours to correct. Announcements at the stations were made in Italian, and the signage only listed the starting and ending stations, not the station in the middle that was indicated on their itinerary.

In Alba, the truffle festival filled the pedestrian malls with vendors, and all the shops were giving away wine and appetizers to draw in people. The piazzas were packed with locals enjoying Renaissance-style games staffed by vendors dressed in medieval garb. All the prizes were bottles of local wine. For dinner, they chose pork roasted on a wood-burning spit, complemented by some of the local Nebbiolo—delicious!

Upon embarking on their walking journey, Barry was enthralled with the vistas and valley views as they ascended and descended countless hillsides and trekked through vineyards into small villages with architecture that varied from modern to medieval. The trail-route notes proved largely accurate with regard to distance and landmarks, but the maps were useless and completely out of scale. Waypoints were marked with red and white paint stripes, but those varied in frequency and distance, making them unreliable. Each day's journey was 11–20 kilometers, often involving steep and muddy uphill climbs to 850 meters, followed by treacherous descents, and they frequently got lost.

On day six, after spending a fabulous night in Cissone, where they enjoyed a memorable dinner of veal dressed in hazelnut butter and truffle-topped tiramisu, they embarked on the longest walk yet to Cravanzana. They lost their way (again) and grew extremely tired. Upon stopping for a rest and a glass of wine in a little town, they debated whether to tackle the remaining 10 kilometers of hills or hire a taxi. As it turned out, hiring a taxi was more difficult than imagined. The only one was located in Alba, and they would have to pay for it to travel both ways. In the end, they decided it was worth paying for the taxi because they still had another day of walking ahead of them before they would reach their final destination, Cortemilia. They did not regret their expensive decision in the least.

On their final day, they chose to take the "alternate" route suggested in the trail-route notes to avoid a path that was suspected of being washed out by a recent mud slide. The alternate route turned out to be a poorly maintained trail that was swallowed by an overgrowth of blackberry bushes. For several hours, the two

Image 7.4 Games at the truffle festival in Alba, Italy
Source: Kelly McMahon

battled through thorns down a steep embankment riddled with sinkholes and slick with mud. They gave each other high-fives when they reached pavement, feeling as though they had narrowly escaped death by a thousand cuts.

Image 7.5 Self-guided walking tour meanders through vineyards in Italy
Source: Kelly McMahon

The small hotel in Cortemilia was by far the most decadent of all. The proprietors served a fabulous meal, with a special glass of sparkling white wine that had the deep minerality of a red Borolo. For dessert, they were served a special plate of hazelnut ice cream covered in fondant and inscribed with their names written in chocolate sauce.

Kelly definitely got her workout—often more than she had bargained for. The food, wine, panoramic views, and accommodations were all fantastic beyond expectation—locally grown, seasonally ripe, and drenched in historic significance. Walking through vineyards, hazelnut groves, and truffle forests by day and eating meals from the fruits of those vistas each night was a sensually rich and gastronomically rewarding experience, although frequently exhausting and frustrating.

Questions

1 Explain the expectations, motivations, and level of satisfaction Kelly and Barry experienced. Do you think these travelers were satisfied enough to choose a similar trip in the future? What could the tour operators do differently to improve the overall experience of their travelers?

2 Describe Kelly and Barry's tourist typology. Are they neophobes or neophiles? Would these travelers recommend this trip to other neophobes or neophiles?
3 How authentic do you think their trip was? Why?

CASE STUDY 7.2

Rice for life: Exploring Thai culture through rice tourism

Tracy Berno

Rice is fundamental to every aspect of Thai culture and cuisine. More than just food, rice is essential to the Thai economy, and it forms the basis for many Thai festivals, rituals, and customs. Rice cultivation has shaped the country's landscape. "[Rice] has created a society, culture and cuisine that are uniquely Thai. ... Rice has made the Thai Thai" (Thompson, 2002, pp. 98–99).

To understand Thai culture, one needs to understand rice. But how can tourists understand rice other than through consuming it? And how does this then help tourists understand Thai culture more deeply?

Food, cuisine, and food traditions all have their roots in local agriculture. Agricultural tourism can provide a foundation for introducing and exploring a new culture. Understanding the systems within which agricultural practices act and how both culture and environment interact within a certain social and geographical space provides tourists with a deeper appreciation of a culture. Agricultural tourism allows culture to be experienced through food as a total process—one that includes production, preparation, and consumption.

Phrao is a small town located in northern Thailand in a region that was once known as the Lanna Kingdom, which in English means "kingdom of a million rice fields." Even today, the local economy comprises 98% agriculture, primarily rice production. Some of the best jasmine rice in Thailand (called khao dok mali rice) is grown in the surrounding area. There is very little tourism in Phrao District, and there are limited employment opportunities outside of agriculture. However, one agritourism operation is developing "rice tourism," combining rice and tourism to provide a unique opportunity for tourists to learn more about Thai culture by learning about rice.

The focus of rice tourism is to provide an authentic Thai cultural and educational experience for tourists based on the Phrao District's most important agricultural product. This is achieved by engaging tourists in a range of agritourism activities focused on rice production, preparation, and consumption over two or three days.

Production

Guests first take a bicycle trip through the countryside, which is dominated by rice paddies, to visit a village market. Several stops allow tourists to view and participate in the various stages of rice production. Tourists are encouraged to go into the paddies and work alongside locals to better understand the labor-intensive nature of rice cultivation. Farmers show guests how to transplant rice. It is hot, backbreaking work.

This experience is complemented by a stop at a local shop selling farm tools, supplies, and rice seed. The owner of the shop, who is also a farmer, provides information about the history of Thai rice and different species and properties of rice in the region. This educational experience is enhanced through an on-site museum with interpretive materials on the history and significance of rice cultivation, different species of Thai rice, and tools and equipment used in the rice fields.

Image 7.6 The author participating in rice cultivation in northern Thailand
Source: Tracy Berno

Preparation

Following the market visit, guests tour the gardens to learn about ingredients used in the regional cuisine followed by a cooking class on Northern Thai cuisine that utilizes products purchased that day at the local market and products harvested from the accommodation's gardens. Learning how to prepare different types of rice and rice dishes is central to the experience.

Consumption

After learning about and preparing the rice and its accompaniments at the cooking school, guests share a meal. Rice is enjoyed as part of each course in a variety of forms, including traditional steamed rice, rice noodles, and rice paper wraps. Even the dessert is rice-based—Thailand's famous *khao niaow ma muang* (Thai coconut sticky rice and mango).

Through participating in rice tourism, tourists gain a deeper appreciation of Thai culture through one of its essential elements, seen through the lens of host-guest interactions, hands-on experiences, and interpretation that offers opportunities to learn about Thai culture through its agriculture and cuisine. Visitors come away appreciating that, in Thai culture, rice is everything.

Questions

1 The concept that underpins rice tourism is "rice for life." Based on the case study, what does "rice for life" mean?
2 How does participative learning about the heritage and the special character of Northern Thailand as experienced through its rice tourism and cuisine facilitate a deeper and more authentic experience of Thai culture?
3 What other activities could enhance the visitors' understanding of the role rice plays in Thai culture?

References

Thompson, D. (2002). *Thai Food*. Camberwell, Vic.: Penguin.

References

Bardhi F., Östberg, J., and Bengtsson, A. (2010). Negotiating cultural boundaries: Food, travel, and consumer identities. *Consumption, Markets, & Culture, 13*(2), 133–157.

Barr, A., and Levy, P. (1985). *The official foodie handbook*. New York: Arbor House.

Cairns, K., Johnston, J., and Baumann, S. (2010). Caring about food: Doing gender in the foodie kitchen. *Gender & Society, 24*(5), 591–615.

Chang, W., and Yaun, J. (2014, June 14–16). *Tourists' characteristics and motivations in attending festivals and events: A study in Texas*. Paper presented at the 47th Travel and

Tourism Research Association Annual International Conference, Vail, CO. Retrieved from scholarworks.umass.edu/cgi/viewcontent.cgi?article=1347&context=ttra

Croce, E., and Perri, G. (2010). *Food and wine tourism: Integrating food, travel and territory.* Wallingford, UK: CAB International.

Enright, M., and Newton, J. (2005). Determinants of tourism destination competitiveness in Asia Pacific: Comprehensiveness and universality. *Journal of Travel Research*, 43(4), 339–350.

Green, E., and Kline, C. (2013). Are you a foodie? Food related travel study (Technical report). Charlotte, NC: 7th Street Public Market.

Hall, C.M., and Sharples, L. (2003). The consumption of experiences or the experiences of consumption? An introduction to the tourism of taste. In C.M. Hall, E. Sharples, R. Mitchell, N. Macionis (eds.), *Food tourism around the world: Development, management and markets* (pp. 1–24), Oxford: Butterworth-Heinemann

Heckhausen, H. (1989). *Motivation and action* (2nd ed.). (P.K. Leppmann, trans.). Berlin: Springer-Verlag.

Hermosillo, J. (2012). Loncheras: A look at the stationary food trucks of Los Angeles (Unpublished master's thesis). University of California, Los Angeles, CA.

Lee, S., Jeon, S., and Kim, D. (2011). The impact of tour quality and tourist satisfaction on tourist loyalty: The case of Chinese tourists in Korea. *Tourism Management*, 32(5), 1115–1124.

Lee, T.H. (2012). Developing policy strategies for Korean cuisine to become a tourist attraction. In *Food and the Tourist Experience: The OECD-Korea Workshop* (pp. 101–110). OECD Studies on Tourism. Paris: OECD Publishing.

MacLaurin, T., Blose, J., and Mack, R. (2007, October 13–14). *Marketing segmentation of culinary tourists.* Paper presented at the 7th Association for Business & Economics Research Global Conference on Business & Economics, Rome, Italy.

Pliner, P., and Hobden, K. (1992). Development of a scale to measure the trait of food neophobia in humans. *Appetite*, 19(2), 105–120.

Plog, S. (2001). Why destination areas rise and fall in popularity: An update of a *Cornell Quarterly* classic. *Cornell Hotel and Restaurant Administration Quarterly*, 42(3), 13–24.

Remmington, M., and Yuskel, A. (1998). Tourist satisfaction and food service experience: Results and implications of an empirical investigation. *Anatolia*, 9(1), 37–57.

Sánchez-Cañizares, S.M., and López-Guzmán, T. (2012). Gastronomy as a tourism resource: Profile of the culinary tourist. *Current Issues in Tourism*, 15(3), 229–245.

Shenoy, S. S. (2005). Food tourism and the culinary tourist (Unpublished doctoral dissertation). Clemson University, Clemson, SC.

Sims R. (2010). Putting place on the menu: The negotiation of locality in UK food tourism, from production to consumption. *Journal of Rural Studies*, 26(2), 105–115.

Sohn, E., and Yuan, J. (2013). Who are the culinary tourists? An observation at a food and wine festival. *International Journal of Culture, Tourism and Hospitality Research*, 7(2), 118–131.

Swarbrooke, J. (1999). *Sustainable tourism management.* Wallingford, UK: CAB International.

Swarbrooke, J., and Horner, S. (1999). *Consumer behaviour in tourism.* Oxford: Butterworth-Heinemann.

Symons, M. (1999, February). *Gastronomic authenticity and the sense of place.* Paper presented at the 9th Australian Tourism and Hospitality Research Conference for Australian University Tourism and Hospitality Education, Adelaide, South Australia. In *CAUTHE 1999: Delighting the senses* (pp. 401–408). Canberra, ACT: Bureau of Tourism Research.

UN World Tourism Organization. (2012). *Global report on food tourism.* Madrid: UNWTO.

Chapter 8

Identifying food tourism markets

Overview

To effectively operate a food tourism enterprise or organize a popular destination, it is imperative to design activities, products, or events that appeal to specific groups of tourists. To identify target tourist types or a target market for a business, the larger tourism market must be segmented and defined by geographic, demographic, psychographic, and product-related commonalities. This chapter discusses the importance of identifying a target market and explains the various factors by which markets can be segmented. An overview of tourism data collection and analysis methods is provided, including a detailed description of the advantages and disadvantages of common survey methods.

Learning Objectives

This chapter will enable students to:

1. Understand the importance of identifying a target market for the tourism product.
2. Define target markets though geographic, demographic, psychographic, and product-related segments.
3. Compare and contrast primary versus secondary data.
4. Discuss the advantages and disadvantages of the various survey methods.
5. Understand how statistical tools, such as cluster analysis and factor analysis, can be used to identify and explain target markets in tourism.

Market segmentation

As discussed in Chapter 7, identifying tourist typologies is essential to the success of any operation and an important part of the planning process. A business can use these typologies to establish a target market for a specific food tourism experience or destination. A **target market** consists of a group of consumers or tourists within the larger market who share similar demographics, interests, behaviors, or lifestyle characteristics and have either a need or want for the product or an identified demand. A clear understanding of the target market, their expectations and motivations, and their budget allows the operation to design new events and activities that serve customer needs, estimate potential visitor numbers, and set appropriate pricing. It also aids in the implementation of effective and targeted promotional strategies, the ability to cater to repeat customers and those who spend more, and select support services valued by the target market.

Market segmentation is the process of dividing a broad market into subsets of consumers or target markets with common needs, interests, and priorities and then designing and implementing strategies to attract them to a business or destination. Markets can be segmented using geographic, demographic, psychographic, or product-related information.

Geographic segmentation groups potential tourists based on their physical locations or place of origin. This may be the area in which they live or, in relation to food tourism, the location they are visiting. For example, Singapore uses geographical segmentation to encourage visitors from nearby countries, such as Australia and New Zealand (Enright & Newton, 2005). Local restaurants or food festivals use geographic segmentation to advertise to visitors interested in exotic cuisines or specific culinary delights after they arrive in the country. People from the same geographic area may have similar food preferences (discussed in Chapter 7), such as Asians, who traditionally eat very little dairy at home. They may not be a good target market for a cheese-making facility, whereas others, say Europeans, may find the experience of eating locally made butter to be the highlight of their trip.

Demographic segmentation is based on specific attributes of tourists, such as age, profession, income level, occupation, ethnic background, education level, household size, and family situation. Destinations may wish to market to a specific demographic. For example, Disney theme parks use family size and situation (married with children) and income to segment their markets. Many farms and farm shops are adding play structures or petting zoos to encourage more families with children to visit. Wineries generally promote their products to adults without children, as children can distract from the vineyard ambience, and parents who are supervising children tend to drink (and purchase) less alcohol. A couple on their honeymoon may want a romantic, locally sourced meal, while university students on semester break may be more interested in local beers.

Psychographic segmentation uses lifestyle choices, hobbies, interests, and values to group tourists. Values and interests might include environmental protection, preserving agricultural open space, health concerns, or food safety. Ecotourism is an example of promoting nature-based travel to groups that value the environment, and research has shown links between nature tourists and increased interest in food tourism (Slocum & Curtis, 2015). People traveling to explore cultural activities may also be inclined to experiment with local recipes. This category might include both neophiles and neophobes. Understanding the interests and values of the target tourist can assist in identifying proper promotional channels (such as magazines or internet sites they consume) as well as establishing corporate responsibility initiatives—such as sustainability, fair trade, low-water usage, or waste reduction—that appeal to a certain customer type.

Lastly, **product-related segmentation** groups tourists by what kinds of attributes they want and need in a particular good or service (how they use it), destination and activity preferences, and preferred communication methods and spending habits. For example, a food tourism business may distribute fliers at a local hotel, but knowing which hotels cater to leisure travelers and which to business travelers increases the effectiveness of the promotional strategy. Knowing whether visitors purchase value-added foods as snacks

Image 8.1 Main Street store in Kueka Lake, New York, USA
Source: Susan L. Slocum

while traveling or to take them home as souvenirs helps determine the types of packaging and the best retail outlets for the product. Other examples may include beach holidays versus ski holidays, organic versus conventional, and locally made versus imported.

Tourism data collection

Data on current tourists or potential tourists can be collected through a number of methods. For existing food tourism operations, a wealth of consumer information can be obtained from previous transactions, online bookings, and past communications. Online booking forms can be customized to provide detailed customer information and preferences. Customer appreciation events are commonly used to test new products or experiences or obtain feedback through unstructured interviews, as is staging a competition, where entrants must provide contact information and a few other details such as demographics to win the contest.

Many businesses regularly collect data. For example, it is common for restaurants to use customer satisfaction cards to evaluate the quality of the food, the service, or the ambiance. However, these simple surveys do not help to determine target market characteristics. Adding additional questions such as "Did you try food that you had never tasted before?" or "Did you order a regional specialty?" can help determine psychographic traits of the customer. Other simple questions that can be included are "Where are you from?" (geographic segmentation), "What other places are you visiting on your trip?" (geographic segmentation), "Are you traveling with children?" (demographic segmentation), or "Why did you choose our restaurant?" (product-related segmentation). It is also important to include open-ended question, such as "Why or why not?", "What did you like best?", or "How can we improve your experience?" in order to understand the deeper meanings behind responses. Rating food as a "3" (average) does not help the restaurant understand how to improve the food, but asking "why" provides problem-solving information.

In the case of new food tourism ventures or activities, target market data might be obtained from data and reports from third parties such as governments, universities, trade associations, banks, Destination Marketing Organizations (DMOs), or other non-governmental organizations. Reports and consumer-panel data may also be available (at a price) through market research organizations. This type of data is usually available in published or electronic format and is referred to as **secondary data** because it was collected previously for a specific purpose. Secondary data were collected, analyzed, and presented to answer different questions or to solve different problems than what you may use it for and so may have limited application. However, using secondary data for market research saves both time and money, as collecting data is labor intensive. Data published by government agencies is readily available and free of charge, while data collected and analyzed by private companies may require permission for use. Secondary data for tourism operations may be available through a local Convention and Visitors Bureau or DMOs. These organizations normally have information on the number and types of visitors that come to the area, their origin, why they are traveling, and their general demographic information.

If funding and time are available to collect tourist data specific to an operation or destination, **primary data** are best. Primary data are collected to address specific problems or to investigate tourism trends; this research is conducted by the food tourism operator or by a marketing firm or university researcher. Primary data may be collected using surveys, focus groups, in-depth interviews, or experiments such as taste tests (Curtis, 2008).

Surveys are perhaps the most common method of primary data collection. Data can be collected in a variety of ways, including over the telephone, face-to-face, online, and using dot surveys. Less formal methods may also include observation and informal interviews. The choice of which survey method to use depends on many factors, including the number of respondents the surveyor desires, the time frame in which the data must be collected, the characteristics of the population to be surveyed, and, of course, the budget. Below are just a few of the advantages and disadvantages of the different survey methods. It is important to note that these data-collection methods use stated data, meaning that an individual may say that they are willing to participate in a given activity, visit a specific destination, or pay a certain price, but that does not mean they will follow through.

Telephone surveys

Telephone surveys are conducted by calling individuals and having them answer questions over the phone. While telephone surveys allow the interviewer to encourage the person to complete the survey, and responses can be analyzed immediately, people wishing to conduct market research on a small budget may find the wage paid to the interviewers prohibitive. Conducting a large-scale telephone survey requires access to large, random samples of contact numbers. For a smaller firm with budget considerations, a list of people to call can be made up from an online directory or from a personal list of regular customers. One drawback to this method is that many individuals now only use unlisted cell phone numbers, and some countries have laws against using cell phone numbers for solicitation calls.

Face-to-face surveys

Face-to-face or in-person surveys have some of the same advantages and disadvantages of telephone surveys. In-person surveys can be an effective way to obtain fully completed surveys, which can then be analyzed immediately. Another potential benefit is that a very specific population can be targeted using in-person interviews. For example, if individuals who frequent a specific farmers' markets or a food-based event are the population of interest, then the interviews can be conducted in front of, inside, or near the venue. However, it is necessary to have permission to conduct surveys in public spaces and on private property, such as a grocery store. On the negative side, conducting in-person surveys can be costly, and some individuals may be put off by being approached for a survey or may not be willing to reveal some information about themselves to a stranger.

Internet surveys

Internet surveys are conducted using online survey software. An email or postcard is most often sent to potential respondents inviting them to complete the survey online. Internet surveys are only useful when the target population has Internet access. Advantages of Internet surveys include fast and complete responses, which are immediately available for analysis. Internet surveys can be very affordable, as web-based survey sites are generally inexpensive. For example, many wineries or farms may have electronic newsletters that are sent to regular customers when new wines are released or when certain vegetables come into season. Also, many businesses have Facebook or Twitter accounts with many followers. An invitation to a web link can be distributed through these avenues as well. If respondent email addresses need to be purchased, that will increase the cost. The local DMO often collects email addresses when potential visitors contact them for information.

Image 8.2 Conducting in-person surveys at a renaissance festival in
Austin, Texas, USA
Source: Susan L. Slocum

Additionally, some survey providers have data-analysis tools, simplifying the process for those without prior experience or statistical knowledge. Disadvantages to Internet surveys include the potential difficulty in assembling a target population contact list as well as motivating those individuals to complete the survey once they have been contacted. And as with some of the other survey methods, some individuals may be skeptical about providing sensitive information (such as annual household income, the amount of money spent on groceries, etc.) over the Internet.

Dot surveys

Dot surveys, or posters, are used to focus on only a few important questions (Lev et al., 2004). The dot survey technique consists of a limited number of questions (usually no more than four) displayed on easels in public locations, such as farmers' markets or urban restaurant districts. Participants indicate responses by using colorful round stickers (i.e., dots) in the columns that represent their responses. For example, a dot survey at a farmers' market may ask respondents to indicate their county of residence, which they would do by placing a sticker in the proper category. Dot surveys are an alternative to traditional survey techniques, like written questionnaires and oral interviews, and have been found to increase response rates over alternative techniques. However, a major drawback of dot surveys is that respondents can see the responses other respondents have given and may therefore be swayed by what they see. Dot surveys also only allow you to collect responses to a limited number of questions and do not allow an opportunity to ask open-ended questions.

Informal interviews and observation

Informal interviews and observations provide **qualitative data**, which approximates or describes a tourist's characteristics. Qualitative data collection allows visitors to expand on an answer, similar to open-ended questions asked on surveys. A structured question may ask where visitors traveled before arriving at a venue. A survey may provide a list of destinations visited, but an interview allows you to understand which destinations they liked, which they did not like, and why. If the interviewer is patient, it may even be possible to obtain stories or anecdotes that provide a rich understanding of why a person is satisfied or unsatisfied with an experience.

In **focus groups**—where a group of individuals is asked a set of specific, open-ended questions together—participants often play off of one another and one comment can trigger a memory that would have been forgotten in a one-on-one interview. Often, data from qualitative studies can be used to design a full survey, allowing the questions to be designed around the visitor's experience rather than the business's expectations. For example, a bed-and-breakfast that uses organic produce in the meals they provide their patrons but does not use certified organic due to cost could ask current customers how they feel about organic produce and whether or not they would be willing to pay more for meals made from produce certified organic by a third party.

Observation simply consists of observing consumers and taking note of their behavior. Observations allow access to subtle behavioral information that the visitor may not even be aware of. For example, watching families interact as they choose a food booth at a festival can provide insight into who makes the final decision (it may be the mother or the child), what drew them to their final selection (Dad says, "Ooh, look at that sandwich"), or the attributes they deem important ("Do they have cold beer?"). Qualitative data is best used to understand and define complex problems in more detail than quantitative data allows.

Analyzing tourism data

Obviously, the methods chosen to analyze tourism data depends on the type of data gathered, such as surveys or focus group interviews, and the information needed from the analysis. In the context of defining and understanding target tourist types and their desired food tourism activities and products, two common survey analysis methods are discussed here.

The first method is **cluster analysis**. Cluster analysis groups **quantitative data** from surveys, in this case responses to a tourism survey, based on information in the data that numerically defines the respondents and their relationships, such as age, income, destination preferences, etc. The goal of cluster analysis is to end up with clusters or groups whose members are similar or related to one another and distinctly different from members of other clusters. For example, breaking groups into foodie types may be done through cluster analysis. Several types of clustering techniques can be used to achieve the end goal

Image 8.3 Conducting a focus group in Moab, Utah, USA
Source: Kynda R. Curtis

of the analysis. Common statistical analysis software, such as Microsoft Excel or SAS, allows the user to choose among various clustering techniques.

As an example, Curtis et al. (2015) used cluster analysis to understand common types of tourists traveling to Utah (USA). Data were collected from 700 in-person tourist (non-Utah resident) surveys at 12 sites in Utah, including tourist information centers in gateway cities, entrances to national parks, airports, ski areas, and convention and visitor centers. Tourists were then grouped according to similar demographics, interests, and trip characteristics. Four clusters, or tourist types, emerged from the analysis and are described in Table 8.1. The results provide an overview of the demographics, psychographics, and travel-related preferences of each group. These results can be used to customize promotional activities and offerings for each group. For example, Internet-based and social media efforts would be most useful to effectively promote a destination to "Sophisticated Food Travelers." This group is also very interested in trying local recipes and locally sourced foods, so locally sourcing restaurants, local food markets, and perhaps cooking classes would appeal to this group. Since this group likes to visit national parks, highlighting local food events or destinations near the parks would increase the quality of their experience.

A form of product-related segmentation called factor analysis was used to understand how different types of food- and agriculture-related tourism activities were linked in the minds of tourists. This type of analysis allows us to determine which food tourism

Table 8.1 Four clusters or tourist types resulting from Utah, USA tourist survey

Cluster 1: Large family trip (9%)	Cluster 2: Outdoor enthusiasts (29%)	Cluster 3: Sophisticated food travelers (30%)	Cluster 4: Food and family pilgrimage (22%)
• Average age: 52 • 67% married • 44% graduate degree—well-educated comparatively • Party size: 4.8 people—largest group • Stay length: 5 days and travel to the area often • Most use the Internet in trip planning and unlikely to use brochures • Unlikely to participate in outdoor recreation or visit national parks • Most likely to participate in agritourism activities when traveling • Most likely to participate in canning, composting, and gardening (DIY) when home	• Average age: 48 • More likely male and least likely to be married • Party size: 2.8 people—smallest group comparatively • Least educated group • Stay length: 4.7 days—the least amount of time comparatively • The most likely group to use a brochure in trip planning • Most interested in outdoor recreation • Less interested in food-related activities at home or when traveling comparatively and spend the least per person on their trip	• The oldest group and most likely to be married • 60% graduate degrees—the most educated group • 74% use the Internet in trip planning • Stay length: 14.3 days • The most likely to travel for business reasons • Most likely to visit national parks • Spend a lot per person ($695) and visit often • The most likely to seek out local foods when traveling, such as buying local foods, visiting farmers' markets, and cooking at accommodations • Participate in food-related activities at home such as cooking and buying local foods, and sustainable behaviors, such as recycling	• Average age: 42—the youngest group • Married and more likely female • Most-educated in terms of bachelor and graduate degrees • Party size: 3.8 • Make annual or traditional visits, don't use outside resources • Most likely to visit culture and heritage sites • Stay length: 10.5 days and spend most per person ($960) • Most likely to seek out food experiences (try new foods, local recipes) and buy food gifts • More likely to belong to beer and wine clubs, purchase organic foods, and visit farms and farmers' markets at home

activities a specific target market wants to do while on vacation. This information is incredibly helpful when designing a complete tourism destination. **Factor analysis** is used to describe variability among observed, correlated variables in terms of a potentially lower number of unobserved variables called factors. The key concept of factor analysis is that multiple observed data types have similar patterns of responses because they are all associated with an underlying characteristic that is not directly measured. For example, people may respond similarly to questions about income, education, and occupation, which are all associated with unobserved socioeconomic status. Factor analysis is available through most common statistical software, including Microsoft Excel and STATA.

Table 8.2 Food and agriculture activities at home and while traveling

Activities at home	Activities while traveling
Local foods	**Food tourism**
Shop at farmers' markets	Try new foods
Buy organic produce	Try local recipes
Visit farms	Buy food-related gifts
Food experiences	**Agritourism**
Try new foods/recipes	Spend a night at a farm
Eat ethnic foods	Agritourism activities
Try new/unknown produce	Visit farms
Do it yourself	**Local foods**
Gardening	Buy local foods
Canning/Preserving	Cook at accommodations
Composting	Shop at farmers' markets
Food connections	
Recycling	
Cook at home	
Buy local foods	

Table 8.2 shows the factors that emerged from the analysis of food- and agriculture-related activities at home and while traveling. Tourists focused on food experiences at home often try new foods/recipes, eat ethnic foods, and try unusual or unknown produce items. The analysis also shows that tourists interested in agritourism generally visit farms and participate in agritourism activities but are also interested in "farm stays" or on-farm accommodations. Thus, an agritourism venue offering corn mazes, wagon rides, etc., may also want to offer overnight accommodations, such as cabins or a bed and breakfast on site to accommodate those looking for a complete experience. This type of offering would increase visitor satisfaction and provide an additional revenue stream for the operation.

Summary

Identifying and understanding target tourist markets is essential for successful product design and promotion for any food tourism enterprise. Finding target markets within the larger tourism market can be done through market segmentation, grouping individuals with similar demographics, interests, behaviors, or lifestyle characteristics. In order to identify commonalities, data on the array of geographic, demographic, psychographic, and product-related characteristics of potential food tourists must be collected. Tourist data is most often collected through surveys or interviews or obtained from government sources, local tourism or destination marketing organizations, or other online resources.

Surveys may be conducted through a number of mechanisms, including phone, online, and in-person, and each mechanism has advantages and disadvantages. The survey type chosen depends on the number of respondents desired, the time frame in which the data must be collected, the characteristics of the population to be surveyed, and the budget for conducting the survey. Once the data are available, a number of statistical methods can be used to understand tourist types. Cluster and factor analysis are two common methods employed to group tourists. Cluster analysis groups all tourist survey respondents into specific groups, while factor analysis reduces the data so that underlying commonalities can be assessed.

Obviously, the end result of any customer or tourist data collection and analysis effort is to ensure a quality experience for the tourist. A quality experience increases the probability of operation or destination success as a result of repeat visits and positive word-of-mouth promotion to family and friends (Wang, 2004).

Study Questions

1 You have been hired by a local farmer to segment their target market to find an appropriate mix of bed and breakfast visitors. What steps do you need to complete? What type of data collection method would be best?
2 Envision the perfect food tourist for a summer food festival in your hometown. List potential customers' geographic, psychographic, and demographic traits. What product-based segments should be considered?
3 What type of analysis on local tourism survey data would be best to identify various events or activities needed to provide a successful destination for visitors?
4 How might a listing of the psychographic characteristics of a target tourism market aid in developing a promotion plan for your destination?
5 Give two situations in which secondary data might be preferable to collecting primary data.

Definitions

Cluster analysis—a statistical method used to group a set of objects such that objects in the same group (called a cluster) are more similar (in some sense or another) to each other than to those in other groups (clusters).
Demographic segmentation—grouping potential tourists based on specific attributes such as age, profession, income level, occupation, ethnic background, education level, household size, and family situation.
Factor analysis—a statistical method used to describe variability among observed, correlated variables in terms of a potentially lower number of unobserved variables called factors.
Focus group—a qualitative method in which a group of individuals is asked a set of specific, open-ended questions together.
Geographic segmentation—grouping potential tourists based on physical location or place of origin.
Market segmentation—the process of dividing a broad market into subsets of consumers or target markets with common needs, interests, and priorities and then designing and implementing strategies to attract them to a business or destination.

Primary data—data originally obtained through the direct efforts of a researcher using surveys, interviews, or direct observation.

Product-related segmentation—grouping potential tourists by their wants and needs regarding the attributes of a particular good or service or destination and activity preferences as well as preferred communication methods and spending habits.

Psychographic segmentation—grouping potential tourists based on lifestyle choices, hobbies, interests, and values.

Qualitative data—data that approximate or describe the characteristics or properties of a subject.

Quantitative data—data, usually in numerical form, that define the characteristics or properties of a subject.

Secondary data—data collected by someone other than the researcher.

Target market—a group of customers within the larger market who have similar demographics, interests, behaviors, or lifestyle characteristics that a business has decided to aim its product and marketing strategies at.

CASE STUDY 8.1

Food tourism in businesses' markets: Green meetings and conventions

Susan L. Slocum and Kynda R. Curtis

Many national and international corporations are embracing sustainability to entice new socially and environmentally minded consumers. As part of this process, many organizations are conducting "green" meetings and conventions in order to reduce their carbon footprint, reduce waste, and save money. Common elements of green meetings include recycling, using public transportation, and sourcing local food. Evidence suggests that meeting planners, who organize events for organizations, consider it important to incorporate sustainability and corporate social responsibility practices into meetings to enhance a company's image and to add value to a company's marketing efforts (Gecker, 2009).

Meetings generally require long hours of concentration without any physical activity. Healthy food has been shown to improve attention span and is increasingly being ranked as highly important for attendees' satisfaction with meetings (Kapetanaki et al., 2014). Food is commonly provided during meetings and plays an important part in the social networking commonly encouraged at meeting events. Additionally, meeting attendees are increasingly concerned about food and beverage sustainability, including buying food from local vendors who use locally

the sophisticated, eco-elegant choice

As the highest rated green caterer in the metropolitan area, Catering by Seasons is dedicated to improving the environmental impact of every event. We believe in the importance of informing our customers about the sustainable services we offer and the methods behind them. Through our green initiatives and education programs, it is our goal to further improve our environmental impact while creating the freshest, most delicious menu for your next event.

At Catering by Seasons, we strive to:

- ❖ Partner with local, sustainable farms to bring our customers fresh, healthy foods

- ❖ Organically grow vegetables in our own urban garden at our headquarters in College Park, Maryland

- ❖ Offer seasonal farm-to-table menus and event options

- ❖ Compost thousands of pounds of food trimmings each week, reducing our waste sent to the landfill

- ❖ Reduce waste through our company-wide recycling program

- ❖ Use 100% wind energy to power our kitchens

- ❖ Train all staff on environmental responsibility, empowering them to contribute and work towards a healthier and more sustainable lifestyle in and out of the office

Catering by Seasons
5105 Berwyn Road, Suite 101
College Park, Maryland 20740
www.cateringbyseasons.com

Event Number: 95303558
Phone: (301) 477-3515
Fax: (301) 220-4489

Image 8.4 Sustainable meeting menu, Virginia, USA
Source: Susan L. Slocum

grown produce and shorter distribution channels (CVENT, Inc., 2012). Meeting planners play a substantial role in meeting-related purchasing decisions, including purchasing of food and beverage.

Washington, DC, is ranked fourth among U.S. metro areas in the number of professional, scientific, and technical services businesses. Neighboring Virginia supports the country's fifth-largest meeting and convention destination (U.S. Bureau of Labor Statistics, 2013). It is estimated that 7% of all tourists, or 1 million people, travel to Washington, DC, for meetings and conventions (Virginia Tourism

Corporation, 2013). Moreover, Washington, DC, has launched a new sustainability campaign to promote sustainable development, including local purchasing, among city residents and visitors.

A quantitative online survey of meeting planners in the Washington, DC, metropolitan area was distributed in March 2014 in order to determine support for sustainability in local meeting-planning food and beverage options. A total of 77 surveys were completed. Using descriptive analysis, it was determined that 71% of the meeting planners hosted events at a variety of different venues rather than supporting a single conference facility. Seventy-six percent of respondents did not have a food-sourcing contract, so they had full autonomy to choose the food for their events. Price, location, and the capacity of the venue were the most important attributes when choosing where to host an event. Sustainable meeting options were somewhat important. When asked which sustainability options were most important, respondents cited recycling and eliminating waste as their highest priorities. Supporting sustainable food scored a 3.3 on a 5-point scale, meaning it was somewhat important.

In relation to food concerns, food quality and food safety were most important to the respondents. There was strong support for vegetarian and vegan meal options as well as concerns related to food allergens (shellfish, gluten, peanuts). Serving international food was ranked the lowest, followed by the ethical treatment of animals in the food chain and offering organic food.

Using cluster analysis, common traits were determined in order to assess viable target markets for locally sourced food in the meeting-planning industry in Washington, DC. Respondents were grouped by the type of organization for which they worked: associations (49% of the respondents), corporations (23.4%), government agencies (5.2%), and other (not-for-profit, universities, 9.1%). The results showed that:

- Associations were most supportive of sourcing locally and were more likely to pay extra for locally sourced food—especially local seafood. This could be in part to their strong preference for healthy food. Additionally, they were likely to support energy-efficient meeting venues, donating to local charities, and recycling.
- Corporations were less concerned with cost and were moderate supporters of sourcing locally. They showed the highest willingness to pay for specialty goods, such as fresh bread and pastries. They were less inclined to pay for fresh produce (fruits and vegetables). They were more concerned than the other clusters with venue attributes such as meeting location, size, and capacity. They also supported energy efficient venues and the elimination of waste.
- Government agencies and businesses categorized as "other" were the most cost-conscious and least likely to support locally sourced food options or to pay extra for specialty food items. They were more likely to support reduced waste and the use of public transportation.

Questions

1 If you were a conference center in Washington, DC, which cluster would best support a sustainable meeting planning package? Why?
2 How best could you incorporate local food into your sustainable meeting package? What concerns should you consider?
3 What other research could you do to find a market for your sustainable-meeting package? How would you go about conducting this research?

References

CVENT, Inc. (2012). Green meetings made easy. Retrieved from www.cvent.com/en/event-management-software/greenmeetings-made-easy.shtml

Gecker, R. (2009). How companies that are cutting back keep their meetings green. Retrieved from meetingsnet.com/checklistshowto/green_meetings/0701-companies-managing-budgetcuts

Kapetanaki, A.B., Brennan, D.R., & Caraher, M. (2014). Social marketing and healthy eating: Findings from young people in Greece. *International Review on Public and Nonprofit Marketing, 11*(2), 161–180.

U.S. Bureau of Labor Statistics. (2013). Occupational employment and wages May 2013: 13–1121 Meeting, convention, and event planners. Retrieved from www.bls.gov/OES/current/oes131121.htm

Virginia Tourism Corporation. (2013). Travel profile to Virginia. Retrieved from www.vatc.org/uploadedFiles/Research/AllTripProfileFY2013TravelsAmerica.pdf

CASE STUDY 8.2

The power of the interview: Understanding farm shops in the UK

Susan L. Slocum and Kynda R. Curtis

A farm shop is a permanent structure where both unprocessed and processed local food items are available for purchase. They are generally open all year and are located near farming communities. Farm shops have gained popularity in Europe but have not been a primary development path for local food distribution in the United States. Instead, the United States has seen a number of farm stands, temporary structures that allow a single farm to sell excess produce on or near their property. One of the advantages of a farm shop over a farm stand is that farm

Image 8.5 Farm shop specializing in meats, Leicestershire, UK
Source: Kynda R. Curtis

shops offer larger and more permanent facilities through which local foods can be sold. They provide an opportunity for farmers to work together and develop social capital within a community.

The research

To better understand the farm shop model, including the networks between farmers and retailers, and to examine potential distribution challenges, research was conducted in England to understand the farm shop system in the hope of customizing these organizations to U.S. farming communities and customers. Since very little research was published on farm shop operations, developing a survey was out of the question. Instead, in-person interviews with farm shop managers and owners were conducted to obtain a deeper understanding of the situation.

The researchers read numerous articles, policy briefs, and industry papers to develop interview questions. It was determined that asking semi-structured questions—those that allow respondents to elaborate on their answers—would be best. These questions open up the conversation to short anecdotes or stories that may better describe the challenges managers face. Specific questions included:

1 What types of marketing methods are most common? Is marketing done individually by shop and/or through cooperative/membership organizations?
2 What types of activities/services do the membership organizations provide? How are they paid for?

3   What types of activities/services does your local tourism authority provide? How are they paid for?

4   What common types of regulations (safety, signage, parking, entrance, etc.) and licensing do farm shops face?

5   How is farm shop ownership commonly structured? Are they owned by a single person (entity) or are multiple entities/farms more common?

6   Who is buying from or visiting farm shops and why? How is customer feedback collected, analyzed, and used?

7   What types of product origin labeling are required and what quality standards are used? Who governs labeling and quality standards?

8   How has farm/food tourism economically impacted your area?

9   What resources (financial, tax incentives, etc.) and training/education opportunities are available for farm/food tourism operators and/or new start-up operations?

Initial farms shops were chosen from a United Kingdom farm shop directory. These initial contacts were followed by snowball sampling, or interviewee-suggested farm

Image 8.6 House of Honey farm shop and café, Swan Valley, Australia
Source: Kynda R. Curtis

shops nearby which could be interviewed. In total, 9 interviews were conducted, each taking about an hour to complete.

The interviews were recorded and then transcribed so that the researchers had a complete text version of the conversation. Using the text, specific themes—things that repeatedly came up in the conversations—were noted. These themes included merchandising and diversification, operations, networking, regulations, and tourism. From these themes, a set of best practices was developed that could be used in the United States. Best practices refer to long-term strategies that encourage profitability (Slocum & Curtis, 2017).

Best practice

This study provides a detailed understanding of the many challenges facing farm shops in England and a list of best practices that could be transferred to the United States. These best practices include (Curtis & Slocum, 2017):

- innovative and distinctive inventory;
- constant reassessment of inventory to maintain a fresh image;
- careful scrutiny of profitable goods and services that fit with individual definitions of "local";
- hands-on involvement with suppliers;
- non-food-related activities geared toward customers' lifestyles;
- clear presence of locally sourced items;
- knowledge exchange between local food suppliers and farm shops;
- involvement with regional tourism associations;
- buy-in support from local government agencies; and
- proximity to tourist attractions for tourism participation.

Questions

1 What other questions could the researchers have asked? What information would these additional questions have provided?
2 How could the set of best practices be turned into a quantitative survey for U.S. farmers who want to establish a farm shop?
3 If you started a farm shop for tourists, what would you do to ensure profitability?

References

Slocum, S.L., and Curtis, K.R. Farm diversification through farm shop entrepreneurship in the UK. *Journal of Food Distribution Research*, 48(2), pp. 35–51.

References

Curtis, K., Slocum, S.L., and Allen, K. (2015). Farm and food tourism: Exploring opportunities. Logan, UT: Utah State University Extension. Retrieved from diverseag.org/htm/farm-and-food-tourism

Curtis, K.R. (2008). Conducting market research using primary data. In Western Extension Marketing Committee, *Niche markets: Assessment and strategy development for agriculture* (Technical report UCED 2007/08-13). Reno, NV: Western Extension Marketing Committee. Retrieved from valueaddedag.org/nichemarkets/07conductingmarketresearch.pdf

Enright, M., and Newton, J. (2005). Determinants of tourism destination competitiveness in Asia Pacific: Comprehensiveness and universality. *Journal of Travel Research*, 43(4), 339–350.

Lev, L., Brewer, L. and Stephenson, G. (2004). *Tools for rapid market assessments* (Technical report 6, revision V). Corvallis, OR: Oregon State University Extension Service. Retrieved from nyfarmersmarket.com/wp-content/uploads/2014/08/toolsforRMA.pdf

Slocum, S.L., and Curtis, K.R. (2015). Assessing sustainable food behaviours of national park visitors: domestic/on vocation linkages, and their implications for park policies. *Journal of Sustainable Tourism*, 24(1), 153–167.

Wang, D. (2004). Tourist behavior and repeat visitation to Hong Kong. *Tourism Geographies*, 6(1), 99–118.

Chapter 9

Developing a food tourism destination

Overview

This chapter describes the role of destination marketing and management and brand creation in the success of a food tourism destination. Destination management requires collaboration and networking to ensure stakeholder involvement in the development process, while destination marketing involves communication strategies that encourage tourism visitation. Food has the potential to support or even enhance a destination's image to both domestic and international tourists, as long as food-related messages are consistent with other destination attributes. A full overview of destination branding is provided, including developing sense of place and marketing aspects that should be considered.

Learning Objectives

This chapter will enable students to:

1 Appreciate the role of destination marketing and management organizations.
2 Understand the important role that food can play in destination success.
3 Describe attributes, benefits, and attitudes as they relate to successful branding awareness.
4 Understand brand development in relation to destinations.
5 Describe the elements of a successful food tourism destination.
6 Discuss the use of various marketing and branding distribution channels.

Destination marketing and management organizations (DMOs)

Tourism is an industry that must be marketed; as it grows, it must be managed if it is to be sustainable in the long run. Destination marketing encourages tourists to visit by developing and communicating the characteristics of a destination. Like many industries, tourism is highly competitive, with many destinations offering similar products. At the same time, a destination must be managed so that it attracts the appropriate types of businesses to fulfill the needs of its visitors. The organizations responsible for these tasks are usually called **destination marketing and management organizations** (DMOs).

DMOs can be structured in many different ways and include a variety of stakeholders. In some countries, the DMO is a government organization housed within the Ministry of Tourism or other federal legislative body. In other regions, the DMO may be a local government organization funded with tax money (such as accommodation taxes) with board members from the tourism industry who oversee its operations. DMOs may be membership organizations, such as a Convention and Visitors' Bureau (CVB), where participating organizations pay dues to support the overall promotion of a destination. DMOs are as diverse as the destinations that support them, but they all have a common goal: to ensure that tourists are aware of their destination by communicating the businesses, events, attractions, and opportunities available in their area; to encourage tourists to choose their destination over others; and to ensure that the destination has the amenities to satisfy its customers.

As management organizations, DMOs are often tasked with finding consensus among a variety of stakeholders, all with different visions for how a destination should be perceived by the traveling public. **Stakeholders**, individuals or groups with an interest in tourism and who have great influence over tourism (Savage et al., 1991), can consist of tourism businesses, local and regional governments, tourists, suppliers, and community members. **Collaboration** is the process of joint decision-making among autonomous key stakeholders of an inter-organizational community to manage and resolve complex planning problems (Gray, 1989). Achieving a collaborative environment is much more challenging than it seems. With limited resources available to develop and promote tourism, stakeholders often compete with one another.

Networking is the channels or relationships through which collaboration is achieved. For example, if a restaurant wants to source local, organic ingredients, the chef might ask a neighbor whether she knows anyone with a farm. That neighbor may call her friend from church, who may recommend her brother's boss, who owns a small farm close by. These relationships allow the chef to obtain produce to support the desires of the tourists that visit the restaurant.

DMOs are responsible for establishing and maintaining networks, not only internal to the destination, such as linking tourism businesses together, but also with external stakeholders like tour companies, airlines, and travel promotional media (see Figure 9.1). These networks make it possible for destination marketing and management to become an inclusive process that values the opinions of all members of a community. Collaboration and networking are difficult tasks because most people have very different ideas on how a destination should be run; having an organization dedicated to ensuring that tourism is a positive economic engine to a region helps reduce barriers to tourism development.

In order to establish a culinary or food destination, DMOs need to establish collaborative partnerships and a common message that is, in turn, communicated to tourists. But not all food tourism messages are the same. France is a well-known wine region with a long history of producing fine wines. Canada, specifically in southern Ontario, has only recently begun to develop wine regions. These distinctly different regions naturally have very different communication strategies. In France, the message should promote the history and reputation of French wines.

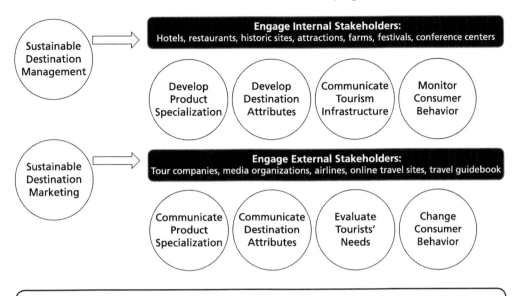

Figure 9.1 Internal and external stakeholders in tourism

Bordeaux has long had a reputation as a town that takes itself very seriously—too seriously perhaps—but no more. The history and culture are still here but UNESCO classified Bordeaux has shed her dowager frocks and the city of wine has become fun, lively and an award winning holiday destination. … The Bordelais love their wines, and it shows. It's a city that lives and breathes wine—from the towering new temple to world wine—the Cité du Vin—to tiny restaurants dedicated to matching food with the perfect claret—you're never more than a step away from the urban wine trail.

(www.bordeauxwinetrip.com/)

Since Canada is not as well known for wine production, the message should educate tourists on regional specialties and unique growing conditions that give rise to exceptional quality wine.

Since the early 1990s Canada has been internationally known for the consistent quality of its Icewine. Produced in every Canadian wine producing region, Ontario produces over 90% of this delicious and quintessentially Canadian product which is made from grapes that have been naturally frozen on the vine. Winter temperatures and freezing concentrate the sugar, acid and berry extracts in the grape, resulting in highly concentrated flavours and the complex intensity for which Canadian Icewines are known. While Canada continues to be proud of its Icewine story, it remains somewhat undiscovered for the quality of its table and sparkling wines. Each of Canada's wine regions have unique growing conditions that allow key varieties to shine and be expressive of their place of origin.

(winecountryontario.ca)

The marketing message should focus on the uniqueness of a destination.

Image 9.1 Local cheese supports the Swan Valley's wine tourism marketing messages in Western Australia
Source: Kynda R. Curtis

Destination branding

Marketing a destination is quite different from marketing a consumer product. A tourist destination comprises many different products, including accommodations, restaurants, attractions, events, and personal interactions (Boo et al., 2009). In other words, the tourism product is a collection of experiences rather than a particular item with some satisfying use. Tourists are seeking both tangible assets—such as beaches, mountains, historical sites, or outdoor activities—and intangible assets—such as culture, history, customs, or relaxation (Qu et al., 2011). Interaction with a destination and the perceived satisfaction derived from that experience constitutes the **tourism product**. As a destination marketer or manager, achieving consistency within the tourism product is very difficult as each product element is controlled by a separate entity outside the control of a single operation or business (Gartner & Ruzzier, 2011). Moreover, each visitor has different, often unique, expectations.

Branding—a unique name, term, sign, symbol, design, or combination of these that identifies the goods and services of one seller or group of sellers and differentiates them from those of competitors (Keller, 1993)—is an important part of destination marketing. A brand expresses all of the information and feelings a consumer has about a product and derives from a variety of information sources such as advertisements and word of mouth from family and friends. In order to be successful, a brand must create **brand awareness**, that is, the brand must be recognizable, and consumers must be able to recall the image associated with the brand. Brand image is made up of three types of interrelated elements that consumers should associate with a destination. **Attributes** are the descriptive qualities that a visitor believes the destination to have, such as the physical characteristics of a destination (such as beaches, mountains, or great nightlife). These are similar to the tangible assets described above. **Benefits** are the personal value visitors attach to these attributes (such as adventure, relaxation, or learning). **Attitudes** are thoughts or feelings a visitor has about a brand or destination (either positively or negatively). Keller (1993) argues that attitudes are the basis for consumer behavior. For example, a positive attitude (purchasing a vacation) is based on a destination's attributes (beaches and sunshine) and the perceived benefits of these attributes (relaxation).

Destination branding is a critical component of destination management and marketing because many destinations have similar attributes. For example, differentiating among beach vacations in the Caribbean, Southeast Asia, or the Pacific Islands might be easy because a choice may be made based on travel distance, prior experience, or something as simple as a recent conversation over dinner. However, once a geographic region has been selected (the Caribbean, for example), the destination brand determines whether a person chooses Jamaica (a party destination), the Dominican Republic (a water-sport mecca), or Aruba (a romantic getaway). Branding helps differentiate a destination in the minds of consumers and can insulate it from competition in a saturated market. **Differentiation** is the process of establishing a unique image in the minds of consumers. The recognizable symbols and messages of branding support the differentiation of a destination and should include a brand name, logo, symbol, slogan, and packaging that reflect the characteristics of the destination (Tasci & Kozak, 2006).

Developing a food destination

Food can be an important element in building a destination brand. Food is often associated with a destination's social, cultural, and natural characteristics and offers the opportunity to further communicate symbolic cultural meanings of the people and geography of a region (Lockie, 2001). Food communicates a **sense of place**, the special meanings that represent the identity and character of a region that are deeply felt by local residents. Lin et al. (2011) remind us that "the distinctiveness of food in relation to a place plays a significant role in a destination identity" (p. 32). Evidence suggests that many tourists are attracted to regional and ethnic foods because of their desire for unique experiences (Hall et al., 2003) and that food-related experiences contribute to the enjoyment of and satisfaction with a tourism destination (Yuksel & Yuksel, 2002). Furthermore, positive food experiences encourage repeat visitation (Sparks et al., 2003).

Lin et al. (2011) argue that food and drink can make a destination more desirable. Food offers the opportunity for a region to showcase its heritage and traditions within tourism markets. However, a "food identity" must be clearly recognizable, hence more marketable. Lin et al. (2011) claim that seven dimensions (shown in Table 9.1) must be considered in relation to food tourism.

While all destinations have restaurants and other food service establishments, a destination's food offerings must "match" the destination attributes in order for food tourism to be successful. The goal here is to highlight specific local cuisine in a way that

---

Table 9.1 Food identity in relation to destination branding

Type of stakeholders	What degree of importance do you attach to regional cuisine as a distinctive factor of the Schist Villages?	What degree of satisfaction do you feel about the regional cuisine in the Schist Villages?	Difference between satisfaction and importance
Tourists	3.7	3.8	0.07
Local Residents	3.9	3.3	–0.50
Tourism Businesses	3.7	3.2	–0.58
Public Decision Makers	4.0	3.6	–0.45

Values: opinions average on Likert scale of 1 to 5.

Source: inquiries.

---

enhances the experiential component of the tourism product. Food class refers to the type of food and the cooking techniques employed to form an authentic experience for tourists. Using locally grown items and cooking them in traditional ways that include ethnic spices can add to the cultural element of the food experience. DMOs may have to encourage eating establishments to carry traditional foods, as restaurant managers may want to serve food familiar to visitors, such as pizza or hamburgers. The less a tourist knows about local food, the riskier the restaurateur will perceive this strategy to be. For example, traditional Thai food involves the use of a variety of hot peppers for flavoring. If a dish is too hot, customers may be turned away. In remembering that travelers may fall into neophobe or neophile categories, having authentic food choices as well as more globally recognized options may help reduce this risk. Other things that are important in food tourism development include food safety, food establishments that are easy to locate, and a variety of food experiences for every budget.

Offering opportunities for food experiences outside of traditional restaurants is also important. Food festivals and farmers' markets provide more elaborate involvement for visitors. Food or drink trails allow tourists to compare and contrast a variety of different foods (or beverages), cooking techniques, or local produce specialties. Both festivals and trails provide an opportunity for local businesses to build collaborative networks and develop coopetition rather than continuing to compete. The success of a festival or trail requires all businesses to work together to produce a single coherent activity for tourists, where a positive customer experience is the primary focus.

A food destination is about more than access to good food; it is also about communicating the food options in a way that supports the destination brand. This identity must be perceived as authentic in order to be successful (du Rand et al., 2003). It is important to tell the "story" behind the food. Food tourists are interested in learning more about cultures; having information available to explain the history or customary practices surrounding certain foods can improve a tourist's satisfaction. Perhaps developing a food trail map listing local food options—such as restaurants, wineries, or events—can help communicate a unified message. Listing all restaurants together, as is often done on DMO websites, allows the tourist to visualize subtle nuances inherent in a region's culture, such as food traditions, and allows the tourist to pick and choose different experiences over the course of their visit. Adding material about each restaurant's specialties or offering historical information about each farm in a community can help explain the story behind the food.

Starting any new food tourism operation on a small scale helps reduce risk and keeps the project manageable. Local businesses make food-related decisions based on perceived profitability. It is the DMO's job to encourage businesses to think about destination attributes (such as local food) and help businesses implement tourism opportunities in ways that minimize risk. Rather than converting all restaurants or farms into tourist attractions, start by asking a few businesses to offer tourism options. Their successes will encourage other businesses to follow suit. Again, providing food maps or listing local specialties on DMO websites helps ensure that local businesses receive the attention and patronage they need to be successful.

Marketing a food destination

Tourists must actively engage themselves in choosing a destination. There are millions of brochures, websites, blogs, and groupons that encourage travelers to choose one destination over another. Mathieson and Wall (1982) claim that how tourists respond to marketing information depends on the type and credibility of the information source. Tourists use a variety of information sources to develop an image of the destination and put more effort into researching a destination if the destination is farther from home or there is a higher cost associated with traveling there (Beatty & Smith, 1987). Karim (2010) writes, "The success of tourism products can be highly dependent on the type of information available for the customers. …With the current information-rich environment, knowing customers' information search behavior is ultimately crucial for effective marketing campaigns and promotions" (p. 535). But not all travelers access information in the same way.

For example, in a study of visitors to Utah, USA, Curtis et al. (2015) found that different types of food tourists used different marketing channels to choose their travel destination (see example in Chapter 8). Large families were not likely to eat local foods but were most likely to visit agritourism activities, such as visiting farms or pick-your-own establishments. More than half of these travelers used the Internet to book their trips and rarely used brochures. Sophisticated food travelers were more likely to seek out food-based experiences and more likely to participate in sustainable behaviors, such as conserving water and electricity. Almost three-quarters of this group used the Internet for trip planning and to book their holidays. However, a third group, who were more likely to be repeat visitors to Utah and who were most likely to seek out food experiences and buy food-related souvenirs, did not use the Internet when trip planning. Instead, they based trip decisions on past experiences and word of mouth. The group least likely to be food tourists was most likely to use brochures when making travel decisions. Chapter 8 discusses market segmentation in more detail, but the message here is that destinations must use multiple types of marketing to reach a wide range of customers.

DMOs must find the best combination of marketing channels to convey their food tourism brand. Both commercial (private promotion, such as websites) and public information sources (travel agents, local/national tourism offices, travel magazines) are valuable to potential culinary tourists making travel decisions. Agencies must ensure that they communicate all relevant information about the destination and that food tourism marketing messages align with other marketing messages about the destination. Using websites, brochures, social media, and press releases broadens a destination's marketing reach. It is

Image 9.2 Tigelada, a traditional Azorean custard from Portugal
Source: ADXTUR – www.aldeiasdoxisto.pt

important to maintain good relationships with other organizations in marketing distribution channels—such as travel writers, guidebook publishers, and large-scale reservation companies (Expedia, TUI, or the major airlines that serve the destination). It is also important to monitor the image being distributed to ensure that media companies are accurately communicating to target audiences and that the appropriate message is being conveyed.

It is important to note that DMOs are promoting a destination and that local businesses need to market their establishments individually. However, not all small businesses have advertising or marketing experience. DMOs often support local businesses by providing training on website development, social media, and working with other businesses in collaborative efforts. While local businesses may understand the local market, tourism may be a new concept. Therefore, DMOs also conduct research to better understand tourist expectations, which should be shared with local businesses. For example, a farm may highlight activities for visitors but neglect to tell the unique story and history of the farm. DMOs may need to work with small businesses to encourage adding more of the educational materials that tourists seek. Networking also helps small businesses find their particular food tourism niche so that each business offers something unique while maintaining the overall destination image.

Summary

Destination marketing and management is an important step in the success of any food tourism destination. Destination management includes working with stakeholders (both internal and external) to ensure inclusive collaboration that values all opinions and perspectives in a community. Networks are the avenues through which collaboration is built.

Destination management provides the vision and planning that shapes food tourism development into the future. This vision must then be communicated to potential visitors through destination marketing.

Marketing involves developing a unified brand but also includes establishing brand awareness so potential visitors know what to expect when visiting a destination. Communicating sense of place to travelers provides information about the character of a region. Food can provide a sensory experience that connects visitors to local heritage and traditions. It is important to find a unified message that links food with the natural and cultural heritage of a region.

In turn, tourists expect specific benefits that justify the purchase of their holiday. DMOs use a variety of marketing outlets such as websites and social media, but word of mouth is also an important information source for tourists. Ensuring that the marketing message that draws tourists to a destination aligns with tourists' actual experiences can be a valuable source for referrals for future visitors.

Study Questions

1   Who are the primary food tourism stakeholders in your hometown?
2   Think of your favorite food. Where is it from? How would you incorporate this food into a tourism message for this area?
3   How could you develop networks to promote collaboration with community members who are not currently stakeholders?
4   Find the destination website for your hometown or region. What marketing messages does it use? What is the common brand communicated to potential visitors? How does food play into that message?
5   Compare and contrast two destinations that promote cooking-schools as a holiday option. How are they similar or different? Describe their unique brands.

Definitions

Attitudes—thoughts or feelings a visitor has about a brand or destination.
Attributes—descriptive qualities that a visitor believes a destination to have.
Benefits—the personal value visitors attach to destination attributes.
Brand awareness—the ease of brand recognition and brand recall.
Branding—a name, term, sign, symbol, or design, or combination of these, which is intended to identify the goods and services of one seller or group of sellers and to differentiate them from those of competitors.
Collaboration—the process of joint decision-making among autonomous key stakeholders of an inter-organizational community to manage and resolve complex planning problems.
Destination marketing and management organization—the organization responsible for encouraging tourists to visit by developing and

communicating the characteristics of a destination and attracting the appropriate type of tourism businesses.

Differentiation—the process of establishing a unique image in the minds of consumers.

Networking—the channels or relationships through which collaboration is achieved.

Sense of place—special meanings that represent an identity and character that is deeply felt by local citizens.

Stakeholders—individuals or groups with an interest in tourism and who have great influence over tourism.

Tourism product—a visitors' experience of a destination, including tangible and intangible assets, and the perceived satisfaction derived from that experience.

CASE STUDY 9.1

A systemic study of stakeholders in the Rede das Aldeias do Xisto

José Alberto Moutela, Fidel Martínez-Roget, and Vivina Almeida Carreira

Residents of large cities are fascinated by the idea of traveling through the mountains of the interior in search and discovery of small villages and the people who inhabit them. The narrow, meandering roads; waterfalls; the vastness of the forests; herds wandering slowly and carelessly along the tracks and paths; local farmers who cultivate their land and enjoy an exotic, aromatic, and tasty cuisine—all are elements of the collective imagination of urban dwellers.

Rural tourism has evolved in recent years toward the creation of authentic experiences in which the simple activity of enjoying the local food is one of the most promoted experiences. A region's typical cuisine is one of its primary tourist resources, portraying its identity and distinction. We traveled to the center of Portugal to visit the region known as the "Network of Schist Villages" (RAdX), where we discovered its natural resources, landscapes, customs and traditions, and importantly, its regional cuisine.

This RAdX includes 27 small population centers distributed throughout central Portugal. The villages are part of a local sustainable development program with a high regional tourism potential, distinguished by exceptional architecture, culture, traditions, and cuisine. The leaders and promoters of this tourist region market to visitors the excellent regional cuisine, entrusting the residents and the economic

Image 9.3 Roasted kid in Portugal
Source: ADXTUR—www.aldeiasdoxisto.pt

and tour operators with a valuable role in the transmission of regional specialties, flavors, and knowledge.

We wanted to know how various stakeholders think and feel about food in RAdX. Our research took place between July and November 2015 and consisted of collecting opinions on the image, motivation, satisfaction, and loyalty that several stakeholders of the RAdX have about this distinctive region.

To evaluate stakeholders' satisfaction and the importance they placed on food, these four stakeholder groups were studied: tourists and visitors; local residents; economic operators; and public and associative decision-makers. All of them were asked a set of questions in order to compare their views, attitudes, and perspectives, including:

1   What degree of importance do you attach to the cuisine of the region?
2   What is your degree of satisfaction with this cuisine?

A Likert scale of 1 to 5, where 1 is not important/satisfied; 2, little important/satisfied; 3, important/satisfied; 4, very important/satisfied; and 5, totally important/satisfied was used to rank their responses. A total of 441 inquiries were made to tourists, 218 to residents, 51 to operators, and 41 to decision-makers or representatives. To analyze and compare the views of stakeholders, averages were calculated for each question across stakeholder groups.

From the data collected, we found that tourists and visitors express a high degree of satisfaction with the food in RAdX (3.8 average), showing an average value greater than the degree of importance (3.7 average). Local residents of RAdX assign a higher importance degree (3.9) than their satisfaction degree (3.3). Economic operators are less optimistic toward both the degree of importance and satisfaction with the local cuisine (3.7 and 3.2 respectively); finally, public and associative decision-makers assign the highest degree of importance to the local cuisine (4.0) but are less satisfied with it (3.6).

Questions

1   What actions should the leaders of the RAdX region take to protect the image and identity of its local cuisine?
2   To what extent can the participation of local residents contribute to the success of systemic and sustainable development programs in the region?
3   How can satisfaction be improved for the stakeholders in this region?

For further information: www.aldeiasdoxisto.pt

CASE STUDY 9.2

The importance of niche product offerings to wine region success

Kynda R. Curtis and Sierra P. Allen

Demand for food and drink tourism is rapidly expanding worldwide, particularly in wine and ale trails and small-scale craft brewery and winery development. As destination marketing becomes increasingly competitive, marketing wine or ale trails alone may be insufficient to sustain regional tourism. Creating a complete destination package by forming partnerships between tourism providers, food establishments, hotels, and other local businesses provides a more satisfying visitor experience. This is especially true when the region is known for unique or ethnic foods or specialty drinks. Niche product offerings vary widely within the food tourism industry, depending on local culture and economy, but may include products such as cheese, honey, chocolate, nuts, coffee, beer, and wine.

Rural areas can benefit from marketing niche products because they generally have unique histories, more intimate producer-to-consumer relationships, and long-standing traditions (Sidali et al., 2015). Here we examine the effect of niche

Image 9.4 Tourist wine trail in Washington, USA
Source: Kynda R. Curtis

products on enhancing food tourism destinations by comparing the Rattlesnake Hills Wine Trail in Washington's Columbia Basin (USA) with the Swan Valley Wine Region just east of Perth, Australia. Both regions offer quality, locally grown wines, but they vary in the number of additional niche products they sell, potentially influencing both regions' individual competitiveness.

The Swan Valley wine region has over 180 years of winemaking history. However, recently the community has improved its offerings and promotional activities by further developing and highlighting additional niche food products. They now market the area as "Perth's Valley of Taste." The Swan Valley experience is not just for wine enthusiasts; there are activities and products suitable for non-drinkers and families with children, including cheese tastings, chocolate confectionaries, local honey, and candy stores. The trail also highlights breweries, unique bars, restaurants and cafés, arts and crafts, and heritage sites. One popular half-day tour by Perth-Tours highlights the region's culinary diversity by combining wine tastings with a pizzeria lunch, local lavender scones, and cheese samplings (Travelocity, 2017).

The Rattlesnake Hills Wine Trail is located just south of Yakima, Washington (USA) and is an established American Viticultural Area (AVA). The first vineyard was established in 1968, and the Wine Trail formally began in 2008. The Wine Trail is traditional, however, in the sense that it offers little with respect to additional products, services, or activities outside of the 17 wineries involved in the trail. The Wine Trail Map and Visitor Passport do not include any other offerings, such as restaurants, bed and breakfasts, or other types of specialty foods or drinks. While the area boasts a selection of unique restaurants, specialty stores, and accommodations, it is apparent that there is little coordination between sectors to promote the region as a destination.

The success of Swan Valley is evident through the large increase in annual visitation. As of early 2016, 3.1 million people were visiting the region annually, contributing AUS$421 million to the local economy, up from 2.1 million visitors

Contents	
🍇 Wineries	12
✖ Restaurants/Cafés	20
🍸 Boutique Bars	25
🍺 Breweries	26
🔺 Distilleries	29
★ Function Centres	29
🎨 Attractions	30
✛ Heritage	34
◒ Arts & Crafts	35
🛍 Shopping	36
🚌 Tours	38
🦜 Accommodation	41
📍 Maps	45
🍯 Local Produce	47
🚶 Picnic Spots & Walk Trails	50
ⓘ Local Information	51

Image 9.5 Swan Valley Wine Trail activity listing in Perth, Australia
Source: Kynda R. Curtis

and AUS$284 million in economic contributions in 2012 (Ardon, 2016). While Rattlesnake Hills is not located near a large population center like Perth, Australia (2.1 million), the area does have a medium-sized population of approximately 400,000, with frequent visitors from the Seattle, Washington, area, which has a population close to 1.5 million. Visitor numbers for the Rattlesnake Hills Wine Trail are not currently available. However, the Walla Walla Valley Wine Region, just 70 miles away, has incorporated a variety of activities and additional products into their regional brand and has experienced increased annual visitation as well.

Creating partnerships between a region's wine, food, and hospitality sectors builds unity and consistency and increases consumer knowledge about the variety of activities in the area. Rural communities and regional governments would be wise to provide technical and financial assistance or incentives to increase niche product development and encourage complementary businesses in wine regions. Preserving traditions, sharing product history, and highlighting the uniqueness of niche products are also essential to creating a deeper and more authentic tourism experience (Sidali et al., 2015).

As an example, Beer et al. (2012) explored methods of increasing culinary tourism to the Black Forest region of southwest Germany. The region is highly visited and is known for gourmet, award-winning restaurants and excellent wines, yet studies found that information on local wineries was difficult to find and poorly marketed. When surveyed, a majority of Black Forest visitors agreed that they would be interested in local cuisine experiences as well as tasting regional products during their stay. Study results suggest creating a marketing strategy for the region that highlights not only the area's fine wine, but also its local niche products. In doing so, visitors would be better informed about the variety of culinary activities available in the region and would have a deeper tourist experience than merely dining at a select scattering of gourmet dining establishments.

Questions

1 Why is it important for a wine region to offer a number of products and services available that appeal to a wide variety of visitors?
2 What are the benefits of creating a complete destination for tourists? What types of partnerships are needed to do so?
3 How can the Rattlesnake Hills Wine Trail enhance the visitor experience? How could they go about partnering with other businesses?

References

Ardon, M. (2016). Swan Valley visitors up by one million. Retrieved from www.communitynews.com.au/avon-valley-gazette/news/swan-valley-visitors-up-by-one-million/

Beer, C., Ottenbacher, M., & Harrington, R. (2012). Food tourism implementation in the Black Forest destination. *Journal of Culinary Science & Technology, 10*(2), 106–128.

Sidali, K., Kastenholz, E., and Bianchi, R. (2015). Food tourism, niche markets and products in rural tourism: Combining the intimacy model and the experience economy as a rural development strategy. *Journal of Sustainable Tourism*, *23*(8–9), 1179–1197.

Travelocity. (2017). Swan Valley food tour with wood-fire pizza lunch and tastings from Perth. Retrieved from https://www.travelocity.com/things-to-do/swan-valley-food-tour-with-wood-fired-pizza-lunch-tastings-from-perth.a411150. activity-details

References

Beatty, S., and Smith, S. (1987). External search effort: An investigation across several product categories. *Journal of Consumer Research*, *14*(1), 83–95.

Boo, S., Busser, J., and Baloglu, S. (2009). A model of customer-based brand equity and its application to multiple destinations. *Tourism Management*, *30*(2), 219–231.

du Rand, G.E., Heath, E., and Alberts, N. (2003). The role of local and regional food in destination marketing: A South African situation analysis. *Journal of Travel and Tourism Marketing*, *14*(3/4), 37–112.

Gartner, W.C., and Ruzzier, M.K. (2011). Tourism destination brand equity dimensions: Renewal versus repeat market. *Journal of Travel Research*, *50*(5), 471–481.

Gray, B. (1989). *Collaborating: Finding common ground for multiparty problems*. San Francisco: Jossey-Bass.

Hall, C.M., Sharples, L., Mitchell, R., Macions, N., and Cambourne, B. (eds.). (2003). *Food tourism around the world: Development, management and markets*. Boston: Butterworth-Heinemann.

Karim, S.A. (2010). Culinary tourism as a destination attraction: An empirical examination of destinations' food image. *Journal of Hospitality Marketing & Management*, *19*(6), 531–555.

Keller, K.L. (1993). Conceptualizing, measuring, and managing customer-based brand equity. *Journal of Marketing*, *57*(1), 1–22.

Lin, Y.C., Pearson, T., and Cai, L. (2011). Food as a form of destination identity: A tourism destination brand perspective. *Tourism and Hospitality Research*, *11*(1), 30–48.

Lockie, S. (2001). Food, place and identity: Consuming Australia's beef capital. *Journal of Sociology*, *37*(3), 239–255.

Mathieson, A., and Wall, G. (1982). *Tourism: Economic, physical and social impacts*. London: Longman.

Qu, H., Kim, L.H., and Im, H.H. (2011). A model of destination branding: Integrating the concepts of the branding and destination image. *Tourism Management*, *32*(3), 465–476.

Savage, G.T., Nix, T.W., Whitehead, C.J., and Blair, J.D. (1991). Strategies for assessing and managing organizational stakeholders. *Academy of Management Executive*, *5*(2), 51–75.

Sparks, B., Bowen, J., and Klag, S. (2003). Restaurants and the tourist market. *International Journal of Contemporary Hospitality Management*, *15*(1), 6–13.

Tasci, A.D.A., and Kozak, M. (2006). Destination brands versus destination image: Do we know what we mean? *Journal of Vacation Marketing*, *12*(4), 299–317.

Yuksel, A., and Yuksel, F. (2002). Measurement of tourist satisfaction with restaurant service: A segment-based approach. *Journal of Vacation Marketing*, *9*(1), 52–68.

Part IV

Food tourism policy and practice

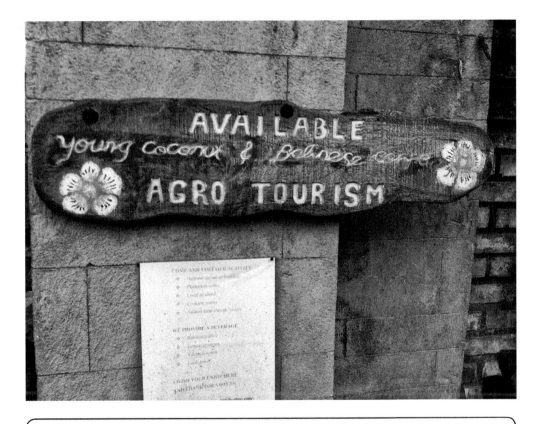

Image IV.1 Agritourism sign in Bali, Indonesia
Source: Kynda R. Curtis

Chapter 10

Food tourism policy and governance

Overview

This chapter investigates the concepts of good governance and policy as they relate to food tourism. The policy cycle, including top-down and bottom-up policy development, is explained. Regional policy instruments—including laws, regulations, and zoning—as well as regressive and progressive taxes are described. International, national, and regional policies and policy organizations are highlighted as is the role that policy plays in the development of food tourism destinations, enterprises, and programs is explored.

Learning Objectives

This chapter will enable students to:

1 Describe the elements of good governance.
2 Describe the policy development process.
3 Understand the difference between progressive and regressive tax policies.
4 Explain international, national, and regional tourism, agriculture, and rural development policy initiatives.
5 Discuss regional policies that affect food tourism development.
6 Appreciate the need to develop and implement effective policies.

Introduction

All development occurs within regulated systems of governance. The goal of governance and policy development is to ensure that certain standards are maintained in order to control growth, sustain communities and environments, and ensure a quality tourism product or experience. For food tourism to be sustainable in the long run, effective planning and policy development are required to guarantee that a destination identifies emerging trends, efficiently and effectively utilizes the community's resources, and meets the needs of consumers and residents alike. Many types of policies—including agriculture, tourism, and rural development—have an impact on food tourism. These policies and programs are conceived of, and implemented at, the international, national, and regional levels. Policies must be "flexible and resilient enough to foster development of new tourism products and services in a rapidly changing world" (Edgell & Swanson, 2013, p. 11). This is accomplished by including food tourism stakeholders in governance and policy development.

From an agricultural perspective, governance usually occurs at a national level and is regulated through formal policies, investments, and international trade negotiations. From a tourism perspective, governance often occurs through public/private partnerships. Almost all countries have agricultural ministries or departments at the federal level, and many countries have established ministries or departments of tourism. Provinces or states may also have agencies responsible for tourism and agricultural development. Often federal ministries will use these regional or local agencies to encourage food tourism development. Coordination among federal, regional, and local agencies is important to ensure two-way communication by allowing federal agencies to communicate long-term strategies to regions and ensure that regions can have a voice in the development of long-term strategies.

Good governance

Governance is a process of leadership that is defined as the coordination of economies, public/private partnerships, and reform objectives aimed at pursuing collective interests (Slocum & Backman, 2011). It lies somewhere between government interventions (policy) and managerial tasks. Governance occurs primarily within a government, but many businesses and organizations have governing principles that determine the vision, goals, and values of a company. Governance can be equated with strategic leadership, in that governance is the process of determining future development paths. For example, a local government may decide that food tourism will support traditional industries in a region. Governance is the process through which this community encourages food tourism business development (such as new restaurants that source locally or a regional food festival), destination marketing resources (such as increased funding for the visitors and convention bureau), infrastructure improvements (such as improved accommodations), and networking (such as developing a farmers' association).

Good governance should include input from all food tourism stakeholders to ensure that a community can support growth. If community members are opposed to an increase in tourist numbers, they may create an unfriendly environment that discourages tourists and the development of tourism businesses. Additionally, many governing agencies are not directly involved with the operation of a food tourism enterprise and may not fully understand the needs of business owners or tourists. By including a variety of different perspectives in the strategic process, many challenges can be avoided. For example, if a tourism board wants to start a wine trail, community members may have concerns about intoxicated driving between wineries. A solution could be to find an entrepreneur who establishes a tour package where visitors travel by bus to each winery and are returned to their hotel at the end of the day. By including business, residents, and local government, drunk-driving concerns are eased, road fatalities are avoided, and new options are available to tourists, which may enhance their experience. Figure 10.1 provides a list of various food tourism stakeholders.

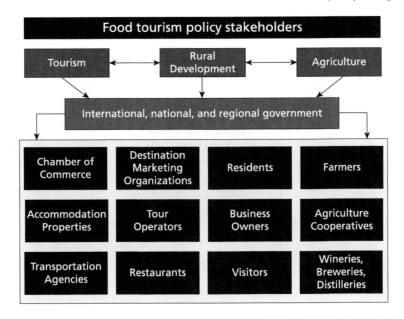

Figure 10.1 Food tourism policy stakeholders

While Figure 10.1 is not inclusive of all food tourism stakeholders, it does cover the major groups that offer food tourism services, are impacted by food tourism development, or are part of the supply chain. For example, farmers may offer on-farm tours, supply food to local restaurants, or chose not to engage in tourism. However, even if they do not engage in food tourism, they may be impacted by tourism's use of distribution points (food hubs), increased traffic from farm deliveries, or increased prices on farm inputs (fertilizer or seeds). The local Chamber of Commerce, DMO, or tour operators are often responsible for marketing food tourism to tourists and have a better understanding of tourist needs than local businesses not experienced with tourism. Their input ensures the success of a new food tourism initiative. Lastly, tourists require other services beyond just food tourism. Including hotels companies, local attractions, and residents in neighboring communities in the planning process may help provide a diverse experience for tourists that encourages them to stay longer and spend more money in the local economy.

The principle of good governance assumes that governments and governing agencies have a responsibility to meet the needs of the general public as opposed to select groups or individuals. Good governance is usually associated with democratic principles. Governance often facilitates the relationships between:

- governments and markets;
- governments and citizens;
- governments and the private or voluntary sector; and
- elected officials and appointed officials.

Good governance is participatory in nature and should allow equitable and inclusive decision-making. This means that all members of a community (the stakeholders) should have a say in the decisions being considered. While not all members of a community may

Consensus Oriented

Participatory

Accountable

Follows the Rule of Law

Good Governance

Transparent

Effective and Efficient

Responsive

Equitable and Inclusive

Figure 10.2 Elements of good governance

agree on the same course of action, good governance implies that the community can come to a general consensus. Certain large entities—such as corporations or influential individuals—should not monopolize the agenda. Potential solutions to problems should create the greatest good. Figure 10.2 highlights elements of good governance.

Good governance also assumes that individuals in positions of power are held to the same standards as the general public. This means that they must follow the rules of law and will be held accountable for their actions. It is also important that those governing agencies have **transparency**, operating such that it is easy for individuals to see and understand the political process, even if they are not directly involved in creating policy. Good governance creates efficient and effective policies that minimize the costs or resources used to effect change.

How policy is developed

Policy is defined as a definite course or method of action selected from a number of alternative actions in light of given conditions that guide and determine present and future decisions. In other words, policy is the set of regulations that communicates appropriate behaviors. For example, agricultural export policy promotes the establishment of international trade partners and encourages farmers to produce commodity crops (corn, wheat, soybeans). As consumers demand more locally grown produce, agricultural policy may change to support the development of farmers' markets. This, in turn, provides new distribution outlets for farmers and encourages them to grow a variety of crops that can be sold directly to consumers. Thus, the policy change results in changed behaviors.

Eight major tasks must be considered when analyzing and developing a new policy (Althaus et al., 2013). These are collectively referred to as the **policy cycle** (see Figure 10.3). Note that policy analysis is a cyclical process of reviewing and reshaping a policy

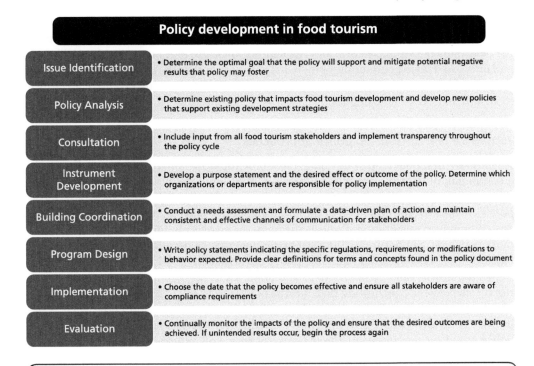

Policy development in food tourism

Issue Identification	• Determine the optimal goal that the policy will support and mitigate potential negative results that policy may foster
Policy Analysis	• Determine existing policy that impacts food tourism development and develop new policies that support existing development strategies
Consultation	• Include input from all food tourism stakeholders and implement transparency throughout the policy cycle
Instrument Development	• Develop a purpose statement and the desired effect or outcome of the policy. Determine which organizations or departments are responsible for policy implementation
Building Coordination	• Conduct a needs assessment and formulate a data-driven plan of action and maintain consistent and effective channels of communication for stakeholders
Program Design	• Write policy statements indicating the specific regulations, requirements, or modifications to behavior expected. Provide clear definitions for terms and concepts found in the policy document
Implementation	• Choose the date that the policy becomes effective and ensure all stakeholders are aware of compliance requirements
Evaluation	• Continually monitor the impacts of the policy and ensure that the desired outcomes are being achieved. If unintended results occur, begin the process again

Figure 10.3 Policy development in food tourism

periodically, such as every 5 to 7 years. When developing a new policy, the most important step is to thoroughly assess the current situation to ensure that the proposed policy will actually address the required behavioral change. All too often, policy documents have no impact on the problem they were designed to solve. It is also important to be aware of other related policies, so that the new policy fits well into the overall goals of the organization or community without contradicting or duplicating existing policies. When policies contradict one another, people do not know which document they should follow (and usually end up following no policy at all).

Let us use a food tourism example to explain. A community may decide that food safety is an issue. This decision may originate from an outbreak of foodborne illness or from a federal government directive to prevent an epidemic of foodborne illness. The community decides to establish a policy to improve food safety, which will include laws and regulations intended to accomplish food safety goals. While the terms "law" and "regulation" are often used interchangeably, they accomplish different goals. **Laws,** or the system of rules designed to regulate certain behaviors, can be established. An example of such a law would be requiring food to be stored a specific way or thrown out after a certain date. **Regulations** govern how the laws are enforced. For example, an agency may be established to inspect restaurants to ensure that they comply with the law. Regulations also stipulate punishments for not obeying the law, such as fines that can be imposed or closing restaurants that repeatedly disobey the law. In assessing the effectiveness of policy, in this case food safety, the policy cycle can help to determine whether the laws are ineffective or if the regulation is the problem. Perhaps safety inspectors are not visiting restaurants frequently enough to ensure that businesses follow the laws.

It is important to seek input from all of the stakeholders throughout the policy cycle. Different stakeholders may see a problem from dissimilar perspectives and can help guide the development of policy, laws, and regulations to ensure that they are enforceable, fair, and effective. Having community buy-in helps to ensure that the community will support the policy. Without this buy-in, a new policy can easily fail or require extensive investment to ensure that everyone complies.

Top-down and bottom-up policy approaches

At the extremes, policies can be created from the top down or from the bottom up, with a continuum of control determining the amount of input individuals have (Figure 10.4). At the citizen control level, all decisions and ownership lie with those most affected by policy changes. At the other end of the spectrum, policy makers can force policies without any community consultation. Projects that actively involve community input and that are more democratic in nature will lead to better governance because they allow for a more participatory, inclusive, and equitable policy environment.

In a **top-down policy** (also known as autocratic leadership), senior executives or officials reach independent conclusions that inform policy decisions. This approach follows the philosophy that government consists of experts or professionals who know what is best for society. In areas where government is elected, governments are tasked with developing policy based on the wishes of the majority of their constituents (those who elected the officials into power). For example, a state official who represents a rural community may

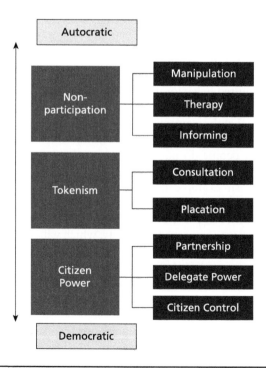

Figure 10.4 Arnstein's ladder of citizen involvement
Source: Adapted from Arnstein (1969)

lobby for agricultural regulations that improve conditions for rural constituents, even if these regulations raise prices for urban citizens. In dictatorships or other totalitarian governments, control is held by a select few who use their power to determine economic development goals regardless of what the citizenry considers appropriate.

Once a plan of action is determined, communities must be convinced of the benefits of policy implementation. One problem with top-down policy is that it is often based on the short-term goals of politicians who need to demonstrate achievable results before the next election cycle. Top-down policy does not usually recognize indigenous knowledge, culture, or local input as valuable contributions to the decision-making process.

Bottom-up policy approaches allow local communities to set their own goals and make decisions about their resources. In effect, bottom-up policies allow individuals and groups most affected by the outcomes of policy to have power and control rather than allowing top officials to make decisions on behalf of a community or industry. Therefore, good governance is important to ensure efficient leadership throughout the process. If bottom-up policy approaches are to be successful, governance agencies must establish avenues to verify that the process is participatory, consensus oriented, equitable, and inclusive (as shown in Figure 10.2).

It is important to note that not all community members have knowledge or experience in policy development. Training is often a key component of many policy documents and can support bottom-up planning by educating community members on issues and potential solutions. Training can include job-specific information, such as food safety procedures, or involve encouraging businesses to develop a united and consistent message that tourists can recognize. There is often a need to train high-quality chefs and encourage both high-end and rustic varieties of restaurants to suit all tourist types. Educating farmers to work with tourists may also be necessary. Finding avenues to source locally and provide viable networks that connect food service professional and agricultural producers can fall within the realm of training and can be one of the largest barriers to successful food tourism

Image 10.1 Local eggs and bacon at a bed-and-breakfast in Harrisonburg, Virginia, USA
Source: Susan L. Slocum

initiatives. Ultimately, the success of food tourism lies in creating a quality product and effectively communicating that quality.

Regional and local food tourism policy

Effective policy can influence many aspects of food tourism, including marketing, labeling, and sustainable growth. Understanding the types of policies that are relevant to food tourism is important to understanding the role that local policy plays in governing food tourism initiatives.

Policy can help address destination marketing challenges. Many regions stress a united leadership structure that usually includes membership organizations that monitor food tourism initiatives to maintain a certain level of quality and uniform marketing messages. These organizations can be spearheaded by the regional government but should include input from stakeholders (as listed in Figure 10.1). The goal is to provide a united message in an effort to reduce confusion in the minds of tourists and create a destination image based on brand identity. Marketing plans are discussed in more detail in Chapter 12, but these plans should incorporate long-term strategic goals that support local policy initiatives.

One increasingly popular policy type is certification schemes, which help tourists recognize local food-related initiatives. **Geographical Indication** (GI) certifications cover agricultural products and foodstuffs that are produced, processed, and prepared in a given geographical area using recognized knowledge or foodstuffs closely linked to that area. Examples include Florida orange juice, Cuban cigars, Bourbon Whiskey, and Roquefort cheese. GI certification has been shown to increase tourism recognition and allows local businesses to charge a price-premium on labeled products. For example, the development of wine routes based on the Stellenbosch geographical indication in South Africa has supported small and medium-sized wineries, increased visitation numbers, and allowed wineries to charge substantial price premiums, resulting in 78% of all business revenues generated through wine tourism activities (including on-site wine purchasing at premium prices) (Bruwer, 2003). While GI certification is discussed in more detail in Chapter 6, from a policy perspective, Stellenbosch's use of GI certification was a wise initiative to support food tourism marketing.

Policy can also be used to control food tourism growth. Many regions find that growth in food tourism creates unintended negative impacts on local residents. **Zoning** is the process of dividing land into areas on which various uses—such as agricultural, residential, or industrial—are permitted or restricted. Zoning ordinances are specifically designed to manage the growth of a community and may include provisions to limit the use of a property (to residential, business, industry, or agricultural use); the type of buildings permitted on the property (size, number of stories, multi-family); parking restrictions (number of parking spaces, prohibiting coaches or RVs); and other land-use limitations. Local government at the town, city, or county level usually regulates zoning. Zoning can be used to ensure that food tourism enterprises are located close to one another, to keep tourism growth away from residential development, or to direct the flow of tourism traffic to specific—often limited—areas of a community.

Regressive and progressive tax policy

Tax policies are relevant to both tourism (in the form of accommodation taxes) and agriculture (in the form of property taxes). Tax policies should be equitable because they affect all residents in a community, not just tourists and tourism businesses.

Regressive taxes place a greater burden (relative to income) on the poor than on the rich. A regressive tax is usually a flat-rate tax, which requires everyone to pay the same rate regardless of income. Sales taxes and gasoline taxes are examples of regressive taxes used in tourism destinations. To see how a regressive tax places a greater burden on the poor, consider the following example: The community you live in has a 20% tax on gasoline. If you make $100 a day but need to spend $10 on gas to get work, you will pay $2 on your gasoline tax, which leaves you with $88 to cover all of your other expenses. You pay 2% of your daily income for the gasoline tax ($2/$100). If you make $500 a day and have the same commute, you have $488 left after paying the gas tax. This means that you pay just 0.4% of your income for the gas tax ($2/$500). The poorer version of you pays a higher percentage of your income on tax (2% versus 0.4%).

Progressive taxes increase as the taxable amount increases. Business taxes are a good example of this. As a company grows and earns more revenue, taxation rates change. As a result, poorer people operating small businesses pay a lower rate of tax than wealthy business owners. If you earn $100 per day at your farm, you may fall into a certain tax bracket, say 10%, in which case you pay $10 in taxes, leaving you with $90 for other expenses. If you make $500 a day, you may fall into the 25% tax rate, which means you pay $125 in taxes and are left with $375. If a community needs a certain amount of tax revenue to operate public services, a progressive tax will reduce the tax burden (lower the amount paid) on poorer members of society.

It is generally assumed that taxes paid by tourists help reduce the amount that local residents need to pay in taxes in order to support the development of roads, schools, and other social services. It is also assumed that tourism taxes are **inelastic**, meaning that an increase in the tax rate for a tourist is not likely to discourage tourism spending, whereas taxes for local residents are considered **elastic**, meaning that an increase in the tax rate will result in locals making fewer purchases. People traveling on vacation tend to be less sensitive to prices than when they are at home, so creating or increasing taxes that impact tourists rather than local residents is generally viewed as a lucrative policy for tourism destinations. However, while tourists buy a number of commodity items that may generate regional sales tax, locals are also affected by increases in sales tax. Therefore, tourism taxes tend to take the form of entrance fees to tourist attractions, accommodation taxes on hotel rooms, travel visa fees, or departure taxes (at airports) for international travelers.

Food tourism policies are not always tax-related. Agencies should use a combination of laws and regulations to ensure positive impacts to communities from food tourism development. Additionally, agencies may develop policies to support other development needs, such as natural resource protection, sustainable development, or small business support.

Food tourism policy organizations

International policy organizations

The most prominent and influential tourism organization is the United Nations World Tourism Organization (UNWTO), which promotes responsible, sustainable, and accessible tourism. The UNWTO encourages growth in tourism to support economies, environments, and communities worldwide in order to achieve the UN's Sustainable Development Goals (adopted in 2015) to end poverty and hunger, improve health and education, make cities more sustainable, combat climate change, and protect oceans and forests (United Nations Development Programme, 2015). The UNWTO published its first Global Report on Food

Tourism, establishing a set of guidelines to support new initiatives in relation to food tourism.

> In this Report, we have attempted to carry out an analysis of the current situation of Food Tourism, through a survey of UNWTO affiliate members and the input of tourism and gastronomy professionals with extensive experience in international organizations, in destination management, tourism enterprises and in the field of training. The aim was to try to obtain a series of conclusions regarding some of the initiatives that are going on worldwide in Food Tourism for possible inclusion in the strategic reflection process being carried out by both the public sector and businesses about policies for development and promotion in this field.
>
> (UNWTO, 2012, p. 5)

This report is arguably the first stage in the policy cycle, as described above, implying that UNWTO is investigating the development of a food tourism policy since food tourism is a growing market segment with implications for rural development strategies. This report has become one of the most influential sources for regions developing both national and regional food tourism policy.

The World Travel and Tourism Council (WTTC) is an international organization of travel industry professionals whose members work with governments to promote and raise awareness about the travel and tourism industry worldwide. Its main goal is to open up international markets, both for travelers and for tourism businesses. While it has not yet embraced food tourism development specifically, the WTTC has become very influential in encouraging pro-investment policies pertaining to tourism infrastructure, particularly in developing counties.

National policy organizations

Agriculture generally has its own cabinet-level entity, but many Western countries do not have large national tourism policy boards. Tourism is usually a part of a larger department or ministry. Table 10.1 shows the key tourism and agriculture policy agencies in a variety

Table 10.1 Agencies governing tourism and agriculture by country

Country	Responsible for tourism	Responsible for agriculture
Australia	Department of Foreign Affairs and Trade	Department of Agriculture and Water Resources
Canada	Minister of Industry	Agriculture and Agri-food Canada
Germany	Federal Ministry for Economic Affairs and Energy	Federal Ministry for Food and Agriculture
Iceland	Ministry of Industry, Energy and Tourism	Ministry of Fisheries and Agriculture
Ireland	Department of Transport, Tourism and Sport	Department of Agriculture, Food, and the Marine
Israel	Ministry of Tourism	Ministry of Agriculture and Rural Development
Italy	Ministry for Cultural Heritage and Activities and for Tourism	Ministry of Agriculture, Food and Forestry

Country	Responsible for tourism	Responsible for agriculture
Japan	Ministry of Land, Infrastructure, Transport and Tourism	Ministry of Agriculture, Forestry and Fisheries
Korea	Ministry of Culture, Sport and Tourism	Ministry of Agriculture, Food and Rural Affairs
New Zealand	Ministry of Business, Innovation and Development	Ministry for Primary Industries
United Kingdom	Department for Culture, Media and Sport	Department of Environment, Food and Rural Affairs
United States	U.S. Department of Commerce	U.S. Department of Agriculture

of developed countries. It is easy to see that tourism and agriculture are often housed in completely different departments or ministries within a government structure, which means that a variety of different, sometimes conflicting, policies may be applied to food tourism development.

Currently, none of these national agencies have formal food tourism policy documents, although many of them have started investigating the impact of food tourism on rural

Image 10.2 Stonetown Market, a government regulated market in Zanzibar, Tanzania
Source: Susan L. Slocum

economies (see case study 1.1), creating the potential for developing national-level policies. However, a number of policy initiatives at the regional or local level bring insight into the growing impact of food tourism. Therefore, many countries and regions around the world may soon develop national food tourism policies.

Summary

This chapter has described the process of policy development. While it has focused on government policies affecting food tourism, the framework of the policy cycle also applies to businesses and other organizations involved in long-term decision-making. Agriculture and tourism often fall under different agencies, each developing policy that can affect food tourism. Good governance must guarantee that policy and the resulting laws and regulations are supportive of food tourism growth while ensuring that communities have a say in how the industry is developed. Inclusive policy, which allows all stakeholders to be actively involved in the policy-development process, is also important. Including stakeholders requires bottom-up planning to ensure that those most affected by food tourism development support long-term goals. Good policy anticipates negative side effects and attempts to eliminate or reduce them so that food tourism development is a positive experience for both residents and tourists.

Study Questions

1   Identify and review two policies in your local community that focus on a common goal. What aspects of these policies support each other? What aspects contradict each other? How would you adapt each policy to make sure that the two policies support common development goals?
2   You have been asked to develop a food tourism policy for your hometown. Who would you consider to be your stakeholders? How would you approach them? How would you implement their different perspectives in the final policy document?
3   Tourism to your area has increased the need for additional law enforcement officers. You decide to implement a food tax to pay for the increased expenses. Using a form of bottom-up policy planning, what steps would you take to ensure good governance? Would your tax be regressive or progressive? Why?

Definitions

Bottom-up policy—a policy that allows local communities to set their own goals and make decisions about their resources in the future.
Elastic good—a good whose price affects the quantity sold of that good; an increase in price reduces the quantity sold and a decrease in price increases the quantity sold.

Geographical Indication (GI)—a certification that covers agricultural products and foodstuffs that are closely linked to a geographical area.

Governance—the coordination of economies, public/private partnerships, and reform objectives aimed at pursuing collective interests.

Inelastic good—a good whose price does not affect the quantity sold of that good; the quantity sold is stable regardless of whether the price increases or decreases.

Laws—a system of rules designed to regulate certain behaviors, which are enforced through penalties.

Policy—a definite course or method of action selected from a number of alternative actions in light of given conditions that guide and determine present and future decisions.

Policy cycle—a process of reviewing and reshaping a policy periodically, such as every 5 to 7 years.

Progressive taxes—taxes that have rates that increase as taxable amount increases.

Regressive taxes—taxes that place a greater burden (relative to income) on the poor than on the rich.

Regulations—a set of rules that govern how laws are enforced.

Top-down policy—a policy created by senior executives or officials independent of those affected by the policy.

Transparency—operating in such a way that it is easy for others to see and understand what actions are performed.

Zoning—the process of dividing land into areas on which various uses are permitted or restricted.

CASE STUDY 10.1

Developing a food tourism destination: Finding common ground in Bedfordshire, England

Susan L. Slocum and Kynda R. Curtis

England has traditionally relied on government support for tourism promotion. After the 2010 economic downturn, the British government moved toward an industry-led approach to destination management and marketing that encouraged regional distinctiveness to promote place-based marketing partnerships. As DMOs lost their primary funding sources and became increasingly responsible for local tourism policy initiatives, new challenges emerged as destinations attempted to redefine their brands and engage tourism stakeholders to contribute both financially and administratively to marketing efforts. Additional challenges included adding management responsibilities to organizations that had primarily specialized in marketing only. The new management tasks include adapting to technological changes, managing tourist expectations, mitigating impacts, confronting new avenues of competition, recognizing creative partnerships, and finding new measures of success.

Bedfordshire is a county one hour north of London with direct train links to St Pancras Station. It offers a number of tourist attractions, including Whipsnade Wildlife Park, Woburn Safari Park, Wardown Park Museum, the Luton Hoo Mansion House, and Body Flight (indoor skydiving). It is also the home of London's Luton Airport, the fifth busiest airport in the UK. Most attractions are located near the two urban centers of Bedford and Luton, but the majority of the county is rural and comprises the drainage areas of the Great River Ouze. The land is fertile and agriculture is prevalent across the landscape. On the southern end of Bedfordshire lies the Chilterns, a series of rolling hills that were designated as an Area of Outstanding Natural Beauty in 1965.

DMOs play an important role in governing tourism destinations because they are uniquely positioned intermediaries between government, industry, and local residents. They are often leaders in tourism development and are responsible for strategic

Image 10.3 Hiking in Bedfordshire, UK
Source: Susan L. Slocum

planning that involves not only attracting tourists but also ensuring an appropriate mix of tourism activities and infrastructure. Bedfordshire's DMO, Experience Bedfordshire (EB) (2017), lists the following mission statement on their website:

> To promote the whole county of Bedfordshire to domestic and international visitors, to protect and enhance leisure, sport and business tourism via an active board (secular and apolitical) that will ensure that Experience Bedfordshire stimulates growth by working closely together with the Bedfordshire Chamber of Commerce, central and local Governments and SEMLEP to deliver value for all its members with a dynamic website, literature, events, exhibitions, positive PR and strong marketing.
>
> (Experience Bedfordshire, 2017)

The first study was conducted to help EB engage industry partnerships and establish a coherent management and marketing policy that aligned with the views of Bedfordshire residents and tourism businesses (Slocum & Everett, 2013). A web-based survey was administered to EB stakeholders, followed by a series of focus groups. Results showed that most tourism stakeholders were frustrated that EB prioritized family and adventure fun rather than the rural nature of the county. They felt that Bedfordshire's strengths lay in their countryside, history, and natural settings. While marketing initiatives such as "Tastes of Bedfordshire" and "Home of Afternoon Tea" were grounded in Bedfordshire's rural setting, mixed messages that promoted high-adrenaline activities (such as skydiving) diluted the overall destination image.

Image 10.4 Chiltern Brewery in Bedfordshire, UK
Source: Kynda R. Curtis

A second study was conducted using in-person interviews to visitors in the county. They were asked to choose words that best described Bedfordshire. The top descriptors were "accessible" (67%), "historic" (57%), "picturesque" (54%), and "cultural" (43%). Only 12% responded "adventurous." These choices have reinforced Bedfordshire's image among the visiting public as a natural attraction.

These two separate research projects highlight the disconnect between the current governance focus in Bedfordshire and the destination attributes prioritized by both local tourism stakeholders and visitors to the area. Slocum and Everett (2013) argue that "the struggle between industry, government and community has refocused power and leadership away from resource assessment toward a market view of destination management that serves big business rather than community" (p. 56). In other words, they suggest that a more inclusive form of governance would encourage the use of the natural attractions (resources) and spread the benefits of tourism around the county rather than strictly seeking financial gains to the largest tourism businesses located in the urban areas.

Questions

1 How can Experience Bedfordshire find a united marketing message that incorporates not only the largest tourist attractions but also the natural beauty of the rural areas?
2 What type of policy could be developed to support the addition of agritourism or food tourism into the tourism product? What are the strengths and weakness of your policy suggestions?
3 How can Experience Bedfordshire better engage tourism and agriculture stakeholders in tourism governance?

References

Experience Bedfordshire. (2017). About Experience Bedfordshire. Retrieved from www.experiencebedfordshire.co.uk/about-experience-bedfordshire
Slocum, S. L., and Everett, S. (2013). Industry, government, and community: Power and leadership in a resource constrained DMO. *Tourism Review, 69*(1), 47–68.

Food waste policy and the role of green certification programs in tourism

Kynda R. Curtis and Susan L. Slocum

Food waste is a global problem. In 2011, 1.3 billion tons of food were wasted, and every year 35% of the total food supply is discarded (Food and Agriculture Organization of the United Nations, 2011). The negative impacts of food waste have prompted governmental organizations and agencies (such as the U.S. Department of Agriculture), non-governmental organizations (such as the Food and Agriculture Organization of the United Nations), and industry partnerships (such as the Food Waste Reduction Alliance) to establish programs and lobby for policies that reduce food loss and reward waste reduction.

Food waste is a primary concern for the hospitality and tourism industry. The cost of food waste in the UK hotel sector was £318 million in 2014. The majority of food waste was generated during food preparation (45%), food discarded by patrons (34%), and spoilage (21%) (Green Hotelier, 2014). The primary impacts of food waste are costly waste-management schemes, increased pests, and wildlife endangerment. For example, a single resort in the Bahamas contributes over a third of the total waste generated on the island (Sealey & Smith, 2014).

Image 10.5 Beach front dining, Brighton, UK
Source: Kynda R. Curtis

Industry and third-party organizations have begun to address the issue of food waste through third-party certification and labeling organizations. In theory, third-party certification programs provide consumers the opportunity to differentiate among goods/services with regard to social and environmental impacts. The higher prices consumers are willing to pay for these products/services create financial incentives for firms to meet certification standards. To be successful, however, certification programs must set sufficient standards, monitor and enforce them, and inform consumers about certified firms and performance history.

Recipe for green certification program success

To be successful, certification programs must be designed so that firms benefit from participating and consumers choose certified tourism operations. Behavioral economics provides decision-making models that seek to change the environment or context in which firms or people make decisions. These contextual changes, or "nudges," lead to improved decision-making. Dolan et al. (2012, p. 266) use "nudge" concepts to formulate a set of effects on behavior they call MINDSPACE cues (Table 10.2).

Program-specific recommendations

The need for salient and easily understandable information requires certification programs to be globally, or at least regionally, recognized. Program details must be

Table 10.2 Behavioral impacts of MINDSPACE cues

Cue	Behavioral impact
Messenger	We are heavily influenced by the communicator/source of information (expertise, trustworthiness, personality)
Incentives	We are motivated by the timing and magnitude of incentives (gifts, coupons, completion certificates, loss of money)
Norms	We are strongly influenced by the actions of others (friends, family, those we respect)
Defaults	We commonly use pre-set options (opting in or out is less likely)
Salience	Our attention is drawn to what is relevant (easy to understand, see, or find)
Priming	Our acts are often influenced by sub-conscious cues (words, pictures, sounds, smells)
Affect	Our emotional associations can powerfully shape our actions (words, images, events)
Commitments	We seek to be consistent with our public promises, and we reciprocate acts
Ego	We act in ways that create a positive self-image

Source: Adapted from Dolan et al. (2012)

easy for consumers, program members (certified firms), and potential new members to obtain. While they should provide streamlined messages and consistent regulations, the processes for achieving certification standards could be tailored to local customs, values, and social norms.

Past performance provides insight into the elements required for a successful certification program, which include a number of behavioral cues for both customers and firms:

- specific certification objectives and their impacts (economic/social/environmental);
- clearly defined program benefits (for firms and consumers);
- measurable achievement indicators or minimum certification standards;
- comprehensive promotion/communication plans and platforms (website, etc.);
- easily recognizable program labels;
- detailed directory of all certified firms;
- transparent member evaluation/monitoring plans and processes;
- specific penalties for non-compliance;
- recertification processes with metrics and timelines;
- dissemination plans for consumer research and results;
- program evaluation plans and implementation budgets.

Firm-specific recommendations

Certification programs can be costly for members due to required record keeping and promotional activities. Financial benefits must offset costs or firms will not participate. Strong financial incentives—such as tax breaks, financial aid, or grants—can help offset these costs and encourage participation. Additional nudges and cues can be used. For instance, a firm is more likely to participate in a program when their competitors also participate (norms cue). Signing a contract to enter the certification program is a priming and commitment cue that can also increase program success. Penalizing firms for non-compliance, as a negative incentive, has also been shown to be highly effective.

Customer-specific recommendations

Norms and ego cues can have strong impacts on consumer behavior. People are influenced by friends and those they respect. Consumers who value environmentally sustainable practices, for example, will be motivated to select certified firms if their friends also choose certified firms. Additionally, selecting these firms can cause consumers to feel good about themselves and feel respected in their social circle. The messenger cue, or information source, also affects how consumers view the information and how quickly they act on it.

When informing consumers, salience and priming cues suggest that certification programs' logos should be easily identifiable on all promotional materials, websites, table cards, menus, etc. Firms should outline the types of activities they are undertaking to meet program standards and the intended social, environmental, and economic impacts to the local and global community (taking advantage of ego and affect cues).

On site, firms can encourage consumers to assist them in achieving the program's sustainability objectives by asking visitors to sign a commitment card outlining the green activities they can participate in during their visit (commitment and priming cues). Firms can provide incentives for completing green activities or opting out of services that waste resources (incentives cue); making green activities the default option, meaning consumer must opt out of the behavior (default cue); or noting the percentage of customers who complete green activities (norms cue).

Conclusions

Reducing food waste and encouraging sustainability, especially in the tourism industry, requires the improvement of certification program design. Using behavioral economic concepts such as "nudges" to influence behavior can lead to greater economic success and environmental responsibility in the tourism industry.

Questions

1 Would you be willing to pay more to stay at a green-certified resort? Why or why not? What kind of information from the certification program would you need to make your decision?
2 What types of "nudges" would help reduce the food you waste while on vacation?
3 How could these concepts be used to establish a food-waste policy for your hometown?

References

Dolan, P., Hallsworth, M., Halpern, D., King, D., Metcalfe, R., and Vlaev, I. (2012). Influencing behavior: The mindspace way. *Journal of Economic Psychology*, 33(1), 264–277.

Food and Agriculture Organization of the United Nations. (2011). Global food losses and food waste. Retrieved from www.fao.org/docrep/014/mb060e/mb 060e00.pdf

Green Hotelier. (2014). Reducing and managing food waste in hotels. *Green Hotelier Know-How Guides*. Retrieved from www.greenhotelier.org/know-how-guides/reducing-and-managing-food-waste-in-hotels/

Sealey, K., and Smith, J. (2014). Recycling for small island tourism developments: Food waste composting at Sandals Emerald Bay, Exuma, Bahamas. *Resources, Conservation, & Recycling, 92,* 25–37.

References

Althaus, C., Bridgman, P., and Davis, G. (2013). *The Australian policy handbook* (5th ed.). Sydney: Allen & Unwin.

Arnstein, S.R. (1969). A ladder of citizen participation. *Journal of the American Institute of Planners*, 35(4), 216–24.

Bruwer, J. (2003). South African wine routes: Some perspectives on the wine tourism industry's structural dimensions and wine tourism product. *Tourism Management*, 24(4), 423–435.

Dolan, P., Hallsworth, M., Halpern, D., King, D., Metcalfe, R., and Vlaev, I. (2012). Influencing behavior: The mindspace way. *Journal of Economic Psychology*, 33, 264–277.

Edgell, D.L., and Swanson, J.R. (2013). *Tourism policy and planning: Yesterday, today, and tomorrow* (2nd ed.). London: Routledge.

Slocum, S.L., and Backman, K.F. (2011). Understanding government capacity in tourism development as a poverty alleviation tool: A case study of Tanzanian policy-makers. *Tourism Planning & Development*, 8(3), 281–296.

United Nations Development Programme. (2015). World leaders adopt Sustainable Development Goals. Retrieved from www.undp.org/content/undp/en/home/sustainable-development-goals.html

United Nations World Tourism Organization. (2012). Global report on food tourism. UNWTO, Madrid. Retrieved from cf.cdn.unwto.org/sites/all/files/pdf/global_report_on_food_tourism.pdf

Chapter 11

Safety in food tourism operations

Karin Allen

Overview

Visitor health and safety are important considerations when developing, expanding, or running a food tourism venue. Food safety is a critical component of the welfare of visitors and guests. When developing and evaluating the food safety practices of a food tourism enterprise, all aspects of food preparation for on-site consumption and food processing for specialty and souvenir products must be considered, as well as the potential for visitor illness resulting from contact with animals.

Learning Objectives

This chapter will enable students to

1 Describe the common types of food-related disease-causing agents and how they can be controlled or minimized.
2 Discuss steps that can be taken to prevent visitor exposure to food-related disease-causing agents.
3 Explain the similarities and differences between food service and food processing operations.
4 Identify the appropriate agencies administering regional food safety policies.

Safe food saves lives

In a first-of-its-kind report published in 2015, the World Health Organization (WHO) estimated that 600 million cases of foodborne illness occurred globally in 2010 (WHO, 2015). That means approximately 1 out of every 10 people worldwide became sick as a result of **microbes** (microscopic life forms that include bacteria, viruses, fungi, and parasites) or chemicals in the food they consumed. Gastrointestinal diseases—primarily attributed to pathogenic viruses and bacteria—were responsible for 550 million of these illnesses. While it is difficult, if not impossible, to determine how many of these illnesses are directly linked to food purchased or consumed in food tourism settings, it is important to recognize that food safety is everyone's responsibility.

Foodborne illness can affect any sector of the food industry in both affluent and poor nations. While the most common causes of foodborne illness vary from country to country, proper food handling and sanitation practices can reduce the incidence of food-related illnesses. **Sanitation** refers to the environmental or operational practices related to cleanliness that reduce or eliminate the spread of disease. Epidemiologists and microbiologists often discuss food safety in terms of "YOPIs" —young, old, pregnant, and immuno-compromised persons. These populations are particularly susceptible to disease-causing agents, and outcomes in these groups are often more severe or even fatal. Many visitors to food tourism enterprises fall into one of these groups, so proper food safety practices are critically important.

Hazards in foods

Food can harbor any number of dangerous biological, chemical, or physical contaminants. A **contaminant** is any unwanted or undesirable material found in food.

Chemical hazards include pesticides; processing chemicals, such as sanitizing agents; and naturally occurring toxins. **Toxins** are chemicals that produce disease in humans. Proper use of agricultural chemicals—such as pesticides, herbicides, and fertilizers—can reduce or eliminate contamination. Sanitizing agents used in food preparation and processing should only be used at concentrations approved by the applicable regulatory agency. Foods that are associated with toxins, such as some mushrooms and puffer fish, should be carefully selected and handled to minimize the risk of chemical contamination.

Physical hazards include: field debris (e.g., rocks), plant components (e.g., nutshells), and processing components (e.g., broken glass, metal shavings). These objects rarely cause illness, but they can result in serious physical injuries such as broken teeth or lacerations of the lips, mouth, or throat. Care should be taken during harvest to remove any field debris, and foods like dried beans should always be sorted carefully before use. Close attention during preparation or processing can eliminate natural plant and processing components. Many jurisdictions prohibit the use of glass containers in food preparation areas and require that glass jars be stored in a separate room from active food processing activities to minimize these risks.

Biological hazards include bacteria, viruses, fungi, and parasites. Fungi, like mold and yeast, commonly cause spoilage and economic loss rather than illness, but certain types of mold can produce toxic chemicals (this is usually a commodity-specific concern). Parasites like *Giardia lambia* and *Cryptosporidium parvum* are often waterborne. They can be deposited on fresh fruits and vegetables through irrigation or washing water but are easily destroyed by proper cooking. Parasites can also be spread by infected animals or food handlers. Viruses and bacteria are the most common biological causes of foodborne illness.

Viruses and bacteria

Sanitation regulations and practices often focus on preventing foodborne illness caused by viral and bacterial microbes. The main source of viral and bacterial contamination is fecal contamination. Fecal microbes can enter irrigation water through animal waste, be deposited directly onto produce by undertreated or untreated manure-based compost, or be transferred to food by infected food handlers who do not practice adequate **hygiene,** defined as personal practices related to cleanliness that reduce or eliminate the spread of disease. Viruses and bacteria can also be transferred to previously uncontaminated foods through cross-contamination, making sanitation practices in processing and preparation areas essential. There are distinct differences in how these microbes grow, so it is important to understand their behavior in order to develop an effective food safety plan. Regardless of the cause, any personnel exhibiting signs of foodborne illness should not work with food until they are symptom-free.

Viruses

Viruses cannot grow or multiply on their own. They must hijack the cells of a living host, such as an animal or human, to grow and cause infection. Viral particles can be deposited on food through contaminated water or infected food handlers. Because viruses cannot multiply on food, steps that are commonly used to control bacteria (such as low-temperature storage) are ineffective. Proper hygiene, use of clean water sources, and facility sanitation are the best strategies to prevent incidents of viral illness.

The most common cause of viral foodborne illness is from Norwalk and Norwalk-like viruses, collectively called noroviruses, which cause what is sometimes referred to as "cruise ship" disease. Between 2010 and 2014, norovirus was the leading cause of foodborne illness outbreaks worldwide (WHO, 2015) and among the top three causes in several countries, including the United States (Scallan et al., 2011), the UK (Tam et al., 2014), and Australia (Kirk et al., 2014). Norovirus can be particularly troublesome in situations where people are in close contact for extended periods of time (such as a cruise ship). Once a person is infected, the virus can be spread directly from person to person by contaminated food or through contact with contaminated surfaces. Symptoms of norovirus include vomiting and diarrhea, which appear within 12 to 48 hours of infection and can last up to 3 days (Food and Drug Administration, 2012).

Bacteria

Bacteria freely multiply on food when environmental conditions are suitable. Many types of bacteria may be present on foods. Some are considered beneficial and may even be used purposely to change the nature of foods, such as those used to culture dairy products (e.g., cheese, yogurt), ferment vegetables (e.g., sauerkraut, some pickles), and produce vinegar. But even beneficial bacteria can contribute to food spoilage. For example, the bacteria necessary to make bleu cheese can also spoil bread. It is important to recognize that food spoilage is not necessarily an indication that the food has become unsafe. **Pathogenic bacteria**—microbes that can cause illness in humans—can still be present in dangerous amounts on foods that appear fresh and wholesome.

In order to grow, all bacteria require an appropriate nutrient source, pH level, atmosphere, access to water, and temperature. The acronym "FAT TOM" is often used to summarize these requirements: food, acidity, time, temperature, oxygen, and moisture. Although these apply to all bacteria, specific requirements for various strains of bacteria can vary considerably. The longer these environmental conditions are maintained, and the closer to ideal the conditions are, the more the bacteria will multiply.

Image 11.1 Fresh meat hanging in a butcher shop, Havana, Cuba
Source: Kynda R. Curtis

Table 11.1 provides a summary of the bacteria of highest concern in foodborne outbreaks. Some of these cause relatively mild symptoms of short duration but affect large numbers of people annually. Others may be responsible for significantly fewer cases but are associated with severe or long-term illness, increased hospitalizations, or a high fatality rate. This information has been summarized from global (WHO, 2015) and select national sources from the United States (Scallan et al., 2011), the UK (Tam et al., 2014) and Australia (Kirk et al., 2014). This is not intended as an exhaustive list, nor should it be inferred that food tourism operators should try to diagnose or provide treatment for foodborne illness associated with specific bacteria.

Regulations concerning food handling and processing are often based on how best to control the pathogenic bacteria most resistant to certain conditions (e.g., high temperatures) or those most likely to be associated with a given type of food or processing method (e.g., bottled foods). These factors as they apply to specific aspects of food preparation and processing are discussed in more detail later in this chapter.

Food safety plans

Each food tourism enterprise should develop a comprehensive food safety plan that includes how staff and visitors will be trained. This may be a regulatory requirement in

Table 11.1 Pathogenic bacteria overview

Bacteria	Common Food Sources	Cause of Frequent Outbreaks?	Typical Illness	Special Considerations
Campylobacter jejeuni	• Undercooked poultry • Raw milk	Yes: #2 worldwide (2013) #1 UK (2012) #1 Australia (2010) #5 US (2011)	Gastrointestinal symptoms lasting up to ten days.	Proper cooking of foods and prevention of cross-contamination is essential to prevent illness.
Clostridium botulinum	• Improperly canned vegetables, beans • Foil-wrapped baked potatoes	No, only sporadic outbreaks related to inadequate processing of specific foods.	Bacteria forms a potent neurotoxin that affects central nervous system. Symptoms vary from mild (dizziness) to severe (paralysis). Can last for months or be fatal.	Spore-forming bacteria. Spores are not destroyed by normal cooking but are controlled by low pH and high concentration of sugar or salt.
Clostridium perfringens	• Improperly handled meat, poultry, meat-based sauces	Yes: #3 US (2011) Not regularly monitored in many countries.	Gastrointestinal symptoms can be intense but rarely last more than one day.	Spore-forming bacteria. Spores are not destroyed by normal cooking, and bacteria will readily grow in improperly held or cooled foods.
Enterohemorrhagic *Escherichia coli*	• Undercooked meat • Raw vegetables • Raw milk	No, only sporadic outbreaks related to specific foods.	Two forms of illness: • Gastrointestinal, lasts up to eight days. • Hemolytic Uremic Syndrome can result in kidney failure, often fatal.	Includes strains like O157:H7 that produce a *Shiga*-type toxin. This toxin is responsible for the more severe symptoms associated with Hemolytic Uremic Syndrome.

Enterotoxic *Escherichia coli*	• Contaminated water • Foods washed in contaminated water	Yes: #1 worldwide (2013)	Gastrointestinal symptoms lasting up to four days.	Common source of traveler's diarrhea. Of special concern to operations serving foreign tourists.
Listeria monocytogenes	• Ready-to-eat refrigerated foods • Deli meats, cheese • Pasta or potato salads • Raw produce • Raw milk	No, only sporadic outbreaks related to specific foods.	Influenza-like symptoms can last for weeks. Can cause stillbirth or miscarriage.	Environmental bacteria that can be found in many types of food. Can grow at low temperatures, so refrigerator storage is not an adequate control.
Salmonella species	• Undercooked eggs, poultry • Raw produce • Low-moisture foods including spices and nuts	Yes: #4 worldwide (2013) #2 US (2011) #3 Australia (2010)	Gastrointestinal symptoms lasting up to seven days. Can lead to long-term health issues.	Includes multiple strains of *Salmonella* bacteria. Illness can also result from handling birds, reptiles, or other infected animals.

some locations. While all employees should be educated about the plan, it can be beneficial to have one person who is in charge of developing and monitoring compliance. When possible, consult with inspectors, academics, or food industry consultants to determine whether the plan is adequate. In many cases, these experts have educational materials that can serve as a starting point, making it possible to personalize a plan for your operation without having to start from scratch.

Worker hygiene and training

All employees who come in contact with food at any point—from harvest to table—should be adequately trained in food safety. This includes information on the foodborne pathogens most likely to cause issues in the type(s) of food they handle as well as the specific sources of contamination common in their work environment. In many regions, food handlers must obtain licensing or certification by satisfying certain training requirements. Licensing and certification may be administered by a national, regional, or local government agency and sometimes vary depending on the specific job function being performed. Table 11.2 lists the main regulatory agencies overseeing packaged and processed foods in several countries (although other agencies may be involved in the regulation of specific commodities, such as meat and poultry). Regional or local government agencies often oversee regulatory enforcement and inspections for packaged food producers as well as for on-site food preparation for immediate consumption.

At a minimum, all employees should be trained on the importance of adequate handwashing. Hands must be washed after eating, drinking, smoking, using restroom facilities, or handling potentially contaminated raw foods. A twenty-second wash with soap in clean, warm, running water is recommended, with subsequent drying using disposable towels or air dryers. Sufficient, dedicated handwashing sinks or outdoor stations should be provided to encourage employees working in all areas of the food tourism enterprise to comply with handwashing requirements. Adequate trash receptacles should be provided next to

Table 11.2 Governmental agencies overseeing food processing activities

Country	Agency with primary jurisdiction over food processing*
Australia	Food Standards Australia New Zealand (FSANZ)
Canada	Canadian Food Inspections Agency (CFIA)
Iceland	Ministry of Industries and Innovation
Ireland	Food Safety Authority of Ireland (FSAI)
Israel	National Food Service
Italy	Ministry of Agriculture, Food & Forestry
Japan	Ministry of Health, Labour & Welfare
Korea	Ministry of Food & Drug Safety
New Zealand	Food Standards Australia New Zealand (FSANZ)
Norway	Food Safety Authority
Sweden	National Food Agency
United Kingdom	Food Standards Agency (FSA)
United States	Food and Drug Administration (FDA)

* Specific commodities, such as meat and poultry products, may be regulated by a separate governmental organization.

handwashing stations, and they should be emptied regularly. Antimicrobial rubs or lotions are generally not considered to be adequate substitutes for handwashing. They may be allowed in certain situations, but the appropriate inspection or regulatory agencies should always be consulted to make sure that this substitution is acceptable. Employers should not require employees to work in any job involving food contact when they are sick, especially if their symptoms are consistent with a foodborne illness. It is good business practice to develop policies ensuring that employees are not penalized for requesting time off from work duties due to illness.

Food safety for agritourism

Farm-based operations

Farm layout and design
It is possible to design an agritourism enterprise to minimize the potential for exposure to harmful pathogens. Where possible, visitor areas should be designed to include "clean" pathways leading into and "dirty" pathways leading out of areas that may harbor pathogens, including petting zoos, areas where visitors interact with farm animals, U-pick areas, and general farm tours. Inform guests that they are expected to stay on designated pathways. Double-fencing areas to create a buffer zone between open and off-limits areas can help ensure compliance. Providing sitting areas where guests can change footwear before and after entering a potentially contaminated area limits the chances that pathogens are carried to other areas of the farm. Handwashing stations should be provided at the entrance to areas where guests eat or handle food and at the exit from areas where they come in contact with animals. Signage reminding them of proper handwashing techniques can help ensure compliance. It is also recommended that guests be instructed not to put their hands in their mouths, touch their eyes, or consume foods until after they have washed their hands, especially after handling animals. Many industry organizations and government agencies have signs or posters available for download to help food tourism enterprises with their efforts to encourage handwashing.

U-pick operations, where visitors can harvest fresh produce directly from the field, pose unique safety issues. In some regions only trained employees are legally allowed into areas where food intended for commerce is harvested. This may require designation of specific growing areas that are open to the general public. Always ensure that the operation is in compliance with applicable national, regional, and local regulations regarding public harvesting areas. Handwashing stations and adequate trash receptacles should be provided at the entrance to fields. Visitors should be reminded that picked items cannot be eaten in the field and that they should wash all produce before consumption. Clean, previously unused containers should be provided to guests to safely harvest and transport picked items whenever possible. For larger produce items where this is not practical, properly cleaned and sanitized containers should be provided for their use in the field. Guests who have previously visited animal attractions must clean or change their footwear to prevent the spread of contaminants into areas where produce is grown.

Eating areas should be located away from open fields and animal pens. Handwashing stations and adequate trash receptacles should be provided at convenient locations adjacent to picnic areas. Whenever possible, eating areas should be enclosed or shielded from wild animals. Trash receptacles that do not attract or harbor pests should be used,

205

and they should be emptied often to discourage animals from identifying them as a reliable source of food. Handwashing sinks or stations should also be provided just outside or immediately inside permanent structures, such as farm stores, restaurants, or lodging facilities.

Visitor versus farm responsibilities

Food tourism enterprises may include many on-farm activities—such as U-pick, hay rides, or farm stays—for their visitors. Ultimately, the business is responsible for the safety of its guests. Providing visitors with a brief overview of farm safety policies and procedures is a part of this responsibility, especially for children under 5 years of age who are at particular risk (National Association of State Public Health Veterinarians, 2013; Lange et al., 2014). In some locations there are even requirements to provide visitor training. While it is not possible to educate guests on every aspect of a farm food safety program, it is a good business practice to provide them with specific information on areas where they are allowed, handwashing considerations, and instructing them to read and comply with signage. Visitors should be reassured that the ultimate goal of these instructions is to provide them with a safe and enjoyable experience and that their active participation helps the business meet this goal.

Food safety for food service

Businesses that prepare food on-site for immediate consumption may be referred to collectively as "**food service**" or "catering" operations, depending on local vernacular. These businesses, which may include cafés, delis, or wineries, prepare meals that are served to customers in on-site dining rooms or designated eating areas, minimally packaged foods to be taken by the guest and eaten within a short period of time off premises or as a picnic, and foods that are transported by employees and served to customers off-site. These types of activities are most often regulated by regional or local government agencies and typically require licensing and regular inspections.

Facility design

In many locations, food preparation kitchens must use commercial-grade equipment. Regulations may also require kitchens to use adequate fire suppression systems; grease traps in drains (or other methods of limiting fats and oils from entering waste water systems); and easily cleanable, nonporous materials for floors, walls, and food-contact surfaces. Always check with regional or local regulatory agencies to ensure adequate facility design, especially before beginning new construction or remodeling existing facilities. Dedicated handwashing sinks, where no food preparation or dishwashing take place, should be placed immediately inside the entrance to kitchens. Depending on the size of the kitchen space, additional handwashing sinks placed at convenient locations may be necessary to encourage employees to wash hands regularly during food preparation and service.

Consideration should be given to the type of cold storage equipment used. In operations where a large amount of produce is harvested, larger walk-in refrigerators may be preferable, even though they are more expensive. If fresh produce is frozen for use in meal preparation throughout the year, a larger freezer may be desirable. Blast chillers, though expensive, freeze produce more quickly, resulting in higher quality when foods are thawed for later use. Although dry storage areas do not have the same temperature requirements as cold storage, it should be easy to maintain them at cool room temperatures. They should also be located in areas where pest intrusion is unlikely. For this reason, placing these areas next to an exterior wall is discouraged.

Ingredient monitoring

The best meals are prepared using fresh, high-quality ingredients. To ensure that the quality of fresh ingredients is maintained, the receipt, storage, and use of raw ingredients should be monitored. Internal monitoring should occur daily for stored ingredients, especially for highly perishable produce. In addition to ensuring high quality, this also helps management determine when new ingredients must be harvested or ordered.

Fresh ingredients, whether harvested on-farm or purchased elsewhere, should be carefully examined for signs of spoilage. Produce harvested on-farm should be washed in a separate location before being brought into food service facilities. Produce with clear signs of spoilage, such as mold or sliminess, should be discarded immediately. High-quality produce should be stored under appropriate conditions to maximize shelf life. The ideal storage conditions for tomatoes, apples, and potatoes, for example, are very different both in temperature and humidity. Trained chefs and experienced cooks are often familiar with the individual requirements of different foods, and other kitchen staff can consult culinary or produce industry guides to determine optimal conditions.

Other perishable ingredients, such as dairy products and meats, should also be inspected carefully, regardless of their source. Because unpasteurized milk and dairy products can harbor pathogenic bacteria, their use is not recommended and in some places may even be illegal. Always verify with regional or local regulatory agencies whether these products can be served to customers. Unpasteurized dairy and raw meats should be stored away from fresh produce and other refrigerated items, such as pre-cooked or leftover foods, to prevent cross-contamination.

All fresh ingredients should be inspected daily and checked for signs of spoilage. It is good business practice to establish a stock rotation system where older ingredients are used before newer ones, provided they are still wholesome. In some cases, individual pieces of moldy or spoiled produce (e.g., apples) can be removed without needing to discard the entire container. Mold can also be cut away from some types of food, while others must be discarded. Always ensure compliance with regional or local regulations regarding the handling of spoiled or moldy foods.

Frozen ingredients should be checked for signs of thawing, which can include the presence of ice crystals. While frozen foods have a much longer shelf life than refrigerated foods, they cannot be stored indefinitely. Products such as meat should be checked for signs of freezer burn and must be discarded if found. Refrigerator and freezer temperatures should also be monitored at least daily to ensure that the equipment is functioning properly. Any foods that have been subjected to unsafe temperatures should be discarded immediately.

Food safety for food processing

The strict legal definition of food processing can vary from region to region. **Food processing** can broadly include any activity applied to a food product to make it ready for sale to the public. This includes, but is not limited to:

- cooling, washing, or packing fresh produce;
- peeling, cutting, or packaging ready-to-eat fresh produce;

- combining or assembling fresh produce blends;
- drying or dehydrating whole or cut produce items;
- cooking, bottling, or canning foods;
- slaughtering or butchering animals;
- curing, drying, or otherwise preserving meat or poultry; and
- pasteurizing, fermenting, or otherwise preserving dairy products.

While some of these activities may not be included in the legal definition of processing in a specific region, they all represent a handling step with the potential to introduce or spread contamination.

Facility design

Food processing areas are often specific to the type of food processing that occurs there. For example, processing activities such as making and bottling fruit jam may only require a commercial kitchen. A **commercial kitchen** is a kitchen where food is prepared or processed for resale and is normally regulated through building codes, food safety plans, and regular inspections. Other forms of processing, such as cheese-making or processing animal carcasses, require specific equipment and are more highly regulated in most

Image 11.2 Locally made hot sauces from Hawai'i, USA
Source: Kynda R. Curtis

jurisdictions. Because of the wide variety of processed foods and the complexity and variability of applicable regulations, a detailed discussion of processing equipment and design requirements is beyond the scope of this book (see Marriott & Gravani, 2006, for further discussion). Always check with national, regional, or local regulatory agencies to ensure adequate facility design, especially before beginning new construction or remodeling existing facilities. In all processing areas, dedicated handwashing sinks should be placed immediately inside the entrance to the room. To prevent contaminants from being brought into these areas, create a changing room that employees must pass through before entering the processing floor. It is a common practice to have employees change out of street clothes and shoes before participating in processing activities. Disposable shoe coverings and washable workwear, such as lab coats or aprons, are often used in place of full uniforms.

One of the attractions of many food tourism enterprises is the opportunity for visitors to observe food processing as it occurs. Unfortunately, it is not always reasonable to allow guests who are untrained in specific safety and sanitation policies to enter the processing floor directly. In some localities this would actually constitute a regulatory violation. Enclosed observation decks or balconies can allow visitors to view the processing floor as part of a guided tour. Where space constraints make overhead viewing impossible, observation windows or walls can be installed. Specific regulations and local building codes may limit the size of such windows and require that only certain types of clear materials be used. At a minimum, tempered or safety glass should be used and thoroughly sealed to prevent pests from entering. It is a good idea to discourage visitors from leaning or pressing against windows or observation walls for their own safety.

Product line selection

Facility design is highly dependent on the type of foods processed there. In cases where specific food processing equipment is unaffordable, impractical due to space constraints, or impossible to install correctly due to infrastructure limitations, products should be selected that can be made safely in existing kitchens while still meeting regulatory requirements. Although regulations vary by location, fresh produce items can easily be washed, cut, and packaged in a food service kitchen during times when the kitchen is not otherwise in use. Packaged baked goods—such as fruit pastries, muffins, and cookies or biscuits—can also be made safely in existing kitchen facilities. Dried or dehydrated produce can be made easily in a commercial kitchen. For berry-growing operations, excess or unattractive fruit can be bottled as jams, compotes, syrups, and pastry or pie fillings. Full-sugar versions of these bottled products are typically subject to fewer regulations than low-sugar or sugar-free versions. Refrigerated or frozen fruit-based products—such as fresh salsa or chutney, sorbet, and ices—are also easily made in food service kitchens. These ready-to-eat items could fall under food service or food processing regulations, depending on the other activities being conducted in the operation and the requirements of regional or local regulatory agencies. The difference in how these products are categorized and regulated often depends on the type of packaging used. Regardless of how these products are regulated, consideration must be given to their safe holding and display in the farm or souvenir shop.

Fruit or vegetable juices, bottled pickled vegetables, and fermented products (e.g., sauerkraut) tend to be subject to more specific regulations, though some may still be made safely in a commercial kitchen. Many other bottled, canned, or vacuum-packaged foods pose a greater food safety risk due to *Clostridium botulinum*, a spore-forming bacteria that grows and produces a toxin in oxygen-free environments. **Spores** are the dormant form of a microbe, especially bacteria and fungi, which begin to grow only when environmental conditions are favorable. Spores are often resistant to common food safety and sanitation practices. Generally, spores cannot be destroyed using normal cooking processes, but they cannot "wake up" and actively grow in foods with a pH below 4.6. Because of this, canned fruits, jellies, and syrups are considered safe. Properly acidified vegetables (e.g., salsa and pickles) often require additional licenses or certifications and additional record keeping to ensure that enough acid is added. Canned and bottled foods with a higher pH or no added acid—such as canned vegetables, milk, and meats—must be carefully processed using high pressure and temperature to destroy spores. In many jurisdictions, these products are tightly regulated. Always be sure to receive appropriate licenses and certifications for these foods and follow all applicable regulations.

Milk, cheese, and other dairy products can pose serious health risks due to several types of bacteria if they are improperly pasteurized or handled. These products are also generally subject to specific regulations and inspections. Animal-based products are also considered inherently hazardous. In many areas, the governmental department or ministry overseeing agriculture regulates processed meat and poultry products. Always check with national, regional, or local regulatory agencies to ensure that existing facilities allow safe processing of proposed products.

Image 11.3 Making coconut candy on the Mekong Delta, Vietnam
Source: Kynda R. Curtis

Summary

The variability and complexity of food safety laws and regulations worldwide can be overwhelming. However, the ultimate goal of any food tourism operation should be to ensure the safety and health of its guests. While it is unlikely any two operations are identical, common practices can be applied to reach the common goal. Appropriate training of employees and guests, providing adequate handwashing facilities and reminders through signage or verbal instruction, and proper design of food preparation and processing areas help limit unintentional exposure to foodborne contaminants. Foodborne illness can be especially devastating to young and elderly guests, so extra care should be taken when targeting these populations. Food tourism operators should remember that food safety is everyone's responsibility.

Study Questions

1   What are the three main types of contaminants found in food? What steps can be taken in a food tourism operation to prevent or limit these contaminants?
2   What are the major causes of foodborne illness worldwide? Are they the same as the major causes in your country or region? Where could you go to find this information?
3   What steps should be taken when an employee with food-handling duties shows signs of illness? Are there certain symptoms that are more concerning than others?
4   What design options limit the potential for cross-contamination between animal contact areas and produce-growing areas? Which are easiest to implement? Which seem more likely to be successful with minimal training to guests?
5   What types of processed foods are easiest to produce using an existing food service kitchen? How might using an existing food service kitchen influence your product-line choices?

Definitions

Commercial kitchen—a kitchen where food is prepared or processed for resale and normally regulated through building codes, food safety plans, and regular inspections.

Contaminant—any unwanted or undesirable material found in food. Contaminants may or may not be visible and include physical, chemical, and biological items.

Food processing—broadly, any activity applied to a food product to make it ready for sale to the public.

Food service—a business that prepares food on-site for immediate consumption, also referred to as catering.

Hygiene—personal practices related to cleanliness that reduce or eliminate the spread of disease.

Microbe—a microscopic life form that includes bacteria, viruses, fungi, and parasites.

Pathogen—a microbe that can cause illness in humans. Adjective form is *pathogenic*.

Sanitation—environmental or operational practices related to cleanliness that reduce or eliminate the spread of disease.

Spore—the dormant form of a microbe, especially bacteria and fungi, which begins to grow only when environmental conditions are favorable. Spores are often resistant to common food safety and sanitation practices.

Toxin—a chemical that produces disease in humans. Toxins can be man-made or produced by certain types of plants, microbes, and animals.

CASE STUDY 11.1

On-farm production of apple cider

Karin Allen

A small farm decided it was time to add some activities that would attract tourists to their location. The harvest season for their apple orchard ran through mid-October, but the pick-your-own customers began dwindling by the end of September. In anticipation of adding some autumn-themed tourist activities, they had already dedicated a portion of an empty field to growing pumpkins the previous spring, and the pumpkins were ready to pick. To encourage families to make the drive to the farm to pick pumpkins, they planned to offer hayride tours of the farm, pony rides, and sell fall-themed crafts produced by other small local businesses. Working with a reputable food supplier, they offered flavored popcorn, caramel apples, and bottled water for purchase.

The first year was a great success, but many guests asked why they weren't selling apple cider. This was an apple orchard, after all. The farmer and his family had always made enough cider for themselves using the leftover apples that weren't pretty enough to sell. Their cider wasn't pasteurized, just pressed from the apple, bottled immediately, then stored in their root cellar where it stayed as cold as it would have in the fridge. The flavor was crisp and fresh, just like taking a bite out of an apple right off the tree, much better than any cider they could have purchased at a grocery store. But their production experience was limited to small batches for personal use. If they were going to sell cider, they would need to expand their operation. Before the next growing season had even begun, the farmer had purchased the necessary equipment and was set up to bottle apple cider for sale at the next fall festival.

Image 11.4 Farm fresh apples, USA
Source: Morguefile.com

The second year's autumn activities were a great success, though several guests commented that they wished they could purchase the cider along with the fresh apples the farm sold at the local farmers' market. In the third year, the farmer started pressing apples early in the season, bottling the juice as he always had, and taking it to the farmers' market. That year, however, the local health inspector took notice of his new product. When the farmer was questioned about his cider, it became obvious that he had not obtained the necessary licenses or registrations to make a bottled juice. He was told that he must stop selling his cider immediately and work with the local Department of Agriculture to get his product approved. After their discussion, the farmer decided he would stop selling the cider at the market and let customers know they would have to visit his farm if they wished to buy the product.

The fall festival was becoming a local tradition, and word spread to neighboring areas. The third year's turnout was beyond anything the farmer could have predicted, and his cider was selling just as fast as he could make it. That year an inspector from the local Department of Agriculture came with his family to see what all the buzz was about. When he noticed the apple cider, he questioned the farmer as well, but his inquiries went deeper than those of the health inspector. He

Image 11.5 Double fence to separate cows and tourists, USA
Source: Morguefile.com

informed the farmer that cider and juice production in that jurisdiction required special trainings and licenses, and that any juice product sold to the public had to be pasteurized for safety. The farmer spoke with the inspector and was friendly but had already decided that he would continue to make the cider despite their conversation.

In the following weeks, the bottled cider was still offered for purchase, but the season was drawing to a close and fewer and fewer apples were available for juicing. It became difficult to keep up with demand. Toward the end of that year's events, the farmer received shocking news. Several people who had visited his farm in the previous weeks had fallen ill. Soon after, regulatory officials showed up at his farm with a cease and desist order, demanding that he immediately halt producing or selling cider. The farmer insisted that his cider was not the cause of the illnesses. It had been made following the same procedure his family had used for years, and none of them had ever gotten sick after drinking it. But the regulatory officials demanded that he comply with the court order, and the discussion turned into an argument. Eventually the local police were called to the farm to put an end the situation. By that point, the story had been picked up by local news reporters, and the community became aware of the issue.

The reality behind the story

Though the story above is fictional, it is based on an actual outbreak that occurred in Michigan, USA, between 2011 and 2012. A local farm had obtained approval to make and sell maple syrup but not apple cider. The Michigan Department of Agriculture and Rural Development (MDARD) (2014) requires all apple cider producers to attend a specialized safety training class. Additionally, the U.S. Food and Drug Administration requires that juice producers develop and follow a Hazard Analysis and Critical Control Points food safety plan. The farmer in question had not met either of these requirements and had received repeated warnings from regulatory officials over the course of two years that his unpasteurized apple cider was not being processed safely.

In November 2012, MDARD was notified that several people had fallen ill after consuming the apple cider. The Michigan Department of Community Health conducted a joint investigation with MDARD and found that the cider was contaminated with *E. coli* O157:H7. Four people, two of them children, were hospitalized because of the severity of their illness. Under the Michigan Food Act of 2000, any food producer who knowingly sells food that is improperly processed can serve prison time. The farmer was prosecuted under this law and pled guilty to the felony charges of willful misbranding and adulteration of food products. He was sentenced to 14 to 48 months in prison and required to pay fines and court costs.

Questions

1 How could the farmer have handled the cider production differently?
2 Which agencies or departments would you need to contact in your area before beginning to process a new food product?
3 As an agritourism operator, how would you proceed if you or one of your employees were told to halt production of a specific food product? How would you address any bad press you received as a result?

References

Michigan Department of Agriculture and Rural Development. (2014). Mitchell Hill Farm in Ellsworth receives first-ever felony conviction under Michigan's food law. Retrieved from www.nasda.org/News/statePR/25019.aspx
Michigan Food Act, PA92 of 2000. Michigan Compiled Laws § 289.5107.

References

Food and Drug Administration. (2012). *Bad bug book—Foodborne pathogenic microorganisms and natural toxins* (2nd ed.). Retrieved from www.fda.gov/Food/FoodborneIllness Contaminants/CausesOfIllnessBadBugBook.
Kirk, M., Glass, K., Ford, L., Brown, K., and Hall, G. (2014). *Foodborne illness in Australia: Annual incidence circa 2010.* Retrieved from www.health.gov.au/internet/main/publishing. nsf/Content/ohp-foodborne-illness-aust.
Lange, H., Johansen, Ø.H., Vold, L., Robertson, L.J., Anthonisen, I.L., and Nygard, K. (2014). Second outbreak of infection with a rare *Cryptosporidium parvum* genotype in schoolchildren associated with contact with lambs/goat kids at a holiday farm in Norway. *Epidemiology & Infection, 142*(10), 2105–2113.
Marriott, N.G., and Gravani, R.B. (2006). *Principles of food sanitation* (5th ed.). New York: Springer.

National Association of State Public Health Veterinarians. (2013). Compendium of measures to prevent disease associated with animals in public settings. *Journal of the American Veterinary Medical Association, 243*(9), 1270–1288.

Scallan, E., Hoekstra, R.M., Angulo, F.J., Tauxe, R.V., Widdowson, M.A., Roy, S.L., Jones, J. L., and Griffin, P.M. (2011). Foodborne illness acquired in the United States— Major pathogens. *Emerging Infectious Diseases, 17*(1), 7–15.

Tam, C.C., Larose, T., and O'Brien, S. J. (2014). Costed extension to the second study of infectious intestinal disease in the community: Identifying the proportion of foodborne disease in the UK and attributing foodborne disease by food commodity. Retrieved from https://www.food.gov.uk.sites/default/files/IID2%20extension%20report%20-%20 FINAL%2025%20March%202014_0.pdf.

World Health Organization. (2015). WHO *estimates of the global burden of foodborne diseases: Foodborne diseases burden epidemiology reference group 2007–2015*. Geneva: WHO Press. Retrieved from www.who.int/foodsafety/areas_work/foodborne-diseases/ferg/en/.

Chapter 12

Devising the food tourism product

Overview

Proper planning, including creating a financial feasibility assessment, is essential to success when creating a food tourism product, whether it is a local food market, a wine trail, a beer festival, or other endeavor. This chapter provides an overview of the components of a business plan and a detailed description of each section's contents. Examples of basic financial statements and uses for each statement are provided in addition to specific tools that can be used to estimate the profit potential of a food tourism product in terms of volume and pricing. A discussion of various product pricing strategies and the advantages and disadvantages of each is included.

Learning Objectives

This chapter will enable students to:

1 Understand the importance of prior planning when starting a food tourism operation.
2 Explain the various components of business and marketing plans.
3 Understand the 4 Ps of marketing and the importance of considering the target market in decision-making.
4 Understand the advantages and disadvantages of the primary pricing strategies and the factors that influence consumer sensitivity to price changes.
5 Use basic financial statements to estimate the potential financial feasibility of the food tourism product.
6 Calculate the break-even volume or pricing for a food tourism product.

Importance of business planning

Business and marketing plans are written documents designed to increase the probability that a business, destination, or tourism activity will succeed and provide tools to define organizational goals and objectives, reach a target consumer base, and secure capital. Banks and other lending institutions often require business plans when individuals apply for start-up or capital investment loans. Business plans outline the activities required for an operation to be successful and assess the external and internal environments, looking at competition and defining the unique product or service that appeals to potential customers. Both types of plans continue to provide direction long after the business is established by providing a measure of the business's success. Frequent updates are vital to keep the plan current and useful.

Successful business and marketing plans can highlight new revenue streams and provide access to new markets and customers. While business plans and marketing plans contain much of the same information, a **business plan** focuses on strategic implications such as internal investment, organizational structure, and long-range strategies. **Marketing plans,** on the other hand, focus on defining and accessing a distinct target market and the unique products or services that differentiate the enterprise from its competitors. Marketing plans focus more heavily on the **4 Ps** of marketing (product, price, place, and promotion), also called the marketing mix. While both documents use similar information, the conclusions drawn in each document vary. Either may be used to secure financing, reduce risk in the marketplace, and help agencies adjust to market changes and environmental unknowns. Ultimately, the final audience for which the plan is written determines the most appropriate format. This chapter discusses common elements of business plans, including the mission statement, statement of goals and objectives, SWOT analysis, market plan, competitive analysis, and financial analysis.

Developing the plan

Mission statement

The first step in developing a business or marketing plan is to formulate a central mission statement and articulate enterprise or destination goals and objectives. A **mission statement** is a short, concise statement describing the business's vision and values that broadly outlines the customers, products, and unique aspects of the enterprise or destination.

Example of food tourism mission statements:

> Belmont Estate—Grenada
> We are committed to being recognized as a world leader in superior agritourism products and services, and to being the premier destination of choice for discerning agritourism consumers. We strive to build a successful and dynamic company with a character of sound integrity, exceptional ethical conduct and resolute responsibility to our community, physical environment, staff and associates, and dedicated to generating profits for our stakeholders and superior products and services to our customers.
>
> (www.belmontestate.net)

Sweetgreen Restaurant—Washington, DC, United States
Founded in 2007, Sweetgreen is a destination for delicious food that's both healthy for you and aligned with your values. We source local and organic ingredients from farms we know and patrons we trust, supporting our communities and creating meaningful relationships with those around us. We exist to create experiences where passion and purpose come together.

(www.sweetgreen.com)

Statement of goals and objectives

A **goal** is a purpose toward which an endeavor is directed over a certain time frame. Long-term goals are strategic in nature (5–10 years) while intermediate and short-term goals are tactical in nature (1–5 years). **Objectives** are the specific step-by-step accomplishments required to achieve a given goal. Goals and objectives should be specific, measureable, attainable, rewarding, and timed. Business goals and objectives may be quantified in terms of profit, market share, number of visitors, etc.

Example of goals and corresponding objectives:

Goal—Establish long-term supply-chain partners that source local food.
Objective—Visit and tour each local farm engaged in direct-to-consumer marketing.
Objective—Establish eight contractual agreements for our four major food groups: vegetables and fruit, meat products, dairy, and processed goods.
Objective—Work with each farm under contract to improve the quality and selection of items throughout the year.
Goal—Educate our customers on the advantages of sourcing locally.
Objective—Add information about our food and the farms we source to our menus.
Objective—Seek two public relations opportunities each year that highlight the advantages of sourcing local.
Objective—Support five different community campaigns (in schools, through special events) to grow consumer awareness of the advantages to sourcing locally.
Goal—Hire committed and well-trained employees that support our vision.
Objective—Offer in-house training on local sourcing.
Objective—Visit local community colleges as guest speakers and recruit qualified staff.
Objective—Offer employee incentives (health insurance, training, community involvement opportunities) to retain committed and qualified employees.

SWOT analysis

The second step in business planning is to conduct a **SWOT analysis** (see Figure 12.1). SWOT stands for an operation or destination's Strengths, Weaknesses, Opportunities, and Threats. To understand the strengths and weaknesses of a business, it is important to assess the company's resources, including: 1) human resources, 2) financial resources, 3) technical resources, 4) management resources, and 5) physical resources. Analyzing these internal resources helps operators define their **competitive advantage**, their ability to gain an edge over or perform better than their competition. Without a clear competitive advantage, most businesses become lost in the sea of choices available to tourists. It is important

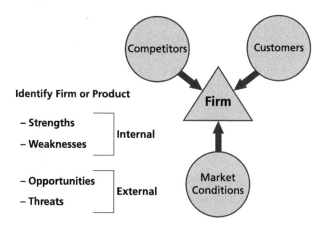

Figure 12.1 SWOT analysis

to recognize that strengths and weaknesses can change with time, as technological and market forces alter the competitive environment. New strengths may become apparent and old strengths may become obsolete. While many weaknesses may not be overcome immediately, acknowledging them is an important first step in directing the efforts required to overcome them in time.

The second part of the SWOT analysis requires assessing opportunities and threats in order to assess the external environment and devise strategies to deal with change. External concerns may include: 1) economic factors, 2) technological changes, 3) changes in government policy, and 4) legal requirements. **Environmental scanning,** the process of monitoring the external environment, should be an integral part of every business or marketing plan. Involvement with chambers of commerce, DMOs, visitor centers, industry associations, state affiliates, and university outreach programs enhances a business's ability to monitor changes industry-wide and respond effectively.

Market plan

The next section in the planning document includes the market plan, which should include a market description that profiles, in as much detail as possible, the target markets the operation, destination, or product seeks to reach. As described in detail in Chapter 8, target markets should be defined by geographic location such as region, province, or county; demographics such as age, income, or number of family members; and, finally, psychographic characteristics including values, interests, and behaviors, such as supporting local farmers, sustainable consumption, outdoor activities, interest in heritage and culture, and concerns about food safety. The food tourism product or the preferences of each target market, including their pricing preferences, should also be described.

The market plan section should also detail marketing objectives. These objectives normally refer to actual sales and/or market share to be achieved or the series of steps taken to accomplish a goal in a set time period. Strategies for achieving each marketing objective should also be described. A detailed set of marketing objectives provides a description of the firm's position in the market (or its desired position), provides direction to employees, and explains the rationale behind marketing decisions.

The market plan must also detail all aspects of the food tourism product, its pricing, promotional strategies, and distribution and sales outlets, referred to as the 4 Ps (product, price, promotion, and place). The target consumer should be at the forefront of all decision-making.

Product

A detailed description of the products and services that will be offered to each target market should be provided. Many food tourism venues offer varied products and services based on resources, seasonality, and market conditions. It is important to detail the benefits of each to the target market and what aspects or attributes of the product or service fulfill their needs. Finding products and activities that complement one another is key to identifying successful combinations. For example, home-baked, locally sourced peach cobbler is not likely to be a successful draw by itself, but may provide an edge over alternatives when combined with a U-pick experience and festival atmosphere filled with fun family activities. It is also important to determine whether the target market will be primarily local (excursionists) or destination consumers. If individuals are looking to travel from one destination to another, activities will need to cater to shorter visits unless overnight lodging facilities are available nearby.

Price

The marketing plan should also include a detailed description of the pricing strategy for each product or service. There are three major pricing approaches: cost-based, demand-oriented, and competition-oriented. Cost-based pricing encompasses both cost-plus pricing, in which price equals total production costs divided by the number of units produced, and mark-up pricing, in which a percentage is added to the production cost of the product. Major drawbacks to cost-based pricing include establishing a price that is not based on customer demand, lack of incentives to reduce costs and operate more efficiently, and the difficulty in adjusting the price when input costs increase. Additionally, service-based products may not have a per-unit cost. For example, the cost of running a food festival does not change based on the number of attendees (it has high fixed costs). Mark-up pricing is straightforward and can be used when there are too many products to effectively estimate consumer demand. Grocery retailers commonly use this type of pricing.

Demand-oriented pricing bases prices on the level of value perceived by the consumer, also called **willingness to pay**. Price skimming is a practice where consumers are initially charged a high price in order to attract consumers with higher willingness to pay as a means to ensure higher initial profits. Gradually, the price is reduced to pick up consumers who are more price sensitive. Conversely, penetration pricing initially sets prices at a low level to capture market share (a large percentage of buyers), which discourages competition, and then the price is increased later when the product has become popular among loyal consumers. Penetration pricing is very common for new food products.

Competition-oriented pricing is ideal when similar products or services exist. Penetration pricing can be used to stimulate interests in the product by setting a price that is lower than the competing product. Parity pricing simply means that the price is set equal to a competing product, and premium pricing sets prices higher than the competing product. Premium pricing is often used to signal quality to consumers and may be a successful strategy for high-quality specialty products.

221

Image 12.1 Menu from 1911 at the Virginia Hotel in Medicine Bow, Wyoming, USA
Source: Susan L. Slocum

The three pricing approaches are not normally used independently. For example, if the price consumers want to pay in the market is less than the cost of producing the product, then a cost-based pricing approach will not be profitable. Instead, premium pricing may be the best strategy for a value-added product to signal high quality so that consumers are willing to pay more. While the price of competing products can be a useful pricing benchmark, it is optimal to design the product or service so that it is somewhat different, or differentiated from, the competition, which may encourage tourists to pay more. For example, if there are many farms offering U-pick opportunities, you may want to offer a petting zoo for children in order to stand out from the competition. Consumers may or

Table 12.1 Determinants of consumer price sensitivity

Effect	Description
Substitution effect	When there are many similar products available, a price increase in one product will cause consumers to switch to one of the less expensive options.
Unique-value effect	Consumers will be less price sensitive if the product or service is unique, has no substitutes.
Switching-cost effect	When consumers face large costs to switch products, such as the time required to seek information or to make an additional stop at a retail outlet, they are less price sensitive.
Difficult-comparison effect	Consumers are less price sensitive when it is hard to compare products or services.
Price-quality effect	Consumer perception that a higher price indicates a higher quality product, reducing the impulse to switch to a less expensive option.
Expenditure effect	Consumers are more sensitive to price changes on large, expensive products rather than small, inexpensive ones.
Fairness effect	Consumers may be willing to pay more for a product if they feel the value or added value provided is higher than competing products.
Inventory effect	Consumers are willing to pay more for a product when it's in season just in advance of a holiday, rather than after the holiday.
End-benefit effect	Consumers may be willing to pay more for products that have an end-benefit, such as protecting the environment, preserving agricultural open space, or supporting family farms.

may not be sensitive to price changes for a variety of reasons. Common effects that determine consumer price sensitivity are provided in Table 12.1.

Place

The distribution strategies the enterprise plans to use to connect to its target market(s) should be detailed in the market plan section. For many food tourism operations, the product or activity may be provided on their own farm, or in their restaurant, which would be considered direct-to-consumer marketing. For others—such as growers who provide local jam, jelly, cheese, or honey to tourists for immediate consumption or as food souvenirs—it would be important to distribute products in retail outlets or other businesses catering to tourists.

Accessing tourism markets can be difficult. Common distribution channels include places where tourists congregate, such as at festivals, near tourist attractions, and in hotel establishments. However, since food tourism is an experiential product, finding innovative ways to connect tourists to your place of business can be difficult. Most likely, food tourism businesses and destinations require the tourist to travel to their facility; therefore, it is through promotional efforts that tourists find information about food-related

223

activities. For example, farms may need signage in order for tourists to know where they are located; restaurants are often promoted in travel guidebooks. Cooking schools or other culinary activities use promotion to connect tourists with food. Tourism is unique in that distribution strategies and promotional strategies must be closely related.

Promotion

The final aspect of the market plan section outlines promotional strategies and includes advertising and other activities that seek to increase tourist awareness about the product, service, or experience. Advertising can be expensive, so a well-thought-out plan can provide efficiency and substantial cost savings. Promotion through business websites, brochures, flyers, and other publications is crucial to reaching tourists. Business or food tourism brochures and flyers can be left with hotels, visitor centers, parks, and resorts. Memberships with local chambers of commerce, visitor/convention bureaus, and local food organizations can be invaluable to promoting activities and establishing multi-entity partnerships and destination marketing campaigns. Advertising or business listings on websites—such as state/regional tourism boards, local food organizations, and Internet trip/vacation booking sites—is highly recommended due to tourists' tendency to find travel information online. Other publications for advertising include local, national, and international tourism publications; heritage/scenic trail maps; and attraction publications at national parks, ski resorts, hunting lodges, etc. Additionally, DMOs specialize in marketing a destination and can be a valuable partner when developing your promotional messages. Marketing strategies for DMOs are discussed more in Chapter 9. Promotional methods need to be customized to the target market to increase effectiveness.

Competitive and financial analyses

The competitive analysis examines other businesses or destinations that may offer similar products, services, or experiences and assesses the firm's comparative strengths and weaknesses. Understanding the strengths and weaknesses of an organization can help you make strategic decisions that align with your strengths and avoid moving in directions where the organization is weak. This analysis uses information and data collected in the SWOT analysis previously described. Strategies to differentiate the business or destination from its competitors should also be detailed here. When conducting a competitive analysis, consider the following:

- How many competitors operate in the market?
- Are competitors large or small? Near or far?
- What types and numbers of products do they sell, or what experiences do they offer?
- What pricing methods do they use?
- Who is their target market?

The final component of the business plan is the financial analysis. Evaluating the financial feasibility of a new product or enterprise is fundamental to the long-term success and sustainability of the enterprise. Depending on the final audience for the business plan, a variety of financial statements may be required. The goal is to provide an accurate analysis that shows the profitability of the enterprise in the long term. **Profit** is a company's revenues minus their expenses. If the plan is for a new business, it is important to address realistic **revenues** (money that is made by a business or organization through product

Image 12.2 Ramen shop in Japan
Source: Susan L. Slocum

sales, investments, etc.) and **expenses** (money that is used to pay the operating costs of a business) or cost estimates, a break-even analysis, and an assessment of profit potential under changing conditions. Ultimately, if the venture cannot demonstrate potential for a successful future, it is unlikely that bankers, governments, or other tourism businesses (such as travel operators or DMOs) will support it.

The steps involved in assessing the financial feasibility of a food tourism operation or product include:

- assessing potential revenues (volume sold and pricing);
- estimating the cost of production or cost to provide; and
- examining break-even volume and/or break-even price.

Completing these steps prior to large-scale investment provides a picture of the potential profitability of the product or service. A detailed financial plan also improves the chances of securing capital funding or access to government grants and loans.

Projected business revenues and costs (or expenses) can be listed on a budget or projected **income statement**, an estimate of the net return (total revenue minus expenses provides an estimate for the profit potential) for one year of production. Figure 12.2 provides an example of a projected income statement. Assessing revenues requires estimating the number of customers who will purchase the product, the amount of the product they will buy, and at what price. To determine the potential number of customers available, the population that falls into the identified target market based on demographics, interests, values, etc. must be estimated. Census data are available in many developed countries and generally provide information on the ages of people in the area, household and family size, income, ethnicity, and more, all of which can provide operations with additional information about the characteristics of potential customers in the local and surrounding area if targeting excursionists. A local DMO will also have some information on the number and types of visitors that come into an area. They will know where tourists originate, why they are traveling (business or pleasure), and their general demographic characteristics. To estimate how much product each customer might purchase, or how

Projected Income Statement	
Revenue	
Sale of Crop Products	$50,000
Sale of Livestock Products	$25,000
Government Payments	$10,000
Total Revenue	*$85,000*
Variable Costs	
Seed	$10,000
Fertilizer	$20,000
Feed	$10,000
Processing	$10,000
Marketing	$5,000
Total Variable Costs	*$55,000*
Fixed Costs	
Interest	$5,000
Depreciation	$10,000
Total Fixed Costs	*$15,000*
Total Costs	*$70,000*
Net Projected Profit	**$15,000**

Figure 12.2 Projected income statement example

much they might spend per visit, examining current and historical purchasing patterns can be helpful. DMOs often collect these data as well.

Consider the example of a strawberry grower who wants to turn a portion of an existing strawberry field into a U-pick strawberry operation where visitors can pick their own strawberries. The grower wants to convert a one-acre field, which can produce around 10,000 pounds of strawberries annually. To calculate the market size for this example, the grower must figure out the volume of strawberries that would be necessary to supply all potential customers with a week's worth of strawberries. To calculate this, multiply the acres of strawberries to be grown by the predicted growth per acre and divide this by weekly fresh consumption per capita (assume 8 pounds annually), which is the annual fresh consumption divided by 52, the number of weeks in a year. Using the numbers for this example, the proposed U-pick operation would require a market size of 64,935 consumers (1 acre x 10,000 pounds per acre/(8 pounds per year/52 weeks per year)).

The grower must consider whether enough consumers can be found to consume all the strawberries grown. For example, the grower may be targeting families as excursionists. In this case, it would be helpful to know whether nearby communities have enough families to make up a portion of the 65,000 customers needed to make the U-pick operation feasible. Let us say the U-pick operation is located near Bend, Oregon, USA, which has 26,073 families with an average of 3.5 persons each and hence a potential market of 91,255 customers. To determine the percentage of these families that might visit the strawberry farm, we estimate 40% or 36,502 customers based on recent agritourism studies (Barry & Hellerstein, 2004; Tchetchik et al., 2008). If customers purchased 16 pounds annually—potentially for freezing, canning, or other production—the operation would only need 32,467 customers, which is less than the estimated number that would attend.

Understanding the costs associated with a food tourism venture is critical to planning, pricing, and decision-making. Costs that must be considered include fixed costs, variable costs, total costs, and average costs. **Fixed costs** are not dependent on production; in other words, if no units are produced, the firm must still pay these costs. Examples include leases, manager salaries, and equipment. **Variable costs** are directly associated with production and can include inputs, utilities, support staff, and equipment repair. **Total costs** are the sum of variable costs and fixed costs and must be covered for a firm to break even. **Average costs** are the total costs divided by the number of units produced, or the per unit cost of production.

As an example of determining the financial feasibility of a food tourism product or service, let us again consider the U-pick strawberry operation. A total of 10,000 pounds of strawberries are produced per acre at a total cost of production of $22,000 ($2.20 per pound). Total expenses include the cost of production for the strawberries (variable costs such as seeds, fertilizer, and farm staff) as well as other costs, such as visitor services (another variable cost based on the number of visitors), permits (a fixed cost), loan payments (fixed cost), etc. If the grower can sell the strawberries at $2.36 per pound, then they will receive $23,600 in revenue per acre of strawberries. If the average consumer picks 8 pounds per visit, then the grower can expect $18.88 in revenue for each person visiting the U-pick (8 x $2.36).

While calculating revenues and costs for a projected income statement is relatively simple, many factors should be considered before making a final pricing decision. For example, visitors may purchase more strawberries if they are attending the U-pick as a family outing or if they are interested in canning or freezing berries to make jams or pies later. Additionally, visitors may be willing to pay more if the strawberries are a specialty item. For example, 2013 prices for organic strawberries were 47% higher per pound than conventional strawberries. Growers need to examine what the target market plans to do while at the farm and what they are willing to pay for the experience.

A **break-even analysis** shows the number of units that must be produced for a business to break even (that is, the minimum amount required to make a profit). Production above this level produces a profit, and production below this level results in a loss. A break-even analysis can also be used to determine the minimum price needed to break even. Break-even analysis is usually done across a range of quantity and price levels to illustrate the pricing or production requirements required to earn a profit under varying market conditions.

Consider the following example. Table 12.2 provides a projected income statement for locally grown and produced pomegranate juice to be sold to marina visitors. The business plans to produce an initial quantity of 20,000 8 oz. bottles and sell them for $2.49 each. This represents revenue of $49,800 (20,000 X $2.49). The profit, defined as revenue minus expenses ($33,350), is $16,450. The break-even price is calculated as total expenses divided by the number of units. In this case, total expenses are $33,350 and 20,000 bottles are sold. Therefore, the break-even price is $1.67 per bottle. The break-even quantity is calculated as total expenses divided by price, in this case $33,350/$2.49, or 13,394 8 oz. bottles. Any price above $1.67 or selling a quantity above 13,394 represents a profit for the company. Anything less will be a loss.

Table 12.2 Projected income statement for pomegranate juice (US$)

Income/cost	Total	Total per unit (8 oz. bottle)
Revenue (quantity X price)		
Total sales	$49,800	$2.49
Expenses		
Variable (packaging, fruit, etc.)	$23,350	$1.17
Fixed (machinery, rent, etc.)	$10,000	$0.50
Total expenses	$33,350	$1.67
Net income	$16,450	$0.82

The final financial statement to consider is the **balance sheet**. A balance sheet is a snapshot of the financial condition of a business at a point in time and changes on a day-to-day basis. Balance sheets are normally completed annually (in some cases monthly). A balance sheet includes a list of **assets** (the property owned by the business), **liabilities** (the debts a business is legally responsible to pay back), and owner equity (see Figure 12.3). **Owner equity** reflects all owner investments, including the sum of profits and losses over previous years and any money they have invested in the company. Assets less liabilities less equity should equal zero (it should balance). Assets should be valued at their current

Balance Sheet			
As of December 31, 2017 (000s)			
Assets		**Liabilities**	
Cash	481	Accounts Payable	625
Marketable Seurities	1,346	Current Portion L-T Debt	1,021
Accounts Receivable	1,677	Taxes Payable	36
Inventory	2,936	Accrued Expenses	157
Prepaid Expenses	172	**Total Current Liabilities**	1,839
Other Current Assets	58		
Total Current Assets	6,670	Long-term Debt	2,332
		Total Liabilities	4,171
Gross Value of Property & Equipment	2,019	**Owner's Equity**	
Accumulated Depreciation	−664	Capital Stock	194
Net Property & Equipment	1,355	Retained Earnings	4,009
		Total Owner Equity	4,203
Note Receivable	349		
Total Assets	8374	**Total Liabilities and Equity**	8,374

Figure 12.3 Balance sheet example

market value, meaning that capital equipment should be listed at the purchase price less any accumulated depreciation.

Summary

This chapter emphasizes the importance of creating a formal business plan with detailed market and financial analysis prior to starting a food tourism enterprise or developing a food tourism product. Business plans provide a road map for owners, managers, and employees and increase the probability of business success by outlining a shared vision and set of values. Business plans are often required to obtain financing, such as start-up or operating loans, which can be essential to maintaining cash flow and sustaining the business in the long run.

Understanding the operation's target market is essential for market planning in terms of the product's attributes, how the product is promoted and distributed, and the price at which it is sold (the 4 Ps). The various pricing strategies have their advantages and disadvantages, and consumers may be sensitive to price changes depending on several factors, such as the availability of similar products and the value they expect to receive.

Image 12.3 Local restaurant at a tourist guesthouse in La Mosquitia, Honduras
Source: Susan L. Slocum

Food tourism policy and practice

Creating a projected income statement that includes estimated revenues and expenses provides a measure of the potential financial feasibility of the food tourism endeavor. Using a break-even analysis to gauge minimum quantity or pricing levels required to make a profit is suggested and should be compared with the potential customer base and consumer willingness to pay for the product.

Study Questions

1   Outline the components of a SWOT analysis. Which are internal and which are external to the organization?
2   What is the main purpose of a mission statement and why would such a statement be important to tourists? Write a mission statement for a food tourism enterprise.
3   Describe the four P's of marketing and how each should be customized to the products' target markets.
4   List four potential fixed costs and four potential variable costs of a cooking school.
5   You plan to purchase a food truck and serve lunches to brewery visitors across the summer season. Your total cost to operate the truck and serve 7,000 meals in one season are $58,000. What do you need to price each meal in order to break even? If you price meals at $9.49, how many meals would you have to sell to break even? If you decide to raise your price by $1.50 per meal, would customers decrease their purchases? Why or why not?

Definitions

4 Ps—the key components of a marketing strategy: product, price, promotion, and place.
Asset—the property of a person, association, corporation, or estate applicable or subject to the payment of debts.
Average cost—the production cost of each unit: total cost divided by the number of units produced.
Balance sheet—a statement of financial condition of a business on a given date.
Break-even—either the number of units that must be produced for a business to make a profit or the price that must be charged at a given level of production in order to make a profit.
Business plan—a plan that focuses on strategic implications such as internal investment, company structure, and long-term strategies.
Competitive advantage—a firm's ability to gain an edge over, or perform better than, its competition.
Environmental scanning—the process of monitoring the external environment, including economic factors, technological changes, changes in government policy, and legal requirements.

Expense—money that is used to pay the operating costs of a business.

Fixed cost—a cost of doing business that is not dependent on the number of units produced, such as rent.

Goal—a purpose toward which an endeavor is directed over a certain time frame.

Income statement—a financial statement that shows the profitability of a business over a given time period.

Liability—the debt a business is legally responsible to pay back.

Marketing plan—a plan that focuses on defining and accessing a target market and the unique products or services that differentiates the business from its competitors.

Mission statement—a short, concise statement describing a business's vision and values.

Objective—the specific step-by-step accomplishments required to achieve a given goal.

Owner equity—all owner investments, including the sum of profits and losses over previous years and any money they have invested in the company.

Profit—revenue minus expenses.

Revenue—money that is made by a business or organization through product sales, investments, etc.

SWOT analysis—an assessment of a company or destination's strengths, weaknesses, opportunities, and threats.

Total costs—the sum of variable costs and fixed costs.

Variable cost—a business cost directly tied with the number of units produced, such as packaging.

Willingness to pay—the level of value perceived by the consumer, represented by the maximum price they will pay for a good or service.

CASE STUDY 12.1

Tierra del Sol

Eric T. Micheels and Savannah Gleim

After living for several years in South America, John and Barb Cote returned to their home province in Canada to begin a new chapter in their lives. John and Barb were looking over their new plot of land, aptly named Tierra del Sol, located minutes south of the city of Saskatoon, Saskatchewan, on Valley Road. Valley Road is a vibrant hub of agribusinesses that provide agricultural services and experiences to urban consumers. With firms already established in the U-pick, nursery, restaurant, and gift spaces, Tierra del Sol had to find its own niche in this competitive market.

Image 12.4 Tierra Del Sol, Saskatchewan, Canada
Source: Eric Micheels

As they are located next to a city center, home to over 250,000 people, the Cotes are able to see trends in locally produced food and beverages. Saskatchewan's first microbrewery was founded in Saskatoon, several food trucks now operate in the city, and the Saskatoon Farmers' Market is home to over 75 vendors who market locally sourced food several days each week.

Based on market trends, they decided on three potential areas where they could achieve desired returns on invested capital. Their first idea was to capitalize on the growing trend toward agritourism to develop a business around a harvest festival and pumpkin patch. The second idea, a U-pick cut-flower business, utilized Barb's skills in flower arranging and horticulture. Finally, John thought a distillery might enable him to utilize his skills in grain production while also tapping into the market for locally produced spirits. Given the amount of capital he and Barb had invested into Tierra Del Sol, John realized that they needed to develop a business model that provided a reasonable cash flow for their living expenses while also enabling them to build equity for retirement.

With these ideas in hand, John got to work putting together three separate business plans, which he would then use to decide on the future direction of Tierra Del Sol. For the flower venture, John and Barb knew that they probably couldn't compete with the traditional cut-flower players located in Ecuador and Nigeria. However, for local consumers who wanted to have a fresh bouquet of lilies, peonies, gladiolas, or cornstalks for fall decorating, the flower business would provide a nice point of differentiation from mass-market players. However, they needed to consider that they were located a few miles away from the city center, where demand might be highest; given the harsh Saskatchewan climate, they would not have any fresh flowers for the key flower holidays like Valentine's Day or Mother's Day.

John also felt that the other businesses operating on Valley Road provided a great opportunity. Several thousand cars passed Tierra Del Sol every day on their way to the Berry Barn (a restaurant and Saskatoon berry farm), Moon Lake Golf Course, and Crickle Creek (a mini golf course and fun zone). However, John thought a more agriculturally based business would do well in Saskatoon, as many in the city were only a generation removed from living on a farm and liked the idea of being able to experience agriculture with their families. John thought a pumpkin patch would provide all of these amenities to the urban consumer, but there were risks associated with this agritourism venture. For one, their pumpkins would likely be higher priced than those at big box stores like Walmart. Weather was also a risk, as a frost could wipe out the crop and limit the revenue that could be generated.

Finally, John and Barb thought a distillery would combine both the past and the present. Given the growing number of local craft brewers and distillers already operating in Western Canada, the competition in this space was increasing. Without specific knowledge of the distilling process, combined with the fact that producing

Image 12.5 Grain storage facility, Saskatchewan, Canada
Source: Eric Micheels

whiskey is a time-intensive process, this venture faced several hurdles. However, the market for craft spirits seemed to be growing, and the transportability of the finished product could enable them to expand to other markets across Western Canada.

After John had developed his business plans, he thought about them further. John and Barb had a good idea which plan made the most sense to them, but they wanted to get additional feedback. John shared some ideas with a few contacts who worked in finance, marketing, and strategic planning. One Friday in September, they all decided to meet for a working lunch to discuss the three plans. John wondered if his contacts had the same thoughts as he did. In a few minutes, he would find out.

Questions

1 How should John and Barb account for the trend in agritourism and the interest in local food production? Saskatoon is not a huge urban center like Toronto or Vancouver. Is it large enough to sustain an agritourism venture?
2 Which plan provides the most opportunity for John and Barb? Which plan carries the greatest risk?
3 What other ideas might be feasible for John and Barb?

References

Barry, J.J., and Hellerstein, D. (2004). Farm recreation. In H.K. Cordell (principal author), *Outdoor recreation for 21st century America. A report to the nation: The national survey on recreation and the environment* (pp. 149–167). State College, PA: Venture Publishing.

Tchetchik, A., Fleischer, A., and Finkelshtain, I. (2008). Differentiation and synergies in rural tourism: Estimation and simulation of the Israeli market. *American Journal of Agricultural Economics*, 90(2), 553–570.

Glossary

4 Ps—the key components of a marketing strategy: product, price, promotion, and place.

Agriculture—the science or practice of farming and ranching including cultivation of the soil for the growing of crops and the rearing of animals to provide food and other products.

Agritourism—rural tourism conducted on working farms where the working environment forms part of the product from the perspective of the consumer.

Asset—the property of a person, association, corporation, or estate applicable or subject to the payment of debts.

Attitudes—thoughts or feelings a visitor has about a brand or destination.

Attributes—descriptive qualities that a visitor believes a destination to have.

Authenticity—the idea that something is true, accurate, or real.

Average cost—the production cost of each unit: total cost divided by the number of units produced.

Balance sheet—a statement of financial condition of a business on a given date.

Benefits—the personal value visitors attach to destination attributes.

Bonding social capital—social networks of homogeneous groups of people with common values and beliefs.

Bottom-up policy—a policy that allows local communities to set their own goals and make decisions about their resources in the future.

Brain drain—a loss of trained or skilled professionals to another area, nation, etc., that offers greater opportunity.

Brand—a name, term, design, or other feature that distinguishes one seller's product from others'.

Brand awareness—the ease of brand recognition and brand recall.

Branding—a name, term, sign, symbol, or design, or combination of these, which is intended to identify the goods and services of one seller or group of sellers and to differentiate them from those of competitors.

Break-even—either the number of units that must be produced for a business to make a profit or the price that must be charged at a given level of production in order to make a profit.

Bridging social capital—social networks of socially heterogeneous groups that include people with different backgrounds.

Business plan—a plan that focuses on strategic implications such as internal investment, company structure, and long-term strategies.

Capital—assets held that can be invested or used to produce goods or services.

Cluster—geographically close group of interconnected companies and associated institutions in a particular industry, linked by shared aims and complementary resources.

Cluster analysis—a statistical method used to group a set of objects such that objects in the same group (called a cluster) are more similar (in some sense or another) to each other than to those in other groups (clusters).

Collaboration—the process of joint decision-making among autonomous key stakeholders of an inter-organizational community to manage and resolve complex planning problems.

Commercial kitchen—a kitchen where food is prepared or processed for resale and normally regulated through building codes, food safety plans, and regular inspections.

Commodification—the process of transforming goods, services, ideas, and people into objects of trade in an effort to support economic growth or profit.

Competitive advantage—a firm's ability to gain an edge over or perform better than its competition.

Consolidation—the merging or joining of groups or companies, leading to a reduction in the total number.

Contaminant—any unwanted or undesirable material found in food. Contaminants may or may not be visible and include physical, chemical, and biological items.

Coopetition—simultaneously cooperating and competing in order to support joint community-building projects.

Cost-benefit analysis—a method for estimating and totaling the equivalent monetary value of a project's benefits and costs within a community to establish whether the project is worthwhile.

Crop rotation—the system of varying successive crops in a definite order on the same ground, especially to avoid depleting the soil and to control weeds and pests.

Culinary tourism—the pursuit of unique and memorable eating and drinking experiences.

Culture—learned knowledge based on material and non-material elements such as beliefs, art, morals, customs, laws, behaviors, values, traditions, and folklore.

Demand—the quantity of a product or service that people are willing or able to buy at a specific price.

Demographic segmentation—grouping potential tourists based on specific attributes such as age, profession, income level, occupation, ethnic background, education level, household size, and family situation.

Destination Marketing and Management Organization—the organization responsible for encouraging tourists to visit by developing and communicating the characteristics of a destination and attracting the appropriate type of tourism businesses.

Differentiation—the process of establishing a unique image in the minds of consumers.

Direct effects—changes in local economic activity resulting from businesses selling directly to tourists.

Direct market sales—sale of farm products to consumers at farmers' markets, farm stands, and through community supported agriculture (CSA) and sales to local restaurants and grocery stores (as opposed to sales to wholesalers and other middlemen).

Discount rate—the interest rate used to discount the value of future earnings or costs.

Diversification—the reallocation of resources—such as land, capital, infrastructure, and labor—into new activities as a means of avoiding risk.

Drink tourism—tourism focused on beverages rather than food as the key element of experience.

Dumping—selling a product on the open market at a price lower than the domestic price.

Economic impact—the sum of direct, indirect, and induced effects.

Economies of scale—the cost savings gained by increasing levels of production.

Elastic good—a good whose price affects the quantity sold of that good; an increase in price reduces the quantity sold and a decrease in price increases the quantity sold.

Environmental scanning—the process of monitoring the external environment, including economic factors, technological changes, changes in government policy, and legal requirements.

Excursionists—visitors who use tourism services, but live within close proximity to the destination and who only stay for a short period of time (a few hours to a single day).

Expectation—a strong belief that something will happen.

Expense—money that is used to pay the operating costs of a business.

Exports—goods produced domestically and sold abroad.

Externalities—costs or benefits that affect a party who did not choose to incur them.

Factor analysis—a statistical method used to describe variability among observed, correlated variables in terms of a potentially lower number of unobserved variables called factors.

Factors of production—resources—such as land, labor, and capital—that can be used to produce goods and services.

Fallowing—the practice of leaving a field unused for one season to manage pests or soil fertility.

Fixed cost—a cost of doing business that is not dependent on the number of units produced, such as rent.

Focus group—a qualitative method where a group of individuals is asked a set of specific, open-ended questions together.

Food hub—a centrally located facility with a business management structure that may aggregate, store, process, distribute, and/or market locally or regionally produced food products.

Food miles—the distance food is transported from the time of its production until it reaches the consumer.

Food or drink trail—a linear route primarily intended for recreational and educational travel involving the consumption of local food or drink.

Food processing—broadly includes any activity applied to a food product to make it ready for sale to the public.

Food service—businesses that prepare food on-site for immediate consumption, also referred to as catering.

Food tourism—a tourist's desire to experience a particular type of food or the produce of a specific region.

Food tourist—a person keenly interested in travel to explore food.

Food-based attraction—a permanent structure that draws tourists and operates all year.

Food-based events—special events focusing on food or drink that include food festivals, farmers' markets, wine regions, and food trails.

Foodie—someone with a long-standing passion for eating and learning about food but who is not a food professional.

Foodways—the cultural, social and economic practices relating to the production and consumption of food.

Genetic engineering—the direct manipulation of an organism's genome using biotechnology.

Geographic segmentation—grouping potential tourists based on physical location or place of origin.

Geographical Indication (GI)—a certification that covers agricultural products and foodstuffs that are closely linked to a geographical area.

Globalization—the process of international integration as a result of the exchange of worldviews, products, and ideas.

Goal—a purpose toward which an endeavor is directed over a certain time frame.

Governance—the coordination of economies, public/private partnerships, and reform objectives aimed at pursuing collective interests.

Human capital—the stock of knowledge, habits, social, and personality attributes, including creativity, embodied in the ability to perform labor to produce economic value.

Hygiene—personal practices related to cleanliness that reduce or eliminate the spread of disease.

Imports—goods produced abroad and brought in to sell domestically.

Income statement—a financial statement that shows the profitability of a business over a given time period.

Glossary

Indirect effects—changes in sales, income, or employment within a region in industries supplying goods and services to tourism businesses.

Induced effects—changes in expenditures within a region as a result of household spending of the income earned in tourism and supporting industries.

Industrialization—the large-scale introduction of manufacturing, advanced technical enterprises, and other productive economic activity into an area, society, or country.

Inelastic good—a good whose price does not affect the quantity sold of that good; the quantity sold is stable regardless of whether the price increases or decreases.

Input/output modeling—a quantitative economic technique that represents the interdependencies between different branches of a national economy or different regional economies.

Laws—a system of rules designed to regulate certain behaviors which are enforced through penalties.

Leakages—the revenue lost to an area when inputs are purchased outside the local economy or newly acquired currency is spent on buying foreign (as opposed to local) goods for resale to tourists.

Liability—the debt a business is legally responsible to pay back.

Local sourcing—sale of local agricultural products to tourism establishments such as restaurants, hotels, and conference centers.

Locavore—a person whose diet consists principally of locally grown or produced food.

Market segmentation—the process of dividing a broad market into subsets of consumers or target markets with common needs, interests, and priorities and then designing and implementing strategies to attract them to a business or destination.

Marketing plan—a plan that focuses on defining and accessing a target market and the unique products or services that differentiates the business from its competitors.

Mechanization—the use of machines or equipment to replace labor requirements in agriculture.

Microbe—a microscopic life form that includes bacteria, viruses, fungi, and parasites.

Mission statement—a short, concise statement describing a business's vision and values.

Monoculture—the agricultural practice of producing or growing a single crop, plant, or livestock species, variety, or breed in a field or farming system at a time.

Motivation—a general desire or willingness to do something or go somewhere.

Multinational corporation—a corporate organization that owns or controls production of goods or services in one or more countries other than the home country.

Multipliers—captures the size of the secondary effects, usually as a ratio of total effects to direct effects.

Neophile—a person who is more likely to try something new that is either unfamiliar or may not be available at home.

Neophobe—a person who is less likely to be adventurous and prefers familiar experiences and food items.

Net present value—a comparison of discounted future cash inflows to present cash outflows.

Networking—the channels or relationships through which collaboration is achieved.

Objective—the specific step-by-step accomplishments required to achieve a given goal.

Oligopoly—a market where there exist few sellers, which as a result can greatly influence price and other market factors.

Oligopsony—a market where there exist few buyers, which as a result can influence the price they pay for products.

Organic—cultural, biological, and mechanical production practices that support recycling resources, promote ecological balance, and conserve biodiversity.

Owner equity—all owner investments, including the sum of profits and losses over prior years and any money they have invested in the company.

Pathogen—a microbe that can cause illness in humans. Adjective form is pathogenic.

Policy—a definite course or method of action selected from a number of alternative actions in light of given conditions that guide and determine present and future decisions.

Policy cycle—the process of reviewing and reshaping a policy periodically, such as every 5 to 7 years.

Primary data—data originally obtained through the direct efforts of a researcher using surveys, interviews, or direct observation.

Principle of absolute advantage—the ability of a provider of goods or services to produce goods more efficiently than all of its competitors, such that its total cost per unit of output is lower.

Principle of comparative advantage—the ability of an individual, company, etc., to produce a good or service at a lower cost and more efficiently than another entity.

Product-related segmentation—grouping potential tourists by their wants and needs regarding the attributes of a particular good or service or destination and activity preferences as well as preferred communication methods and spending habits.

Productivity—output per unit of input.

Profit—revenue minus expenses.

Progressive taxes—taxes that have rates that increase as taxable amount increases.

Psychographic segmentation—grouping potential tourists based on lifestyle choices, hobbies, interests, and values.

Qualitative data—data that approximate or describe the characteristics or properties of a subject.

Quantitative data—data, usually in numerical form, that define the characteristics or properties of a subject.

Regressive taxes—taxes that place a greater burden (relative to income) on the poor than on the rich.

Regulations—a set of rules that govern how laws are enforced.

Revenue—money that is made by a business or organization through product sales, investments, etc.

Rural development—the process of improving the quality of life and economic well-being of people living in relatively isolated and sparsely populated areas.

Sanitation—environmental or operational practices related to cleanliness that reduce or eliminate the spread of disease.

Satellite accounting—a quantitative economic technique that estimates the interdependencies between economic activities that are not defined as industries in their own right.

Satisfaction—deriving pleasure from the fulfillment of one's wishes, expectations, or needs.

Secondary data—data collected by someone other than the researcher.

Sectorial development—development that depends on a single economic sector or industry as the primary economic driver.

Self-sufficiency—the ability to supply one's own needs without external assistance.

Sense of place—special meanings that represent an identity and character that is deeply felt by local citizens.

Social capital—the links, shared values, and understandings that enable individuals and groups in a society to trust each other and so work together.

Souvenirs—commercial objects usually purchased during travel that remind people of past experiences and places visited.

Specialization—restricting activity to one specific or unique action.

Spore—the dormant form of a microbe, especially bacteria and fungi, which begins to grow only when environmental conditions are favorable. Spores are often resistant to common food safety and sanitation practices.

Stakeholders—individuals or groups with an interest in tourism and who have great influence over tourism.

Strong sustainability—the belief that the existing stock of natural capital must be maintained and enhanced because the functions it performs cannot be duplicated by manufactured capital.

Supply—the amount of a product available for sale at a given price.

Sustainable consumption—the purchasing of products and services that support health and environmental well-being.

Sustainable development—development that meets the needs of the present without compromising the ability of future generations to meet their own needs.

Sustainable tourism—tourism development that meets the needs of the present tourists and host regions while protecting and enhancing opportunities for the future.

SWOT analysis—an assessment of a company or destination's strengths, weaknesses, opportunities, and threats.

Target market—a group of customers within the larger market who have similar demographics, interests, behaviors, or lifestyle characteristics at which a business has decided to aim its product and marketing strategies.

Tariff—the tax or duty imposed by a government on imports or exports.

Territorial development—development that integrates multiple sectors or industries in a specific region.

Top-down policy—a policy created by senior executives or officials independent of those affected by the policy.

Total costs—the sum of variable costs and fixed costs.

Tourism—the temporary movement of people to destinations outside their normal places of work and residence, the activities undertaken during their stay in those destinations, and the facilities created to cater to their needs.

Tourism product—a visitors' experience of a destination, including tangible and intangible assets, and the perceived satisfaction derived from that experience.

Tourism satellite account—a detailed analyses of all the aspects of demand for goods and services associated with the activity of visitors; to observe the operational interface with the supply of such goods and services within the economy; and to describe how this supply interacts with other economic activities.

Tourist typologies—the classification of tourists by their behavior.

Toxin—a chemical that produces disease in humans. Toxins can be man-made or produced by certain types of plants, microbes, and animals.

Tragedy of the commons—a situation where individuals, acting independently and rationally according to their individual self-interest, behave contrary to the best interests of the whole group by depleting a resource.

Transparency—operating in such a way that it is easy for others to see and understand what actions are performed.

Triple bottom line—the economic, natural, and social resources that must be protected in sustainable development.

Urbanization—a population shift from rural to urban areas.

Value-added products—products that have experienced some type of post-harvest processing that adds value to the basic food item.

Variable cost—a business cost directly tied with the number of units produced, such as packaging.

Voluntourism—holidays that involve working alongside local residents, usually in an effort to give back to communities or help alleviate poverty.

Weak sustainability—the philosophy that man-made capital is more important than natural capital.

Welfare—the well-being of an economy, country, etc.

Willingness to pay—the level of value perceived by the consumer represented by the maximum price they will pay for a good or service.

Yield—the quantity or amount of a crop that is produced, harvested, etc.

Zoning—the process of dividing land into areas on which various uses are permitted or restricted.

Index

Page numbers in **bold** indicate references to tables or figures. Page numbers in *italics* indicate references to case studies.

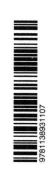

9781138931107